Real-Time C++

Christopher Michael Kormanyos

Real-Time C++

Efficient Object-Oriented and Template Microcontroller Programming

 Springer

Christopher Michael Kormanyos
Reutlingen
Baden-Württemberg
Germany

ISBN 978-3-642-34687-3   ISBN 978-3-642-34688-0 (eBook)
DOI 10.1007/978-3-642-34688-0
Springer Heidelberg New York Dordrecht London

Library of Congress Control Number: 2013931231

ACM Computing Classification (1998): C.3, D.2, C.5, B.1

Printed on acid-free paper

Springer is part of Springer Science+Business Media (www.springer.com)

To those who pursue the art of technical creativity

Preface

This book is a practical guide to programming real-time embedded microcontroller systems in C++. The C++ language has powerful object-oriented and template features that can improve software design and portability while simultaneously reducing code complexity and the risk of error. At the same time, C++ compiles highly efficient native code. This unique and effective combination makes C++ well suited for programming microcontroller systems that require compact size, high performance, and safety-critical reliability.

The target audience of this book includes hobbyists, students, and professionals interested in real-time C++. The reader should be familiar with C or another programming language and should ideally have had some exposure to microcontroller electronics and the performance and size issues prevalent in embedded systems programming.

About This Book

This is an interdisciplinary book that includes a broad range of topics. Real-world examples have been combined with brief descriptions in an effort to provide an intuitive and straightforward methodology for microcontroller programming in C++. Efficiency is always in focus, and numerous examples are backed up with real-time performance measurements and size analyses that quantify the true costs of the code down to the very last byte and microsecond.

Throughout the chapters, C++ is used in a bare-bones, no-frills fashion without relying on any libraries other than those specified in the language standard itself. This approach facilitates portability.

This book has three parts and several appendices. The three parts generally build on each other with the combined goal of providing a coherent and effective set of C++ methods that can be used with a wide range of embedded microcontrollers.

- Part I provides a foundation for real-time C++ by covering language technologies. Topics include getting started in real-time C++, object-oriented methods, template programming, and optimization. The first three chapters have a particularly hands-on nature and are intended to boost competence in real-time C++. Chapter 6 has a unique and important role in that it is wholly dedicated to optimization techniques appropriate for microcontroller programming in C++.
- Part II presents detailed descriptions of a variety of C++ components that are widely used in microcontroller programming. These components can be either used as presented or adapted for other projects. This part of the book uses some of C++'s most powerful language elements, such as class types, templates, and the STL, to develop components for microcontroller register access, low-level drivers, custom memory management, embedded containers, multitasking, etc.
- Part III describes mathematical methods and generic utilities that can be employed to solve recurring problems in real-time C++.
- The appendices include a C++ language tutorial, information on the real-time C++ development environment, and instructions for building GNU GCC cross compilers and a microcontroller circuit.

C++ is a rich language with many features and details, the description of which can fill entire bookshelves. This book, however, primarily concentrates on how to use C++ in a real-time microcontroller environment. Along those lines, C++ language tutorials have been held terse, and information on microcontroller hardware and compilers is included only insofar as it is needed for the examples. A suggested list of additional reading material is given in Chap. 17 for those seeking supplementary information on C++, the C++ standard library and STL, software design, C++ coding guidelines, the embedded systems toolchain, and microcontroller hardware.

When units are needed to express physical quantities, the MKS (meter, kilogram, second) system of units is used.

Companion Code, Targets, and Tools

The companion code includes three introductory projects and one reference project. The introductory projects treat various aspects of the material presented in Chaps. 1 and 2. The reference project is larger in scope and exercises many of the methods from all the chapters.

The companion code is available at

https://github.com/ckormanyos/real-time-cpp

The C++ techniques in this book specifically target microcontrollers in the *small-to-medium* size range. Here, small-to-medium spans the following approximate size and performance ranges:

- 4 kB ... 1-MB program code
- 256 byte ... 128-kB RAM
- 8 bit ... 32–bit CPU
- 8 MHz ... 200-MHz CPU frequency

Most of the methods described in this book are, however, scalable. As such, they can be used equally well on larger or smaller devices, even on PCs and workstations. In particular, they can be employed if the application has strict performance and size constraints.

A popular 8–bit microcontroller clocked with a frequency of 16 MHz has been used as the primary target for benchmarking and testing the code samples in this book. Certain benchmarks have also been performed with a well-known 32–bit microcontroller clocked at 24 MHz. An 8–bit microcontroller and a 32–bit microcontroller have been selected in order to exercise the C++ methods over a wide range of microcontroller performance.

All the C++ examples and benchmarks in the book and the companion code have been compiled with GNU GCC versions 4.6.2 and 4.7.0. Certain examples and benchmarks have also been compiled with other PC-based compilers.

The most recent specification of C++11 in ISO/IEC 14882:2011 is used throughout the text. At the time this book is written, the specification of C++11 is brand-new. The advent of C++11 has made C++ significantly more effective and easy to use. This will profoundly influence C++ programming. The well-informed reader will, therefore, want to keep in touch with C++11 best practice as it evolves in the development community.

Notes on Coding Style

A consistent coding style is used throughout the examples in this book and in the companion code.

Code samples are written with a `fixed-width font`. C++ language keywords and built-in types use the same font, but they are in boldface. For instance,

```
constexpr int version = 7;
```

In general, the names of all symbols such as variables, class types, members, and subroutines are written in lowercase. A single underscore (_) is used to separate words and abbreviations in names. For instance, a system-tick variable expressed with this style is shown in the code sample below:

```
unsigned long system_tick;
```

Using prefixes, suffixes, or abbreviations to incorporate type information in a name, sometimes known as *Hungarian notation*, is not done. Superfluous prefixes, suffixes, and abbreviations in Hungarian notation may obscure the name of a symbol, and symbol names can be more intuitive and clear without them. For example,

---

```
std::uint16_t name_of_a_symbol;
```

Names that are intended for use in public domains are preferentially long and descriptive rather than short and abbreviated. Here, clarity of expression is preferred over terseness. Symbols used for local subroutine parameters or private implementation details with obvious meanings, however, often have terse or abbreviated names.

The global subroutine below, for example, uses this naming style. It returns the **float** value of the squared Euclidean distance from the origin of a point in two-dimensional Cartesian space $\mathbb{R}^2$:

```
float squared_euclidean_distance(const float& x,
                                 const float& y)
{
  return (x * x) + (y * y);
}
```

C++ references are heavily used because this can be advantageous for small microcontrollers. Consider an 8–bit microcontroller. The work of copying subroutine parameters or the work of pushing them onto the stack for anything wider than 8 bits can be significant. This work load can potentially be reduced by using references. In the previous code sample, for instance, the floating-point subroutine parameters x and y, each 4 bytes wide, have been passed to the subroutine by reference (i.e., **const float&**).

Fixed-size integer types defined in the std namespace of the C++ standard library such as std::uint8_t, std::uint16_t, and std::uint32_t are preferentially used instead of plain built-in types such as **char**, **short**, and **int**. This improves clarity and portability. An unsigned login response with exactly 8 bits, for instance, is shown below:

```
std::uint8_t login_response;
```

Code samples often rely on one or more of the C++ standard library headers such as <algorithm>, <array>, <cstdint>, <limits>, <tuple>, <vector>, etc. In general, code samples requiring library headers do not explicitly include their necessary library headers.

The declaration of login_response above, for example, actually requires <cstdint> for the definition of std::uint8_t. The library file is, however, not included. In general, the code samples focus on the core of the code, not on the inclusion of library headers.

It is easy to guess or remember, for example, that `std::array` can be found in `<array>` and that `std::vector` is located in `<vector>`. It can, however, be more difficult to guess or remember that `std::size_t` is in `<cstddef>` or that `std::accumulate()` is in `<numeric>`. With assistance from online help and other resources and with a little practice, though, it becomes routine to identify what standard library parts can be found in which headers.

In cases for which particular emphasis is placed on the inclusion of a header file, the relevant **#include** line(s) may be explicitly written. For instance,

```
#include <cstdint>

std::uint8_t login_response;
```

Namespaces are used frequently. In general, though, the **using** directive is not used to inject symbols in namespaces into the global namespace. This means that the entire namespace must be typed with the name of a symbol in it. This, again, favors non-ambiguity over brevity.

The unsigned 16–bit counter below, for example, uses a type from the `std` namespace. Since the "**using namespace** std" directive is not used, the name of the namespace (`std`) is explicitly included in the type:

```
std::uint16_t counter;
```

Suffixes are generally appended to literal constant values. When a suffix is appended to a literal constant value, its optional case is uppercase. For example,

```
constexpr float pi = 3.14159265358979323846F;

constexpr std::uint8_t login_key = 0x55U;
```

Certain established C++ coding guidelines have strongly influenced the coding style. For the sake of terseness and clarity, however, not every guideline has been followed all the time.

One clearly recognizable influence of the coding guidelines is the diligent use of C++-style casts when converting built-in types. The following code, for instance, explicitly casts from **float** to an unsigned integer type:

```
float f = 3.14159265358979323846F;

std::uint8_t u = static_cast<std::uint8_t>(f);
```

Even though explicit casts like these are not always mandatory, they can resolve ambiguity and eliminate potential misinterpretation caused by integer promotion.

Another influence of the coding guidelines on the code is the ordering of class members according to their access level in the class. The communication class below, for example, represents the base class in a hierarchy of communication objects. The members in the class definition are ordered according to access level. In particular,

```cpp
class communication
{
public:
  virtual ~communication();

  virtual bool send(const std::uint8_t) const;
  virtual bool recv(std::uint8_t&);

protected:
  communication();

private:
  bool recv_ready;
  std::uint8_t recv_buffer;
};
```

C-style preprocessor macros are used occasionally. Preprocessor macros are written entirely in uppercase letters. Underscores separate the words in the names of preprocessor macros. The MAKE_WORD() preprocessor macro below, for example, creates an unsigned 16–bit word from two unsigned 8–bit constituents:

```cpp
#define MAKE_WORD(lo, hi) \
          (uint16_t) (((uint16_t) (hi) << 8) | (lo))
```

Acknowledgements

First and foremost, I would like to thank my wife and daughter for encouraging me to write this book and also for creating a peaceful, caring atmosphere in which I could work productively. Thank you for your time. You have my gratitude.

I would also like to express appreciation to family, friends, and associates, too numerous to list, who contributed to this project with their innovative ideas, support, friendship, and companionship.

Thanks go to the members of the C++ standards committee, Boost, the volunteers at GCC, and all the developers in the vibrant C++ and embedded systems communities. Through your efforts, oftentimes for no pay whatsoever, C++ has evolved to an unprecedented level of expressiveness, making object-oriented and generic programming more effective and easier than ever.

Working with Springer Verlag was a delightful experience. I thank my editor, who first identified the merit of this work and supported me throughout the writing process. I also thank the copyediting team and all the staff at Springer Verlag for their professionalism and capable assistance.

- ATMEL® and AVR® are registered trademarks of Atmel Corporation or its subsidiaries, in the USA and other countries.
- *Real-Time C++: Efficient Object-Oriented and Template Microcontroller Programming* is a book authored by Christopher Michael Kormanyos and published by Springer Verlag and has not been authorized, sponsored, or otherwise approved of by Atmel Corporation.
- ARDUINO® is a registered trademark of the Arduino Group.
- SPI™ is a trademark of Motorola Corporation.
- The circuit of the target hardware described in this book and depicted in Chap. 2 and Appendix D was designed and assembled on a solderless prototyping breadboard by Christopher Michael Kormanyos.
- The photographs of the target hardware described in this book and depicted in Chap. 2 and Appendix D were taken by Christopher Michael Kormanyos.

Reutlingen, Germany   Christopher Michael Kormanyos
Seattle, Washington, USA

Contents

Acronyms

ADC	Analog-Digital Converter.
AUTOSAR	AUTomotive Open System ARchitecture, is a worldwide cooperation of automotive manufacturers and companies supplying electronics, semiconductors and software that cooperates on, among other things, a standardized architecture for automotive microcontroller software.
AWG	American Wire Gauge.
binutils	Binary Utilities, are the GNU binary utilities for GCC.
C	C, is the C programming language.
C99	C99 is the C language specification in ISO/IEC 9899:1999.
C++	C++, is the C++ programming language.
C++03	C++03 is the C++ language specification in ISO/IEC 14882:2003.
C++11	C++11 is the C++ language specification in ISO/IEC 14882:2011.
C++98	C++98 is the C++ language specification in ISO/IEC 14882:1998.
CPU	Central-Processing Unit.
ctor	Constructor of a class object in object-oriented programming, is a special subroutine that is called when an object is created.
DIL	Dual In-Line electronic packaging.
DSP	Digital Signal Processor.
dtor	Destructor of a class object in object-oriented programming, is a special subroutine that is called when an object is destroyed or deleted.
FIR	Finite-Impulse Response, is a kind of digital filter.
FLASH	Flash Memory, is a nonvolatile computer memory that can be electrically written and erased, commonly used as an alternative to ROM.
FPU	Floating-Point Unit.
GAS	GNU Assembler, is the GNU assembler.
GCC	GNU Compiler Collection, is a collection of free compilers for several popular programming languages including, among others, C and C++, ported to a wide range of targets.
GMP	GNU Multiprecision, is the GNU multiprecision library.

GNU   Is a *nix-like computer operating system consisting entirely of free
            software.
GUI   Graphical User Interface.
HEX   Hexadecimal representation, is a base–16 numerical representation
            commonly used in computer engineering.
ICE   In-Circuit Emulator, is a hardware device used to debug embedded
            microcontroller software with an emulated bond-out processor.
ISP   In-System-Programming, is the act of programming the program
            code of a microcontroller using a communication interface while the
            microcontroller is fitted in the application, rather than as a standalone
            non-soldered component.
ISR   Interrupt Service Routine.
JTAG   Joint Test Action Group, which was later standardized as IEEE
            1149.1, is a protocol and hardware interface used for printed circuit
            board testing, boundary scan and recently more and more for debug-
            ging embedded systems.
LED   Light-Emitting Diode, is a semiconductor-based light source used in
            diverse applications such as lighting, consumer electronics and toys.
MCAL   Microcontroller Abstraction Layer, is a low-level layer in a layered
            software architecture (such as AUTOSAR) that consists of partially
            non-portable components that access microcontroller peripherals and
            their registers, such as a PWM signal generator or a serial UART
            interface.
MinGW   Minimalistic GNU, is an open-source programming toolset that
            emulates *nix-like environments.
MKS   Meter, Kilogram, Second, is a system of units used to express
            physical quantities.
MPC   Multiple-Precision Complex, is a GNU C library for the multipreci-
            sion arithmetic of complex numbers.
MPFR   Multiple-Precision Floating-Point with correct Rounding, is the GNU
            multiprecision floating-point library.
MSYS   Minimalistic System, is a collection of GNU utilities that enhance
            and extend the MinGW shell.
newlib   Newlib is a free implementation of the C standard library intended
            for use with embedded systems and ported to a variety of CPU
            architectures.
nop   No Operation Code, is a commonly arising assembly instruction that
            simply does no operation, and one or more of which are often used
            for ultra low-level functions such as creating a short delay or cleaning
            an instruction pipeline.
opcode   Operation Code, is a machine language instruction containing the
            operation to be done.
PPL   Parma Polyhedra Library, is a software library for abstract geometri-
            cal polyhedron representations.

PWM	Pulse-Width Modulated signal, is a square wave that usually has a fixed period and a variable duty-cycle.
RAM	Random Access Memory, is computer memory with nearly constant access time regardless of address or memory size and is volatile in the sense that data are lost when the power is switched off.
ROM	Read-Only Memory, is a class of computer memory that, once written, cannot be modified, or can only be modified slowly or with external programming tools and has permanent character in the sense that data are retained throughout power on/off cycles.
SPI™	Serial Peripheral Interface bus, is a four-wire serial communication interface commonly used for communication between a microcontroller and one or more off-chip devices on the printed circuit board.
STL	Standard Template Library, is part of the C++ standard library containing a vast collection of generic containers, iterators and algorithms.
TO–220	Transistor Outline electronic packaging, number 220.
TR1	C++ Technical Report 1, includes the standard library extensions that are specified in ISO/IEC TR 19768:2007, that are now predominantly integrated in C++11 (ISO/IEC 14882:2011).
UART	Universal Asynchronous Receiver/Transmitter, is an asynchronous receiver and transmitter commonly used for serial communication between a PC and a microcontroller.

Part I
Language Technologies for Real-Time C++

Chapter 1
Getting Started with Real-Time C++

C++ programs combine class types that encapsulate objects with procedural subroutines in order to embody the functionality of the application. This chapter presents these main language elements of C++ using a short, intuitive program that toggles an LED on a microcontroller output port pin. In addition, other language features are introduced including the syntax of C++, namespaces, the C++ standard library and optimization with compile time constants. This chapter uses our target system with the 8–bit microcontroller.

1.1   The LED Program

A simple microcontroller application is shown in Fig. 1.1 on the following page. The circuit in this figure has one LED connected to a digital output port pin on the microcontroller over a resistor to ground. Switching the port pin to high drives current through the resistor and the LED, and thereby switches the LED on. Setting the port pin to low stops current flow through the resistor and the LED, subsequently turning the LED off.

The LED circuit shown in Fig. 1.1 is part of the circuit belonging to our target system with the 8–bit microcontroller. Further details on the entire circuit in this application and its electrical components can be found in the figure here and also in Appendix D.

An object-oriented C++ program designed to control the LED circuit in Fig. 1.1 is shown below. It is called the *LED program*. In the LED program, an `led` object called `led_b5` is created on `portb.5`. The LED object `led_b5` is subsequently toggled from low to high and vice versa indefinitely without pause, break or return in an iterative loop in the `main()` subroutine.

C.M. Kormanyos, *Real-Time C++*, DOI 10.1007/978-3-642-34688-0__1,
© Springer-Verlag Berlin Heidelberg 2013

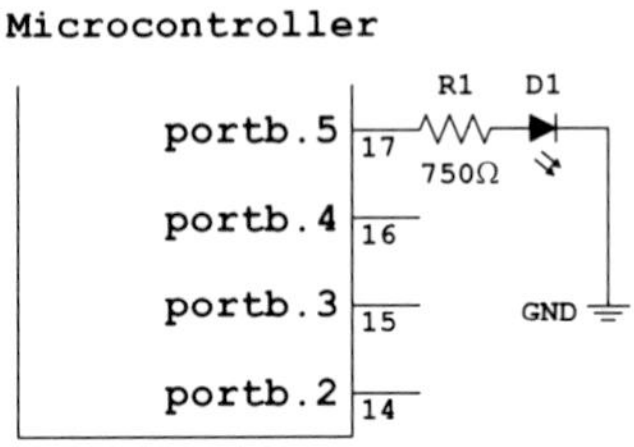

Fig. 1.1 The circuit of the
LED D1 on our target with
the 8–bit microcontroller is
shown. D1 is connected to
portb.5 on microcontroller
pin 17 over a 750 Ω resistor
R1 to ground

Microcontroller

```
portb.5 |17  R1   D1
portb.4 |16  750Ω
portb.3 |15       GND
portb.2 |14
```

```cpp
// The LED program.

#include <cstdint>
#include "mcal_reg.h"

class led
{
public:
  // Use convenient class-specific typedefs.
  typedef std::uint8_t port_type;
  typedef std::uint8_t bval_type;

  // The led class constructor.
  led(const port_type p,
      const bval_type b)  : port(p),
                            bval(b)
  {
    // Set the port pin value to low.
    *reinterpret_cast<volatile bval_type*>(port)
      &= static_cast<bval_type>(~bval);

    // Set the port pin direction to output.
    *reinterpret_cast<volatile bval_type*>(port - 1U)
      |= bval;
  }

  void toggle() const
  {
    // Toggle the LED via direct memory access.
    *reinterpret_cast<volatile bval_type*>(port)
      ^= bval;
  }

private:
  // Private member variables of the class.
```

```
  const port_type port;
  const bval_type bval;
};

namespace
{
  // Create led_b5 on portb.5.
  const led led_b5
  {
    mcal::reg::portb,
    mcal::reg::bval5
  };
}

int main()
{
  // Toggle led_b5 in a loop forever.
  for(;;)
  {
    led_b5.toggle();
  }
}
```

The LED program uses various C++ language elements. These include classes, namespaces, type definitions, C++ cast operators, direct memory access and even a little bit of the C++ standard library.

In particular, the predominant parts of the LED program are:

- The inclusion of header files with **#include**.
- The led class.
- The led class constructor and class members that encapsulate the initialization and toggling of the LED via direct memory access.
- The anonymous **namespace** containing the led_b5 object.
- The main() subroutine that toggles the led_b5 object indefinitely in a never-ending for(;;)-loop.

In the following sections of this chapter, we will investigate in detail how each one of these parts of the LED program is written and how each one works. Along the way, we will briefly discuss many aspects of the syntax of C++ and efficient ways to use the C++ language with real-time embedded systems.

1.2 The Syntax of C++

The syntax of C++ is similar to that of C. In fact, C++ is based on C. With a few minor exceptions, nearly all valid C language constructs can also be used in a C++ program.

As with C, the C++ language uses curly braces {...} to delimit scope. Parenthesizing and operator priorities are the same in C++ and C. The C++ language has familiar built-in types such as **char**, **short**, **int**, **long**, **float**, **double**, etc. C++ also supports C's well-known **#include** syntax for inclusion of header and library files. C++ uses C's iteration statements for, **while** and **do-while**. Source-level comments in C++ can be written in either slash-slash form (//...) or block form (/* ... */). Most C++ developers, however, preferentially use slash-slash comments instead of C-style block comments. See Item 4 in Meyers [4].

1.3 Class Types

Classes, structures (structs) and unions are collectively known as *class types* in C++. The LED program has a class called led. In particular,

```
class led
{
  // ...
};
```

Class types allow for object-oriented programming in C++ because they group data together with functions operating on them in a self-contained *encapsulated* unit. For example, the led class encapsulates the real LED hardware by grouping the LED's port pin with its toggle function.

Classes, structs and unions can have any mixture of data, functions and overloaded operators called *members*. For example, the public interface of led has a class *constructor* (also known as a ctor) and a member function called toggle().

A class constructor has the same name as its containing class. Constructors can have any number of input parameters. The constructor of led has two input parameters that characterize the address of the port data register and the output port pin of the LED hardware.

Class initialization code can be placed in the body of the constructor. In particular, the port hardware of the LED is initialized in the body of the led constructor.

```
class led
{
public:
  // The led class constructor.
  led(const port_type p,
      const bval_type b)  :  port(p),
                             bval(b)
  {
    // Set the port pin value to low.
    *reinterpret_cast<volatile bval_type*>(port)
      &= static_cast<bval_type>(~bval);

    // Set the port pin direction to output.
    *reinterpret_cast<volatile bval_type*>(port - 1U)
      |= bval;
  }
  // ...
};
```

Note that the address of the LED's port *direction* register is calculated from the address of its port *data* register. Also note that the port direction register is set before the port data register is written. This strategy eliminates potential spikes on I/O pins. These I/O port characteristics are specific to the microcontroller hardware and need to be modified when porting the led class to another system.

The so-called *constructor initialization list* is placed after the constructor function parameters and a colon, but before the opening brace of the constructor body. In particular,

```
led(const port_type p,
    const bval_type b)  :  port(p),
                           bval(b)
{
  // ...
}
```

Constant member variables *must* be initialized in the constructor initialization list. Non-constant member variables *should* be initialized in the constructor initialization list. The order of all member variables present in the constructor initialization list should be identical to their order of appearance in the class definition because the compiler initializes them in the order they are declared (Meyers [4], Item 13).

The implementation of the led class shown above is entirely contained within its definition. Alternatively, part or all of the implementation of a class type can be placed in a separate source file.

The definition of the `led` class, for instance, could be placed in a header file called `led.h`. In other words,

```cpp
// In the file led.h
class led
{
public:
  led(const port_type p,
      const bval_type b);

  void toggle() const;
  // ...
};
```

The corresponding implementation details of the `led` class could be put in the `led.cpp` source file. For example,

```cpp
// In the file led.cpp
#include "led.h"

led::led(const port_type p,
         const bval_type b)  : port(p),
                               bval(b)
{
  // Set the port pin value to low.
  *reinterpret_cast<volatile bval_type*>(port)
    &= static_cast<bval_type>(~bval);

  // Set the port pin direction to output.
  *reinterpret_cast<volatile bval_type*>(port - 1U)
    |= bval;
}

void led::toggle() const
{
  // Toggle the LED.
  *reinterpret_cast<volatile bval_type*>(port)
    ^= bval;
}

// ...
```

When members are defined outside of a class definition, the *scope resolution operator* (::) is used to resolve the class name from the names of members in the implementation file. For example,

```
// The scope resolution operator (::).
void led::toggle() const
{
  // ...
}
```

Including implementation details directly in the class definition can improve optimization via *inlining*. There is no need to explicitly *recommend* inlining to the compiler with the **inline** keyword because a function implemented directly in the class declaration is per default inline. Short, non-virtual subroutines that require the utmost performance may be implemented in the class definition, allowing for potential compiler inlining. Long calculations and polymorphic functions that may be less time critical or rely on the runtime virtual mechanism (Sect. 4.4) should generally be localized in the source file corresponding to the class definition.

1.4   Members

The led class has a member function called toggle(). In particular,

```
void toggle() const
{
  // Toggle the LED.
  *reinterpret_cast<volatile bval_type*>(port)
    ^= bval;
}
```

The toggle() function is responsible for toggling the LED from off to on and vice versa. The toggling of the port pin is carried out with bit manipulation through direct memory access. This, as well as C++'s templated **reinterpret_cast**() operator, will be described in greater detail in Sect. 1.10.

The trailing **const** qualifier means that toggle() is a *constant* member function. A constant member function can not alter the state of any class member variables. A constant function can, however, modify variables qualified with the **mutable** keyword. Here, mutable means capable of being changed. Class member functions that modify member variables should generally be non-constant, see Sect. 4.9.

The led class also has two private constant member variables (data members). These are port and bval. In particular,

```
private:
  const port_type port;
  const bval_type bval;
```

Once set, the value of a constant class data member can not be modified. So after port and bval are set, they retain their values for the lifetime of the class instance. The variable port represents the LED's port address and the variable bval stores the numerical value corresponding to the pin position of the LED on the port.

Both member variables, port as well as bval, have the underlying type of std::uint8_t, which is itself type defined from the built-in type **unsigned char**. For the sake of convenience and intuitive legibility, the types of port and bval have been declared as class-local types using **typedef** statements. The suggestive names port_type and bval_type (as in *bit-value* type) are used.

In C++, members of a class type have one of three *access controls*. These are public, private or protected, whereby protected access has not been used yet. For example,

```
class led
{
public:
  // ...

protected:
  // ...

private:
  // ...
};
```

The public members of a class constitute its user interface because they can be accessed by any part of the program. Private members can only be accessed by the class itself and its *friends*. Class friends are described in Sect. 4.11. Private members make it possible to hide selected data and implementation details when desired. Protected members are useful for code re-use via *inheritance* in class hierarchies (Sect. 4.3). Class inheritance is also subject to access control.

Some C++ programming guidelines recommend ordering the appearance of class members according to access control. Public members should appear first because users of a class type are most interested in the public interface. Protected members should come second because authors of derived classes are also interested in the protected interface. Private members should come last because they are only of interest to the class author.

If left unspecified, the default levels of member access and inheritance are private for classes and public for structures and unions. This is the only non-stylistic difference between classes and structures in C++. Some C++ guidelines do, however, recommend exclusively using classes for objects having member functions and restricting the use of structs to more simple *data* structures that only have data members and possibly a trivial constructor.

1.5   Objects and Instances

A class type is an *object* that represents an actual thing or concept that can be manipulated as a cohesive entity. An *instance* is an occurrence of a class type. A class defines how instances of it behave. In object-oriented programming, *object* is often used interchangeably with *instance of a class*.

In the LED program, led_b5 is an instance of the led class. In other words,

```
const led led_b5
{
  mcal::reg::portb,
  mcal::reg::bval5
};
```

The parameters in the constructor of led_b5 use C++'s *uniform initialization syntax* (Sect. A.2). This convenient braced initialization syntax allows for uniform initialization of, well, *anything* including built-in types, class types, STL containers and C-style arrays alike. Uniform initialization was introduced with C++11.

Here, led_b5 is a constant object that will not be modified for the entire lifetime of the program. As such, it is declared using the **const** keyword. Furthermore, led_b5 is created using constant register values contained in a user-defined namespace called mcal::reg. When the register addresses are resolved, the code of led_b5's constructor is equivalent to the following.

```
const led led_b5
{
  0x25, // The address of portb.
  0x20  // The bit-value of portb.5 (1 << 5).
};
```

The LED D1 on our target with the 8–bit microcontroller is connected to portb.5 on the microcontroller. When the constructor code of led_b5 is executed, the physical address of portb (0x25) is stored in the port member and the pin's bit value (0x20) is stored in the bval member.

Since `led_b5` is a static instance, its constructor requires initialization code that needs to execute before the object is used in `main()`. The compiler takes care of this by automatically generating an internal subroutine for `led_b5`'s constructor that is called from a mechanism in the so-called *startup code*. The startup code executes before the jump to `main()`, ensuring that `led_b5` will be properly initialized before it is used. See Chap. 8 for more information on startup code.

The `led_b5` instance is toggled by calling its `toggle()` member function in the `for(;;)`-loop in `main()`. In particular,

```
led_b5.toggle();
```

Notice, in the way `toggle()` is called, how `led_b5` really does behave like an encapsulated object in the sense of object-oriented programming, see Chap. 4. The toggling is also carried out in real-time on our target with the 8–bit microcontroller, as we will see when we build, flash and run the LED program in Chap. 2.

1.6 #include

Files such as library files or user-defined header files can be included in another file with the **#include** syntax. For example,

```
#include <cstdint>
#include "mcal_reg.h"
```

With these two lines, the standard library header file `<cstdint>` and a project-specific header file called `"mcal_reg.h"` are included in the LED program. Here, the acronym "MCAL" stands for *microcontroller abstraction layer*, inspired by the AUTOSAR [1] software architecture from the Automotive industry. The MCAL directly interfaces with the microcontroller peripherals, and we will be using it in various parts of this book.

Path information uses dots and forward slashes in the *nix-way. In addition to forward slash, C++ compilers also understand backward slash. It is even possible mix forward and backward slash in the same **#include** line. Forward slash, however, is considered standard in C++ and should be used consistently throughout the project.

The C++ compiler has its own specific collection of default include paths including, among others, the location of the standard library headers. It is also possible to add other directories to the compiler's search path using command line options in order to improve coding ease and portability. Angled brackets (<...>) should be used for files that are in the compiler's default include paths. Quotation marks ("...") should delimit the names of user-defined include files that are not in the compiler's default include paths.

1.7 Namespaces

A *namespace* is a collection of related symbol names. For example, the symbols in the C++ standard library are contained in the namespace std. In particular,

```
namespace std
{
  typedef unsigned char uint8_t;

  // Lots of other standard library stuff
  // in lots of files.
  // ...
}
```

Namespaces can be used to create unique names for symbols by adding additional naming information. For instance,

```
namespace this_space
{
  const int version = 1;
}

namespace another_space
{
  const int version = 3;
}
```

In this case, there are two versions of version in individual namespaces occurring in the same file-level scope. However, since the two versions of version are in different namespaces, they are unique. In particular, this_space::version and another_space::version are distinct. There would be a naming conflict if namespaces were not used. The scope resolution operator (::) is used to resolve symbols in namespaces.

The LED program presents another example of a namespace, this time using an unnamed namespace.

```
namespace
{
  const led led_b5
  {
    // ...
  };
}
```

A unnamed namespace is called an *anonymous* namespace. An anonymous namespace limits the scope of anything within itself to file-level. A file-local anonymous namespace guarantees unique names for otherwise same-named symbols occurring in different files. The anonymous namespace is considered superior to C-style **static**. The anonymous namespace is the preferred mechanism for file-level scope localization and reduction of naming ambiguity in C++ projects.

An optional **using** directive may be used to eliminate the necessity to type the namespace prefix. For example,

```
using namespace std;
```

When the "**using namespace** std" directive is present, the code beneath it can use all the symbols in the namespace std without explicitly typing the std prefix and scope resolution operator. In particular,

```
#include <cstdint>

using namespace std;

uint8_t my_u8; // No need for std:: with uint8_t
```

It is also possible to inject individual symbols from a named namespace into the global namespace by using a **using** directive for only that symbol. For example,

```
#include <cstdint>

using std::uint8_t;

uint8_t my_u8; // No need for std:: with uint8_t
```

In this book, however, we generally do not use the **using** directive. We thereby prefer clarity over terseness in style.

1.8   C++ Standard Library

The namespace std contains all the symbols in the C++ *standard library*. The standard library is a vast collection of types, functions and classes that is an essential part of the C++ language. The standard library also contains an extensive set of generic containers and algorithms called the *standard template library* (STL). In this book, we will make considerable use of the C++ standard library and the STL part of it. See Sects. 5.8, and A.6–A.8.

The LED program uses the C++ standard library for std::uint8_t, one of several available fixed-size integer types. Readers familiar with the C99 specification of the C language [2] might have experience with <stdint.h>. This C library file defines identical fixed-size integer types, but in the global namespace. Using C++'s fixed-size integer types can improve portability because potentially non-portable user-defined types such as, say, my_uint8 or my_uint16 no longer need to be defined manually and managed with potentially hard-to-read preprocessor switches. See Sects. 3.2 and 6.10 for additional details on fixed-size integer types.

1.9   The main() Subroutine

The work of the LED program takes place in the main() subroutine. In particular,

```
int main()
{
  for(;;)
  {
    led_b5.toggle();
  }
}
```

Every C++ program is required to have one and only one implementation of main(). In C++, the return type of main() is plain integer, in other words **signed int**. When we just write **int** in C++, we mean **signed int** because the default for integral types if left blank is **signed**, unless explicitly declared as **unsigned**.

The main() subroutine in the LED program lacks an explicit return code. The C++ compiler can automatically generate the return code for main() if needed. If the compiler does generate a return value for main(), its type is **signed int** and its value is zero. The implicit generation of code to return a value is specific to the main() subroutine. Other subroutines which return any type other than **void** must supply explicit return code.

The `main()` subroutine is called from the startup code after the standard initialization mechanisms for RAM and static constructors have been carried out, see Chap. 8.

Two portable definitions of `main()` are allowed according to the C++ standard (Sect. 3.6.1 in [3]):

```
int main()
{
  // ...
}
```

and

```
int main(int argc, char* argv[])
{
  // ...
}
```

The second form is used when program arguments are passed to `main()`. For our embedded microcontroller programs, no arguments are passed to `main()` and the first form is used.

1.10 Low-Level Register Access

Microcontroller programming in C++ requires low-level register access. For example, both the constructor as well as the `toggle()` function of the `led` class manipulate registers via direct memory access to control the LED hardware. See Chap. 7 for further discussions of register manipulation.

In particular, `led`'s member function `toggle()` is responsible for toggling the LED.

```
void toggle() const
{
  // Toggle the LED.
  *reinterpret_cast<volatile bval_type*>(port)
    ^= bval;
}
```

The templated cast operator **reinterpret_cast()** is one of four specialized cast operators available in C++. See Sect. A.1 for a description of C++ cast operators. The **reinterpret_cast()** operator is the one that is designed for casting integral types to pointers and back. Readers familiar with low-level register access in C might find the following equivalence example helpful.

```
// C++ register access.
*reinterpret_cast<volatile bval_type*>(port)
  ^= bval;

// Equivalent C-style.
*((volatile bval_type*) port) ^= bval;
```

1.11   Compile-Time Constant

In the LED program, registers are defined with C++'s generalized constant expression syntax using the **constexpr** keyword. In particular,

```
namespace mcal
{
  // Compile-time constant register addresses.
  namespace reg
  {
    // The address of portb.
    constexpr std::uint8_t portb = 0x25U;

    // The values of bit0 through bit7.
    constexpr std::uint8_t bval0 = 1U;
    constexpr std::uint8_t bval1 = 1U << 1U;
    constexpr std::uint8_t bval2 = 1U << 2U;
    constexpr std::uint8_t bval3 = 1U << 3U;
    constexpr std::uint8_t bval4 = 1U << 4U;
    constexpr std::uint8_t bval5 = 1U << 5U;
    constexpr std::uint8_t bval6 = 1U << 6U;
    constexpr std::uint8_t bval7 = 1U << 7U;
  }
}
```

A generalized constant expression, denoted with the keyword **constexpr**, is guaranteed to be a compile-time constant. In general, using **constexpr** is considered superior to the preprocessor **#define** because generalized constant expressions have clearly defined type information. See Sect. 3.8 for more information on **constexpr** and generalized constant expressions, and also Sect. 7.1 for additional details on register addresses.

An alternative for ensuring that an integral value is a compile-time constant is with a static constant member of a class type. There will be more on static constant integral class members in Sect. 4.10.

Using compile-time constants almost always facilitates optimization in C++. As mentioned previously in Sect. 1.5, for example, led_b5's constructor code is equivalent the following.

```
const led led_b5
{
  0x25, // Address of portb.
  0x20  // Bit-value of portb.5.
};
```

Since the constructor's parameters are compile-time constants, the compiler can directly initialize led_b5's member variables without using the stack or intermediate CPU registers. This efficient kind of optimization is known as *constant folding*, and is often useful in real-time C++ programming. Section 2.6 describes methods for improving performance even further by combining constant folding with C++ templates.

References

1. AUTOSAR, *Automotive Open System Architecture* (2012), http://www.autosar.org
2. ISO/IEC, *ISO/IEC 9899:1999: Programming languages—C* (International Organization for Standardization, Geneva, 1999)
3. ISO/IEC, *ISO/IEC 14882:2011: Information technology—Programming languages—C++* (International Organization for Standardization, Geneva, 2011)
4. S. Meyers, *Effective C++: 55 Specific Ways to Improve Your Programs and Designs*, 3rd edn. (Addison Wesley, Reading, 2005)

Chapter 2
Working with a Real-Time C++ Program on a Board

This chapter presents a complete example of building, flashing and executing a microcontroller C++ program using the LED program. The LED program will be built with GCC cross tools in the MinGW/MSYS [5] environment. Our target microcontroller is an 8–bit ATMEL® AVR® microcontroller [2]. This popular microcontroller has state-of-the-art quality and widespread availability. In addition, there is a well-maintained GCC port for this microcontroller making it well-suited for our example. In the second half of this chapter, we will investigate efficiency aspects and compiler warnings and errors based on the example of the LED program.

2.1 The Target Hardware

Our target hardware is shown in Fig. 2.1. It is a single-chip microcontroller circuit that has been hand-built on a solderless prototyping breadboard. This board uses an 8–bit ATMEL® AVR® microcontroller [2], featuring 32 kB of program code, 2 kB of RAM and 1 kB of EEPROM. The microcontroller is clocked with an external quartz at 16 MHz. The schematic for the circuit of our target hardware and details about building it with discrete components on a solderless prototyping breadboard are given in Appendix D.

Our target hardware uses the same microcontroller and LED port pin as the well-known and versatile ARDUINO® open source project [1, 9]. In addition, an ARDUINO® or an ARDUINO®–compatible board can optionally be used for the exercises in this chapter. Note, though, that our target hardware is not fully ARDUINO® compatible because it lacks the circuitry for the serial UART communication interface that the ARDUINO® uses for communication with its bootloader.

C.M. Kormanyos, *Real-Time C++*, DOI 10.1007/978-3-642-34688-0_2,
© Springer-Verlag Berlin Heidelberg 2013

Fig. 2.1 Our target system built with discrete components on a breadboard is shown

2.2 Build and Flash the LED Program

The workflow for building and flashing a C++ program is shown in Fig. 2.2. The main steps include compiling the sources, linking the object files, extracting the HEX-file and flashing it in the microcontroller. We will build the LED program according to the workflow in Fig. 2.2. We will use traditional *nix-style commands within the MinGW/MSYS [5] environment.[1]

Here, we assume that the GNU GCC cross compiler has been built and installed, and that its path has been added to the PATH variable in the MinGW/MSYS command shell. See Appendix C for details on building and installing a GNU GCC cross compiler.

We will now compile the LED program. The LED program is stored in the file led.cpp in the chapter02_02 directory of the companion code. Navigate to the chapter02_02 directory in the MinGW/MSYS command shell. Identify the source file led.cpp. It can be compiled with the following command:

```
avr-unknown-elf-g++ -mmcu=atmega328p -O3 \
-std=c++0x -I. -c led.cpp -o led.o
```

---

[1] There are tools and methods available for building microcontroller C++ projects. In addition to traditional *nix-style commands, other popular build facilities include GNUmake [3], the Python programming language [8] and SCons [10]. Furthermore, a variety of both cost-free as well as commercial GUIs are available for project management and build.

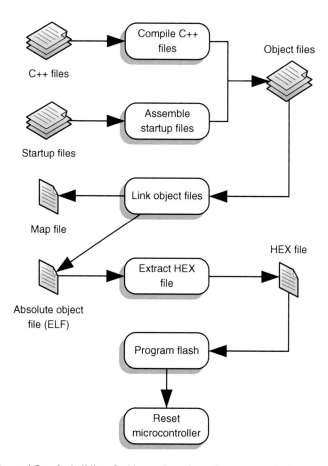

Fig. 2.2 The workflow for building, flashing and running a C++ program is shown

Here, the backslash is used to separate the long command onto two lines. It is not part of the command.

This command means:

- Invoke the cross compiler `avr-unknown-elf-g++` as a C++ compiler. Here, we use the decorated name of `g++` specially built for our target with the 8–bit microcontroller.
- Select the microcontroller architecture with the `-mmcu=atmega328p` flag.
- Use level 3 optimization with the `-O3` flag.
- Use the C++11 language standard with the `-std=c++0x` flag.[2]

---

[2]With GCC version 4.7 or later, the newer flag `-std=c++11` can be used to select the C++11 language standard.

- Include the current directory in the compiler's default include path with the `-I .` flag. This is needed for finding the self-written header file `<cstdint>` present in the `chapter02_02` directory itself.
- Compile `led.cpp` using `-c led.cpp -o led.o`. This produces the object file `led.o`.

We will now link the LED program to create an absolute object file. The precompiled startup code in `crt0.o` will also be linked with `led.o` to create the absolute object file `led.elf`.

In the `chapter02_02` directory, link `led.o` and `crt0.o` with the following command:

```
avr-unknown-elf-g++ -mmcu=atmega328p \
-nostartfiles -Wl,-Tavr.ld,-Map,led.map \
led.o crt0.o -o led.elf
```

This command means:

- Invoke the cross compiler `avr-unknown-elf-g++` as a linker. Here, again, we use the decorated name of `g++` specially built for our target with the 8–bit microcontroller (Appendix C).
- Select the microcontroller architecture with the `-mmcu=atmega328p` flag.
- Use the `-nostartfiles` flag to prevent the linker from linking with the compiler's own startup files. We have provided our own startup code in `crt0.o`.
- Use the memory definitions in the linker input file `avr.ld` and create an output memory map file `led.map` with the flags `-Wl,-Tavr.ld,-Map,led.map`.
- Link the two object files `led.o` and `crt0.o` together to create the absolute object file `led.elf` using `led.o crt0.o -o led.elf`. The absolute object file is in ELF binary format, the Executable and Linkable Format [12].

We will now extract the HEX-file from the absolute object file using the program `objcopy`. In the `chapter02_02` directory, extract the HEX-file `led.hex` with:

```
avr-unknown-elf-objcopy -O ihex led.elf led.hex
```

This command means:

- Invoke object copy `avr-unknown-elf-objcopy`. Here, again, we use the decorated name of the `objcopy` program in the binary utilities that have been specially built for our target with the 8–bit microcontroller (Appendix C).
- Create an output HEX-file in a well-known 16–bit text-based hexadecimal file format with the `-O ihex` flags.
- With the part of the command `led.elf led.hex`, extract `led.hex` from `led.elf`.

We should now have the HEX-file `led.hex` that contains the executable code of the LED program. It is a short, text-based HEX-file that should be similar to the one shown in the listing below.

```
:100000000E940300400011241FBEC0E0D8E0DEBF04
```

```
:10001000CDBF0E9412000E941E000E9427000E9475
:100020003700FFCF11E0A0E0B1E0E2E9F0E002C06C
:1000300005900D92A030B107D9F7089511E0A2E024
:10004000B1E001C01D92A230B107E1F7089510E0C0
:10005000C6E0D0E004C02297FE010E943300C43005
:10006000D107C9F708950590F491E02D0994E09126
:100070000001F0E090910101808189278083FCCF0D
:1000800085E28093000180E2809301012D98259AFA
:020090000895D1
:00000001FF
```

This executable HEX-file file can be flashed into the microcontroller's program
FLASH memory using any of several available free and commercial tools. The
instructions in the chapter02_02 directory show how to flash the HEX-file using
a commercially available JTAG [4] SPI^{TM} flash tool.

Users of the ARDUINO® should, however, note that the bootloader that
comes pre-programmed in the ARDUINO® will be erased when we flash the
LED program. If needed for development in the ARDUINO® environment, the
ARDUINO® bootloader can be re-flashed [1].

When the LED program is executed, the LED D1 should light up because it will
be toggling. The toggling will, however, be extremely rapid, with a frequency of
approximately 2 MHz. This is far too fast for the human eye to resolve. Toggling
can be viewed with a digital oscilloscope if available. Alternatively, the toggling
frequency can be reduced using a delay loop or a timer, as shown in the following
section.

2.3 Adding Timing for Visible LED Toggling

As mentioned above, the LED program toggles the LED too quickly to observe.
Therefore, we will slow down the toggling in another version of the LED program
that uses timing. This version of the program is included in the chapter02_03
project of the companion code and it is partially listed below.

```
// The LED program with timing.

#include <cstdint>
#include <util/utility/util_time.h>
#include <mcal/mcal.h>

class led
{
  // ...
};
namespace
```

```
{
  // Define a convenient local 16-bit timer type.
  typedef util::timer<std::uint16_t> timer_type;

  // Create led_b5 at port B, bit position 5.
  const led led_b5
  {
    mcal::reg::portb,
    mcal::reg::bval5
  };
}

int main()
{
  // Enable all global interrupts.
  mcal::irq::enable_all();

  // Initialize the mcal.
  mcal::init();

  // Toggle led_b5 forever with a 1s delay (0.5Hz).
  for(;;)
  {
    led_b5.toggle();

    // Wait 1s in a blocking delay.
    timer_type::blocking_delay(timer_type::seconds(1));
  }
}
```

The major change here is the inclusion of a 1 s blocking delay following the LED toggle(). In particular, in main(),

```
// Toggle led_b5 forever with a 1s delay (0.5Hz).
for(;;)
{
  led_b5.toggle();

  // Wait 1s in a blocking delay.
  timer_type::blocking_delay(timer_type::seconds(1U));
}
```

This reduces the LED toggling frequency to $1/2$ Hz, allowing the toggling to be observed with the human eye. Of course, multitasking methods (Chap. 11) should be used rather than a 1 s blocking delay. A 1 s blocking delay is done here solely for the example of visible LED toggling, not as a real-world design suggestion.

In order to include timing, we have included more software components. In particular, we have included a timer utility header file `util_time.h` and simplified the code with a convenient **typedef** for a `timer_type`. See Sects. 6.9 and 15.3. We have also initialized a small MCAL in order to create a system-tick, as described in Sect. 9.3.

Try to build, flash and run the LED program with timing in the way previously described for the original LED program. This should result in a program that has visually pleasing LED toggling with a frequency of $1/2$ Hz.

2.4   Run and Reset the LED Program

After the program has been flashed, it stays in flash memory even when the board is powered off and disconnected from the PC or any other electrical supply. When the board is supplied with power, the microcontroller boots and program execution begins. It should not be necessary to push the reset button or do anything else other than simply plug in the power jack.

It may seem remarkable how quickly the microcontroller boots. It only requires a few milliseconds for the target system to boot and work through the startup code (Chap. 8). As a result, the LED will seem to start toggling essentially immediately after power-up.

The program can also be manually reset anytime while it is running using the *reset* button on the board. A photograph depicting the microcontroller reset button on our target system is shown in Fig. 2.3. The reset button gives the microcontroller an electrical soft-boot signal. This results in immediate program reset and subsequent execution of the startup code, etc. just like normal power-up.

It may be helpful to become familiar with both power-on reset using the power jack as well as soft reset using the manual reset button on the board. Try each one out a few times and make sure everything is working as expected.

2.5   Recognizing and Handling Errors and Warnings

Properly handling errors and warnings is an essential part of learning the C++ language. If a mistake in typing or syntax is present in the code, the compiler will report an *error* upon the attempted compilation of it.

We will now provoke an error in order to experience how this works. Consider typing some nonsensical characters such as "asdf" in one of the blank lines of led.cpp in the LED program from Sect. 1.1. For example,

Fig. 2.3 Pointing toward the reset button on our target board is shown

---

```cpp
// The LED program.

#include <cstdint>
#include "mcal_reg.h"
asdf
class led
{
  // ...
};

// ...
```

The led.cpp file now contains an error. If we save the faulty file and try to compile it, GCC will report an error message similar to the one shown below.

```
led.cpp:5:1: error: 'asdf' does not name a type
```

It is easy to interpret the error message within the context of the offending code. The compiler reports an error in line 5 at column 1 of led.cpp.

In addition to errors, the compiler can issue *warnings*. A warning indicates that the compiler has encountered ambiguous code. Warnings should be taken seriously and corrected because the compiler is reporting a potentially false interpretation of the code.

We will now provoke a warning. Consider removing the "**int**" part of the code preceding main() in led.cpp. For instance,

```
// ...

main()
{
   // ..
}
```

When compiling this code with the -pedantic warning option (see below),
GCC issues the following warning.

```
led.cpp(50) :6: warning: ISO C++ forbids declaration
   of 'main' with no type [-pedantic]
```

Here, GCC is warning that the subroutine main() has been declared with no
type. The warning is in line 50 at the beginning of column 6, whereby the beginning
of column 6 is in the middle of the parentheses of the declaration of main().

For GCC, the warning options shown below result in a depth of warning that can
be appropriate for most C++ projects.[3]

```
-Wall -Wextra -pedantic
```

This means:

- Report warnings for *all* normal issues.
- Also report *extra* warnings.
- Issue warnings in a *pedantic* fashion regarding ISO C++ adherence.

Another useful warning option is -Weffc++, which warns about failure to
conform with certain guidelines in Meyers' well-known books [6, 7].

When the compiler encounters one or more warnings, it nonetheless completes
compilation. The warning option -Werror can be used to treat all warnings as
errors, thereby stopping compilation upon warning (well, now an error).

The error and warning messages shown previously are easy to understand. Error
and warning messages can, however, become quite verbose including long symbol
names and recursive file references. This can complicate tracing the origin of the
offending code. In particular, it can be difficult to properly decipher error and
warning messages originating from C++ templates. With a little practice, though,
properly interpreting error and warning messages becomes routine.

Error and warning messages in C++ can be of immense help when trying to
diagnose coding problems. Using a high warning level will also improve the overall
quality of the code.

---

[3]See [11], Chap. 1 in section "Exploring C Warning Messages" and also Appendix A for
comprehensive information on GCC's warning options.

2.6   Reaching the Right Efficiency

C++ is a rich language with powerful features, giving vast control over the implementation details. In order to effectively program microcontrollers in C++, then, developers need to make insightful and sensible design choices.

When considering the `led` class in the LED program of Chap. 1, for example, an experienced microcontroller programmer might be thinking, *That class has a lot of overhead for simply toggling an LED! It may be a poor design choice.*

This astute observation would, in fact, be correct in this particular case. Indeed, the storage requirement alone for `led`'s member variables is at least 2 bytes, possibly even 4 bytes or 8. Depending on the CPU architecture and the memory alignment characteristics of the compiler. Add to this the overhead of a potentially non-inlined call to the `toggle()` function, and the `led` class may be excessively bulky for its modest functionality.

C++ *templates* can be used to remedy this situation. A C++ template is a function or class that can have parameters of different types. See Chap. 5 for more information on C++ templates.

We will now convert the `led` class to a template class. In particular,

```cpp
template<typename port_type,
         typename bval_type,
         const port_type port,
         const bval_type bval>
class led_template
{
public:
  led_template()
  {
    // Set the port pin value to low.
    *reinterpret_cast<volatile bval_type*>(port)
      &= static_cast<bval_type>(~bval);

    // Set the port pin direction to output.
    *reinterpret_cast<volatile bval_type*>(pdir)
      |= bval;
  }

  static void toggle()
  {
    // Toggle the LED.
    *reinterpret_cast<volatile bval_type*>(port)
      ^= bval;
  }
```

```
private:
  static constexpr port_type pdir = port - 1U;
};
```

In the led_template class, the types and member variables present in the original led class have been replaced with *template parameters*. This remarkable method profoundly improves efficiency because template parameters and their corresponding code are entities known at compile time. Templates can improve efficiency and reduce potentially redundant code by providing *scalability*. In this sense, templates offer high performance and strong *generic* character. We will discuss template programming in greater depth in Chap. 5.

Using the led_template class in code is straightforward. For example,

```
namespace
{
  // Create led_b5 at port B, bit position 5.
  const led_template<std::uint8_t,
                     std::uint8_t,
                     mcal::reg::portb,
                     mcal::reg::bval5> led_b5;
}

int main()
{
  // Toggle led_b5 forever.
  for(;;)
  {
    led_b5.toggle();
  }
}
```

In this version of main(), the template instance of led_b5 is used in exactly the same fashion as the non-template instance has been used previously in Sect. 1.1. We see that template classes can also be used to encapsulate objects. It can take a bit of trial-and-error to get accustomed with the syntax of templates and find stylistically appealing ways to write them in code. These issues can, however, readily be resolved with a bit of practice.

This version of the LED program is available in the companion code for Chap. 2. We can build this template version of the program for our target with the 8–bit microcontroller and create an *assembly listing* for the led.cpp file (Sect. 6.4). The assembly listing reveals that the efficiency of the led_template class approaches that of hand-programmed assembler. Remarkably, though, we are programming with a C++ class that utilizes the benefits of object-oriented design and data encapsulation.

Table 2.1 The resources required for led.cpp for both the template as well as the non-template versions of the LED program are shown

Class version	Code size main() (byte)	RAM size led_b5 (byte)	Runtime for(;;) -loop (μs)
Non-template	36	2	0.44
Template	16	0	0.31

We will now investigate how the efficiency and resource consumption of the template version of the LED program compare with those of the non-template version. The storage requirement of the led_template class have been reduced because the member variables port and bval have been replaced by template parameters that are compile-time constants. These template parameters can be eliminated at compile time via constant folding. In addition, the toggle() function has been made **static**. This potentially reduces the call overhead when servicing the toggle() member.

As shown in Table 2.1, the template version of the program is both smaller *and* faster than the non-template one. It is somewhat remarkable, but not uncommon, that template-based design decreases memory consumption while simultaneously improving performance.

Selecting a template or a non-template LED class is an example of a typical design choice in microcontroller C++ programming. Although this is just one small example from infinitely many potential design choices, it does show how decisions about design and implementation can crucially impact efficiency.

References

1. ARDUINO®, *ARDUINO®* (2012), http://www.arduino.cc
2. ATMEL®, *8-bit ATMEL® Microcontroller with 4/8/16/32K Bytes In-System Programmable Flash (ATmega48A, ATmega48PA, ATmega88A, ATmega88PA, ATmega168A, ATmega168PA, ATmega328, ATmega328P)*, Rev. 8271D–AVR–05/11 (ATMEL®, 2011)
3. Free Software Foundation, *GNUmake Version 3.81* (2006), http://www.gnu.org/software/make
4. IEEE Computer Society, *IEEE Std 1149.1—1990: IEEE Standard Test Access Port and Boundary-Scan Architecture* (1990), available at http://standards.ieee.org/findstds/standard/1149.1-1990.html
5. MinGW, *Minimalist GNU* (2012), http://www.mingw.org
6. S. Meyers, *More Effective C++: 35 New Ways to Improve Your Programs and Designs* (Addison Wesley, Reading, 1996)
7. S. Meyers, *Effective C++: 55 Specific Ways to Improve Your Programs and Designs*, 3rd edn. (Addison Wesley, Reading, 2005)
8. Python Software Foundation, *Python Programming Language—Official Website* (2012), http://www.python.org
9. M. Schmidt, *ARDUINO®: A Quick-Start Guide* (Pragmatic Programmers, Raleigh, 2011)

10. SCons, *SCons: A Software Construction Tool* (2012), http://www.scons.org
11. W. van Hagen, *The Definitive Guide to GCC* (Apress, Berkeley, 2006)
12. Wikipedia, *Executable and Linkable Format* (2012), http://en.wikipedia.org/wiki/Executable_and_Linkable_Format

Chapter 3
An Easy Jump-Start in Real-Time C++

Developers new to real-time C++ may want to obtain some useful results quickly before taking the time to master all the intricate details of the C++ language. This chapter addresses this desire by presenting a simple, yet effective, subset of the C++ language specifically designed for those seeking a lightweight and reliable jump-start in real-time C++. The C++ subset in this chapter represents a judicious selection of some of the most easy-to-do things in C++ that can potentially be used in the widest possible range of programming situations. The strategy of this C++ subset is shown in Fig. 3.1.

3.1 Declare Locals when Used

In C++, local variables can be declared where they are first used. They do not necessarily need to be bound to the opening curly brace of a scope. This can improve code readability and facilitate compiler optimization.

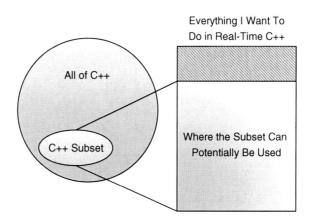

Fig. 3.1 The sketch shows how a small subset of C++ can potentially be used for a wide variety of programming situations

C.M. Kormanyos, *Real-Time C++*, DOI 10.1007/978-3-642-34688-0__3,
© Springer-Verlag Berlin Heidelberg 2013

The code below, for example, conveniently declares integral variables i, j and k near where they are first used in the subroutine.

```cpp
void initialize();
void use_i(const int);
void use_j(const int);
void use_k(const int);

void do_something()
{
  // Initialize someting.
  initialize();

  // Declare i when using it in use_i().
  const int i = 3;
  use_i(i);

  // Declare j when using it in use_j().
  const int j = 7;
  use_j(j);

  // Declare k in the scope of the for-loop.
  for(int k = 0; k < 10; ++j)
  {
    use_k(k);
  }
}
```

3.2 Fixed-Size Integer Types

The C++ standard library has a complete set of portable fixed-size integer types in its <cstdint> library. User-defined types can potentially be clumsy and hard-to-maintain. They can be replaced with standard fixed-size integer types such as std::uint8_t, std::uint16_t, etc. Fixed-size integer types were first introduced briefly in Sect. 1.8.

The code below, for instance, uses variables that have different kinds of fixed-sizes with 8, 16 and 32 bits.

```cpp
#include <cstdint>

// This has exactly 16-bits.
constexpr std::uint16_t value_exact_16 = 0xABCDU;
```

```cpp
// This has at least 32-bits.
constexpr std::uint_least32_t value_at_least32 =
  0xFFFFFFFFUL;

void do_something()
{
  // Use the fastest integer with at least 8-bits.
  for(std::uint_fast8_t i = 0U; i < 10U; ++i)
  {
    // Do something with i.
    // ...
  }
}
```

3.3 The bool Type

C++ includes a built-in Boolean type **bool** that has two and only two possible values, **true** and **false**. In C++, the result of a Boolean test has the type **bool** and its value is either **true** or **false**. Using C++'s built-in Boolean type can improve the clarity of logic and simplify coding.

The code below, for instance, uses C++'s built-in Boolean type **bool** in logical statements.

```cpp
bool valid();
bool login();
void start_session();

void do_something()
{
  // This Boolean test yields true or false.
  const bool session_is_ok = (valid() && login());

  // This tests if session_is_ok == true.
  if(session_is_ok)
  {
    start_session();
  }
}
```

3.4 Organization with Namespaces

C++ supports namespaces. Namespaces can be used for improving program organization and code readability. Namespaces can optionally be employed to correspond to different parts or functional groups of the software. Namespaces were first introduced in Sect. 1.7.

The code below, for example, uses C++ namespaces to organize several parts of the MCAL in the software architecture (Sect. B.2).

```
// Namespace for the microcontroller abstraction layer.
namespace mcal
{
  // The mcal initialization.
  void init();

  // The general purpose timer stuff in the mcal.
  namespace gpt
  {
    void init();
    std::uint32_t get_time_elapsed();
  }

  // The ADC stuff in the mcal.
  namespace adc
  {
    void init();
    std::uint16_t read_value(const unsigned);
  }
}

// Initialize the mcal.
// Note the clean organization with namespaces.
void mcal::init()
{
  mcal::gpt::init();
  mcal::adc::init();
}
```

An unnamed namespace (i.e., an anonymous namespace) can be used for file-level localization. For example,

```
namespace
{
  unsigned local_counter;
}
```

3.5 Basic Classes

It is not difficult to start working with class types in C++. As a first step, simple C-style structures can be replaced with C++ classes or structures having just a constructor, a few data members and possibly some simple functions. To keep things easy at first, it may be preferable to avoid using inheritance and runtime polymorphism. One can, and really should, use these powerful object-oriented features when confident enough to do so to make full use of C++. Additional information on classes and object-oriented programming can be found in Chap. 4.

The class below, for instance, encapsulates an unsigned integer coordinate point in two-dimensional Cartesian space $\mathbb{R}^2$.

```
#include <cstdint>

// An unsigned xy-coordinate point with some geometry.
class point
{
public:
  std::uint8_t x;
  std::uint8_t y;

  point(const std::uint8 x_ = 0U,
        const std::uint8 y_ = 0U) : x(x_), y(y_) { }

  std::uint16_t squared_euclidean_distance() const
  {
    // Squared Euclidean distance from the origin.
    const std::uint16_t x2 = std::uint16_t(x) * x;
    const std::uint16_t y2 = std::uint16_t(y) * y;

    return x2 + y2;
  }
};

point p1;
```

```
point p2 { 31U, 47U };

// The distance d1 is 0.
std::uint16_t d1 = p1.squared_euclidean_distance();

// The distance d2 is 3,170.
std::uint16_t d2 = p2.squared_euclidean_distance();
```

3.6 Basic Templates

C++ templates use the same code for different types. Templates can reduce the
effort for code upkeep and eliminate redundant sources of error. C++ templates
also allow for *scalability*. When beginning with templates, it may be preferable to
keep template depth and subroutine complexity low. C++ templates are described in
detail in Chap. 5.

The code below, for instance, implements a template subroutine for computing
the sum of two objects.

```
template<typename T>
T add(const T& a, const T& b)
{
  return a + b;
}
```

The class below, for instance, implements an xy-coordinate `point` similar to
the one shown in the previous section, but as a template class.

```
#include <cstdint>

// Template version of the x-y point class.

template<typename short_type,
         typename long_type>
class point
{
public:
  short_type x;
  short_type y;

  point(const short_type& x = short_type(0),
        const short_type& y = short_type(0)) : x(x_),
                                               y(y_)
```

```
  {
  }

  long_type squared_euclidean_distance() const
  {
    // Squared Euclidean distance from the origin.
    const long_type x2 = long_type(x) * x;
    const long_type y2 = long_type(y) * y;

    return x2 + y2;
  }
};

point<std::int16_t, std::int32_t> p
{
  -2129U,
   5471U
};

std::int32_t d = p.squared_euclidean_distance();
// 11,647,759
```

3.7 nullptr Replaces NULL

C++ offers the **nullptr** keyword. The **nullptr** keyword eliminates the need for redundant and potentially conflicting definitions of NULL.

The code below uses the **nullptr** keyword to test if a pointer to some object, a something*, is non-zero.

```
class something
{
public:
  something() { }
};

namespace
{
  // Default initialized to nullptr (i.e., 0).
  something* ps;
}
```

```
void do_something()
{
  // Any kind of zero pointer equals nullptr.
  if(nullptr == ps)
  {
    // Initialize ps.
    // ...
  }

  // Do something with ps.
  // ...
}
```

3.8   Generalized Constant Expressions with `constexpr`

Compile-time constants can be defined with **constexpr** or by using integral class members of type **static constexpr** or (the older) **static const**. As briefly mentioned in Sect. 1.11, constants defined this way are known at compile time and have clearly defined type information.

The **constexpr** keyword can be used with a wider variety of things than the original **const** keyword. In particular, **constexpr** can also be used to define compile-time constant floating-point values, subroutines adhering to low-complexity constraints and other objects such as std::arrays (Sect. 3.11).

The code below shows various ways to use the **constexpr** keyword to make compile-time constants.

```
#include <cstdint>
#include <array>

// A compile-time constant version number.
constexpr unsigned int version = 3U;

// A compile-time floating-point value.
constexpr float pi(3.14159265358979323846264338328F);

// A compile-time constant function (low complexity).
constexpr int three() { return 3; }

// A constant array of integers.
constexpr std::array<int, 3U> my_array
{
```

```
   { 1, 2, 3 }
};

namespace mcal
{
  struct reg
  {
    // A compile-time constant register address.
    static constexpr std::uint8_t portb = 0x25U;
  };
}
```

3.9 static_assert()

The C++ compiler can perform checks on Boolean expressions that are known at compile time using the **static_assert**() facility. There are additional details on **static_assert**() in Sect. A.4.

The code below, for instance, uses **static_assert**() to ensure that the program version is high enough. The test with **static_assert**() is performed at compile time.

```
constexpr unsigned int version = 3U;

// Print an error if version is less than 2.
static_assert(version >= 2U, "Version is too low!");
```

3.10 Using <limits>

The C++ standard library includes portable and convenient numeric limits in its <limits> header for obtaining and querying the limits of built-in types. The classes in <limits> are templates and it is also common to implement template specializations of std::numeric_limits for user-defined custom data types. The <limits> library is described further in Sect. A.5

The code below uses some members of std::numeric_limits for integral and floating-point types.

```
#include <limits>

// This is 31 on a system with 4 byte int.
// The sign bit is not included in digits.
constexpr int n_dig = std::numeric_limits<int>::digits;

// This is 2,147,483,647 if int is 4 bytes.
constexpr int n_max = std::numeric_limits<int>::max();

// Compile-time check if float conforms to IEEE-754.
static_assert(std::numeric_limits<float>::is_iec559,
              "float is not IEEE754 conforming!");
```

3.11 std::array

Perhaps the simplest STL container is std::array. In C++, std::array can be used as a drop-in replacement for C-style arrays. Since std::array is a sequential STL container, it offers the benefits of iterators, container size, compatibility with STL algorithms, etc.

The std::array container has the added benefit of size known at compile-time. The compiler can, therefore, allocate storage for an std::array where it needs to—on the stack, in static memory, on-the-fly for an std::array declared as a **constexpr**, etc. Using std::array eliminates concerns about potential memory fragmentation from dynamic memory allocation and allocators (Sect. 10.3).

The code below creates a login key consisting of three 8–bit unsigned integers.

```
#include <cstdint>
#include <array>

// A login key stored in an std::array.
constexpr std::array<std::uint8_t, 3U> login_key
{
  { 0x01U, 0x02U, 0x03U }
};
```

3.12   Basic STL Algorithms

Using STL algorithms in C++ can significantly reduce coding effort and eliminate
potential sources of error from hand-written code sequences. It is easy to get
started with a few intuitive and easy-to-use STL algorithms such as minimax
operations std::min() and std::max(), mutating sequence operations like
std::fill() and std::copy() or non-modifying sequence operations
including std::all_of(), std::for_each(), etc. See Sects. 5.8, 6.17
and A.6–A.8 for more information on STL algorithms.

The code below, for example, initializes (and re-initializes) four unsigned integral
counters in an array using the std::fill() algorithm.

```
#include <algorithm>
#include <array>
#include <cstdint>

namespace
{
  // Four counters.
  std::array<std::uint8_t, 4U> counters;
}

void do_something()
{
  // (Re-)Initialize the counters with std::fill().
  std::fill(counters.begin(),
            counters.end(),
            static_cast<std::uint8_t>(0U));

  // Do something with the counters.
  // ...
}
```

3.13   <numeric>

The STL's <numeric> library has some particularly useful algorithms for microcontroller programming including, among others, std::accumulate() and
std::inner_product() which can be used for things like checksums, vector-
matrix mathematics, etc. The functions in <numeric> can reduce code complexity
and bring the heart of the algorithm at hand into clear focus. See Sect. A.8 for further
information on <numeric>.

The example below computes the inner product of two arrays.

```
#include <array>
#include <numeric>

const std::array<int, 3U> u
{
  { 1, 2, 3 }
};

const std::array<int, 3U> v
{
  { 4, 5, 6 }
};

const int uv = std::inner_product(u.begin(),
                                  u.end(),
                                  v.begin(),
                                  0);
// The result is 32.
```

The result is $4 + 10 + 18 = 32$. Readers familiar with physics or vector mathematics might recognize this as the dot product $\mathbf{u} \cdot \mathbf{v}$ in three-dimensional Cartesian space $\mathbb{R}^3$, the result of which is a scalar.

3.14   atomic_load() and atomic_store()

The C++ standard library includes a collection of safe and portable atomic operations in its <atomic> library. The <atomic> library is large with many functions. It is, however, possible to get an easy start in the <atomic> library with two simple functions, std::atomic_load() and std::atomic_store().

The code below, for example, uses std::atomic_load() to perform a consistent read of the 32–bit system-tick on an 8-bit CPU. Here, it is assumed that system_tick is modified in a timer interrupt service routine, thereby making a consistent read via means such as std::atomic_load() mandatory.

```
#include <cstdint>
#include <atomic>

namespace
{
  // The one (and only one) 32-bit system-tick.
```

```cpp
  volatile std::uint32_t system_tick;
}

std::uint32_t get_time_elapsed()
{
  // Ensure 32-bit consistency on an 8-bit CPU.
  return std::atomic_load(&system_tick);
}
```

Chapter 4
Object-Oriented Techniques for Microcontrollers

Object-oriented programs are built from various class objects that intuitively embody the application through their actions and interrelations among each other. This chapter introduces object-oriented real-time C++ methods using classes for LEDs, PWM signal generators and communication interfaces.

4.1 Object Oriented Programming

Consider the application shown in Fig. 4.1 below.

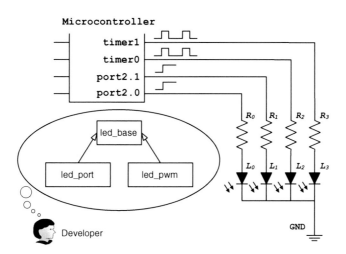

Fig. 4.1 An application with four LEDs is shown

This application has four LEDs and two peripheral timers used as pulse-width modulated (PWM) signal generators. The LEDs L0 and L1 are connected to port

C.M. Kormanyos, *Real-Time C++*, DOI 10.1007/978-3-642-34688-0_4,
© Springer-Verlag Berlin Heidelberg 2013

pins P2.0 and P2.1, respectively. These LEDs have the same circuit as the one shown previously in Chap. 1, Fig. 1.1. They are controlled with bit manipulation of the microcontroller's port P2, as introduced in the LED program of Sect. 1.1.

The LEDs L2 and L3 are connected to PWM signals generated from peripheral timers in the microcontroller. L2 is connected to timer0 and L3 is connected to timer1. Setting the duty cycle of the PWM signal to 0 or 100 % switches the corresponding LED off or on, respectively. Intermediate duty cycles with values greater than 0 % but less than 100 % can be used for dimming the corresponding LED. Dimming is an additional feature that an LED on a simple digital I/O pin does not have.

We will now design a *class hierarchy* for the LED objects in Fig. 4.1. This is the class hierarchy that the developer in Fig. 4.1 is considering. The two types of LEDs can be represented with a *base class* and two *derived classes*. The base class is called led_base. The two derived classes are called led_port and led_pwm.

One potential implementation of the led_base class is shown below.

```cpp
class led_base
{
public:
  virtual void toggle() = 0; // Pure abstract.
  virtual ~led_base() { }     // Virtual destructor.

  // Interface for querying the LED state.
  bool state_is_on() const { return is_on; }

protected:
  bool is_on;

  // A protected default constructor.
  led_base() : is_on(false) { }

private:
  // Private non-implemented copy constructor.
  led_base(const led_base&) = delete;

  // Private non-implemented copy assignment operator.
  const led_base& operator=(const led_base&) = delete;
};
```

The public interface of the led_base class has two *virtual functions*, the virtual toggle() function and a virtual destructor called ~led_base().

In object-oriented programming, a derived class provides its own specific version of a virtual function in its base class. This is called a function *override*. When calling a member function on a base class pointer or reference to an object, the virtual function in the derived class will be used.

This is the virtual function mechanism in C++, and it is an essential part of *dynamic polymorphism* in object-oriented programming.

In dynamic polymorphism, derived classes in a class hierarchy can be manipulated with a common interface yet still exhibit specialized behavior. In our case here, it means that any kind of LED derived from `led_base` can `toggle()` in its own way.

In general, the destructor of a derived class should be virtual. This ensures that the proper derived class destructor is called when destroying an object via a base class pointer.

For more information on virtual function overrides and virtual destructors, consult Eckel [4], Chap. 15, subsection "Virtual Functions" and also section "Destructors and Virtual Destructors".

Another interesting feature of the `led_base` class is its protected constructor. The protected constructor can not be called from any other parts of the program except classes derived from `led_base`. This makes sense because `led_base` is intended to be just that, a base class. No one is actually supposed to create instances of `led_base`. Furthermore, if one were to try, the compiler would forbid it.

Now that we have the `led_base` class, we can derive another class from it called `led_port`.

```cpp
class led_port : public led_base
{
public:
  typedef std::uint8_t port_type;
  typedef std::uint8_t bval_type;

  led_port(const port_type p,
           const bval_type b)  : port(p),
                                  bval(b)
  {
    // ...
  }

  virtual ~led_port() { }

  virtual void toggle()
  {
    // Toggle the LED.
    *reinterpret_cast<volatile bval_type*>(port)
      ^= bval;

    // Toggle the is_on indication flag.
    is_on = !is_on;
  }
```

```
private:
  const port_type port;
  const bval_type bval;
};
```

The `led_port` class is specifically designed to toggle LEDs connected to a port pin. In our case here, this means `L0` and `L1` in Fig. 4.1. The `led_port` class is similar to the `led` class from the LED program in Sect. 1.1. There is nonetheless an important distinction between the two. The `led_port` class is derived from `led_base`.

Take a moment to notice how both `led_base` as well as `led_port` have the virtual `toggle()` function. This is a common interface that is shared by `led_port` and `led_base`.

A virtual override in a derived class does not need to explicitly use the **virtual** keyword, unless this is required for further derived classes. Some developers feel that supplying the optional **virtual** keyword in a derived class is redundant and should be avoided. Others consider it to be a helpful reminder that the function is virtual and is, in fact, overriding a function with the same signature in its base class.

For the LEDs on PWM signal generators in Fig. 4.1, we need an LED class that encapsulates a second kind of LED driver. Instead of manually switching an LED on and off by toggling a port pin, this class controls the brightness of its LED with a PWM signal generator. In particular,

```
class led_pwm : public led_base
{
public:
  explicit led_pwm(pwm* p) : my_pwm(p) { }
  virtual ~led_pwm() { }

  virtual void toggle()
  {
    // Toggle the LED with the PWM signal.
    is_on = (my_pwm->get_duty() > 0U);

    my_pwm->set_duty(is_on ? 0U : 100U);

    is_on = !is_on;
  }

  // This LED class also supports dimming.
  void dimming(const std::uint8_t duty)
  {
    my_pwm->set_duty(duty);
```

```
    is_on = (duty != 0U);
  }

private:
  pwm* my_pwm;
};
```

Just like the `led_port` class, `led_pwm` has its own override of the `toggle()` function. This is `led_pwm`'s specialized way to `toggle()`. Notice in the implementation of the `toggle()` member how the `led_pwm` class uses its private variable `my_pwm` for manipulating the PWM signal generator connected to its corresponding LED.

In addition to the `toggle()` function, `led_pwm` also has a `dimming()` function. As mentioned above, dimming can be used to set intermediate values of LED brightness that lie between 0 and 100 %. There is additional logic in the `toggle()` algorithm that synchronizes dimming with toggling. If the PWM signal has any non-zero duty cycle upon entering the `toggle()` function, then the LED is assumed to be on and it will be switched off by setting the duty cycle to 0 %. If the PWM signal has a duty cycle of 0 %, then `toggle()` switches the LED on by setting the duty cycle to 100 %.

The constructor of the `led_pwm` class is declared with the **explicit** keyword. This ensures that the constructor can only be used if the input parameters are supplied and prevents potential unintended automatic compiler conversion of the class to another type. See also Eckel [4], Chap. 12, subsection "Preventing Constructor Conversion".

The PWM signal generators can be encapsulated with a pwm class. In particular,

```
class pwm
{
public:
  explicit pwm(const int channel) : duty_cycle(0U) { }
  ~pwm() { }

  void set_duty(const std::uint8_t duty)
  {
    // Limit the duty cycle to 0...100.
    duty_cycle = std::min<std::uint8_t>(duty, 100U);

    // Set the duty cycle in the PWM hardware.
    // ...
  }

  std::uint8_t get_duty() const
  {
```

```
    return duty_cycle;
  }

private:
  std::uint8_t duty_cycle;
};
```

The pwm class has a simple public interface consisting of its ctor and two functions, set_duty() and get_duty(). These two functions are designed for setting and retrieving the value of the pwm's duty cycle. In our example here, we assume that the duty cycle can be set from 0 ... 100 % in 101 discrete steps. The microcontroller-specific code sequences required for initializing the PWM hardware and setting the duty cycle are not shown. These are treated in greater detail in Sect. 9.4.

4.2 Objects and Encapsulation

Objects, through their actions and relations among each other (both concrete as well as abstract), compose the functionality of an object-oriented application. Objects for microcontrollers usually encapsulate electronic sub-circuits or control functions such as digital filters, regulation loops, communication devices, measurement equipment, graphical instruments, etc.

The LED class hierarchy and the pwm class, for example, encapsulate the electronic sub-circuits shown in Fig. 4.1 by uniting their respective functionalities with their internal data. In particular, the code sample below shows led_port, led_pwm and pwm objects.

```
namespace
{
  // Two LEDs on port2.0 and port2.1
  led_port led0
  {
    mcal::reg::port2,
    mcal::reg::bval0
  };

  led_port led1
  {
    mcal::reg::port2,
    mcal::reg::bval1
  };
```

```
// Two PWMs on channels timer0 and timer1.
pwm pwm0 { 0 };
pwm pwm1 { 1 };

// Two LEDs connected to pwm0 and pwm1.
led_pwm led2 { &pwm0 };
led_pwm led3 { &pwm1 };
}
```

This code has instances of all four LEDs (L0–L3) and the two PWM signals from Fig. 4.1. The pwm instances, objects themselves, are used to initialize the led_pwm objects.

Now that we have our LEDs, it is straightforward to toggle them. For example,

```
void do_something()
{
  // Toggle L0-L3.
  led0.toggle();
  led1.toggle();
  led2.toggle();
  led3.toggle();
}
```

This code toggles led0–led3. Notice how the uniform toggle() interface makes it convenient to toggle both kinds of LEDs using the same function call. This is an example of object-oriented microcontroller programming in C++.[1]

4.3 Inheritance

Consider class inheritance in object-oriented C++ programming. For example,

```
class led_port : public led_base
{
  // ...
};
```

---

[1]This code does not yet make use of the runtime virtual function mechanism. We will re-examine this example in association with dynamic polymorphism and the runtime virtual function mechanism in Sect. 4.4.

A derived class inherits data members and methods from its base(s) and can use them subject to access control. For example, `led_port` can use `led_base`'s public and protected members. In particular, `led_port` can directly manipulate `led_base`'s protected member `is_on`.

```
class led_port : public led_base
{
public:
  virtual void toggle()
  {
    // Toggle the LED.
    *reinterpret_cast<volatile bval_type*>(port)
      ^= bval;

    // Toggle the is_on indication flag.
    is_on = !is_on;
  }

  // ...
};
```

The `toggle()` function also toggles the state of `is_on` from **false** to **true** and vice versa after toggling the LED. Since `led_port` is publicly derived from `led_base`, it is allowed to manipulate the protected member variable of its base class. Clients of classes derived from `led_base` can query the state of `is_on` by calling the `state_is_on()` method.

Each successively more derived class adds to the inheritance chain. For example, `led_port` and `led_pwm` add their individualized `toggle()` capabilities. In addition, `led_pwm` adds its dimming function. We could potentially derive another kind of PWM-based LED class, say `led_pwm2`, from `led_pwm`. This new class would inherit both the `toggle()` function as well as the `dimming()` function— and could even add other functions of its own.

As mentioned earlier in Sect. 1.4, inheritance has three access controls: public, protected and private. When not explicitly specified, the default inheritance level of a class is private. The default inheritance level of a struct is public. Private inheritance is less common, but can be useful. The `noncopyable` class of Sect. 15.2 shows an interesting example of private inheritance used to control the access level of class copying. The access level of inheritance allows for fine-tuning copy semantics and hiding private data in class hierarchies.

Inheritance runs through the class hierarchy, providing for distribution of program complexity. Armed with the right object granularity and prudent design of class hierarchies, it is possible to build powerful and expressive object-oriented microcontroller programs in C++.

4.4 Dynamic Polymorphism

Dynamic polymorphism, or runtime polymorphism, is one of the most powerful tools in object-oriented C++ programming. Dynamic polymorphism in C++ uses a runtime virtual function mechanism to call methods of a derived class by accessing them from a base class pointer or reference. For example,

```cpp
void led_toggler(led_base* led)
{
  // Use dynamic polymorphism to toggle
  // a base class pointer.
  led->toggle();
}

void do_something()
{
  led_toggler(&led0); // Toggle an led_port.
  led_toggler(&led1); // Toggle an led_port.
  led_toggler(&led2); // Toggle an led_pwm.
  led_toggler(&led3); // Toggle an led_pwm.
}
```

In this code, `led_toggler()` uses dynamic polymorphism on a base class pointer (`led_base*`) to call the `toggle()` function for two different kinds of LED objects (i.e., `led_port` and `led_pwm`). The virtual function mechanism selects the right `toggle()` function at runtime. The compiler has automatically generated a small amount of object code for this.

In the calls to `led_toggler()` above, the compiler automatically downcasts the `led_port` and `led_pwm` pointers to base class pointers. Explicit downcast is possible, and exemplified below.

```cpp
void do_something()
{
  led_toggler(static_cast<led_base*>(&led0));
  led_toggler(static_cast<led_base*>(&led1));
  led_toggler(static_cast<led_base*>(&led2));
  led_toggler(static_cast<led_base*>(&led3));
}
```

According to stylistic preferences and coding guidelines, some developers prefer to supply the explicit downcast. Others consider a non-necessary downcast redundant. They believe that it makes code "over-casted" and reduces legibility.

Dynamic polymorphism also works with a base class reference. For example,

```
void led_toggler(led_base& led)
{
  // Use dynamic polymorphism to toggle
  // a base class reference.
  led.toggle();
}

void do_something()
{
  led_toggler(led0); // Toggle an led_port.
  led_toggler(led1); // Toggle an led_port.
  led_toggler(led2); // Toggle an led_pwm.
  led_toggler(led3); // Toggle an led_pwm.
}
```

The microcontroller programmer needs to be aware that dynamic polymorphism has slight runtime and size costs. When designing classes and class hierarchies, one should be sure that the benefits of dynamic polymorphism are worth its overhead. The following section provides more detail on this.

Dynamic polymorphism and the runtime virtual function mechanism are powerful object-oriented methods. They allow specialized objects that share a common inheritance to be treated identically while still retaining their own specific characteristics. This allows for enormous design flexibility because a uniform interface can be used throughout the entire class hierarchy.

4.5   The Real Overhead of Dynamic Polymorphism

One may wonder how much overhead is associated with dynamic polymorphism and the runtime virtual function mechanism in C++. Since the implementation details of the virtual function mechanism depend on the compiler implementation, there is no exact answer to this question. In general, though, the best compilers in the market have remarkably low overhead for dynamic polymorphism.

We will now examine a scheme commonly used to implement the runtime virtual mechanism in C++. Many compilers store the addresses of virtual functions in a compiler-generated table at a location that could be either in static RAM or program code. A general rule-of-thumb, then, is that each virtual function of a class costs one chunk of memory large enough to hold a function pointer. Consider an 8–bit platform. If a function pointer requires 2 bytes on this platform and a derived class has three virtual functions, then the implementation of the derived class requires 6 bytes of storage for its virtual function table.

Calling a virtual function is fast because all the compiler needs to do is select the proper entry from the virtual function table and call it. This is only slightly slower than a normal function call. In addition, the call overhead of a virtual function remains the same regardless of how many levels of inheritance there are. It is always the same effort for accessing the virtual function table. Readers interested in additional details on the overhead associated with the runtime virtual function mechanism can consult FAQ 20.4 of Parashift [1] or Eckel [4], Chap. 15, section "Under the Hood".

Even though modern C++ compilers have little overhead associated with dynamic polymorphism, low-level drivers that are called very often (e.g. in high-frequency interrupts) may be unsuited for dynamic polymorphism. Procedural methods or static polymorphism (Sect. 5.7) could be better options for extremely time critical code. Functions in the application layer that are less time critical can greatly benefit from well-designed class hierarchies because the advantages of dynamic polymorphism usually far outweigh its modest costs.

4.6 Pure Virtual and Abstract

Examination of the `led_base` class implementation reveals that its `toggle()` function does not have a body. Rather, the `toggle()` function of `led_base` is a so-called *pure virtual* function, implemented with the unmistakably recognizable syntax "`= 0`". In other words,

```cpp
class led_base
{
public:
  virtual void toggle() = 0; // Abstract.

  // ...
};
```

A class that has one or more pure virtual methods is called an *abstract* class. An abstract class is the generalized notion of something, as opposed to a concrete example of a specific thing. As such, the pure virtual functions of an abstract class are not intended to be called. Instead, pure virtual functions define a mandatory interface for derived classes. In other words, pure virtual functions define a sort of *blueprint* for derived classes.

Consider an abstract base class. Any to-be-instantiated class derived from it *must* implement overrides for each pure virtual method of its base(s). Otherwise, no objects of the derived class can be instantiated.

For example, both `led_port` as well as `led_pwm` are derived from the abstract `led_base` class. Therefore, both of them must provide a member override for `toggle()`. In this way, C++ provides clear language semantics for data abstraction.

Say we derive a class called `led_no_toggle` from `led_base` but fail to include the required virtual `toggle()` function. If anyone attempted to instantiate an instance of `led_no_toggle`, there would be a compiler error. In particular,

```
class led_no_toggle : public led_base
{
public:
  led_no_toggle() { }
  virtual ~led_no_toggle() { }

  // Does not have a toggle function.
  // ...
};


namespace
{
  led_no_toggle led_no; // Compiler error!
}
```

As mentioned above, an abstract object is an idealization—not intended to be created. It is usually a good idea to protect the constructor of an abstract class type. This is why the constructor of `led_base` is protected. The protected constructor ensures that no one is able to create `led_base` objects. Yet the constructor is *only* protected, and not private. Publicly derived classes are, therefore, granted access to the base class constructor.

A derived class can, itself, contribute methods to the abstract interface by adding pure virtual functions of its own. However, it is always important to remember that class types with pure virtual functions are not intended to be instantiated and hence will lead to a compiler error.

4.7   Class Relationships

There is a variety of well-known class relationships in object-oriented design. In fact, we have already worked with some of them without even explicitly mentioning them. Possibly the most important class relationship is the *is-a* relationship for which a derived class *is-a* subclass of a base class. In other words, `led_port` *is-a* subclass of `led_base`, and `led_pwm` also *is-a* subclass of `led_base`.

Another special relationship is that of *has-a*, in the sense of *having* something. The `led_pwm` class exhibits the *has-a* relationship with its member variable pwm. In other words, the `led_pwm` class *has* its own PWM signal generator. Since it

has its own pwm object, it can use this for the internal workings of the toggle()
function.

There is also the *uses-a* relationship. The relationship of *using* usually requires
some way to pass the thing-being-used to its user. This can be done, for example, via
function parameter or by accessing an existing instance through pointer or reference.

The difference between *has-a* and *uses-a* can be subtle, but important. In
particular, if led_pwm were to *use* a pwm and not *have* one, then its toggle()
function would need an input pwm pointer or reference parameter. Note, though,
that this would break the uniformity of the toggle() interface within the class
hierarchy.

We will now visualize these important class relationships with a few simple code
snippets.

The led_pwm class *is-a* specialized kind of led_base.

```cpp
class led_pwm : public led_base
{
  // led_pwm is-a led_base.
  // ...
};
```

The led_pwm class *has-a* class-owned pwm.

```cpp
class led_pwm : public led_base
{
  // ...

private:
  // led_pwm has-a pwm.
  pwm* my_pwm;
};
```

Perhaps in a different implementation, the led_pwm class might *use-a* PWM
signal. In this case, a pointer to a PWM signal, in other words a pwm*, could be
used as a subroutine input parameter to the toggle() function instead of being
a class member. Even though this would wreck the uniformity of the toggle()
interface in our example, the *use-a* relationship can be a useful class relationship in
many other cases.

```cpp
class led_pwm : public led_base
{
  // ...

  // This led_pwm uses the use-a relationship
```

```
  // to toggle.
  virtual void toggle(pwm* p)
  {
    // ...
  }
};
```

Careful consideration of class relationships is necessary for successful object-oriented design because class relationships strongly influence the efficiency and cleanliness of the interfaces in a software project. A thorough description of class relationships can be found in Sect. 6.4 in Coplien [2]. Additional information on the *is-a* relationship is available in Eckel [4], Chap. 1, section "Is-a vs. Is-Like-a Relationships".

4.8   Non-copyable Classes

The led_base class has private yet non-implemented declarations of a copy constructor and copy assignment operator. In particular,

```
class led_base
{
public:
  // ...

private:
  // Private non-implemented copy constructor.
  led_base(const led_base&) = delete;

  // Private non-implemented copy assignment operator.
  const led_base& operator=(const led_base&) = delete;
};
```

This means that the led_base class and its derived classes are non-copyable. Declaring a private copy constructor and a private copy assignment operator and qualifying them with the **delete** keyword tells the compiler that a given class and its derived classes should be treated as strictly non-copyable without exception.

When using non-copyable classes, the compiler will issue an error for any code, including compiler-generated code, that tries to copy the class. This technique is often done on purpose in order to eliminate the risk of both intentional as well as unintentional attempts to copy a class instance.

Explicitly making certain classes non-copyable can be particularly useful in real-time C++ because some classes or class instantiations may be intimately linked to a particular hardware unit or peripheral device. For instance, an LED on a port pin, a PWM signal on a timer output or a communication interface such as a serial UART may be bound to a unique microcontroller peripheral resource.

If only one instance of a class should be allowed to use a single resource, then non-copyable semantics can reduce the risk of unintentionally using the resource with multiple class instances. Non-copyable semantics can also improve intuitive clarity in the code by unmistakably indicating if a class is intended to be copied or not.

In fact, the non-copyable mechanism is so widely established that some high-reliability guidelines [8] recommend using it when appropriate. In addition, a standard C++ utility called `noncopyable` in Boost [3] has been invented to simplify the semantics of making a class object non-copyable. See Sect. 15.2 for our own version of the `noncopyable` utility.

Class copying is a rich topic involving issues such as eliminating reliance on compiler generated default copy, deep-copy mechanisms for pointer members, checking for self-assign, etc. For additional information on class copying, see Eckel [4], all of Chap. 11 "References & the Copy-Constructor" and also Chap. 12, section "Overloading Assignment". Meyers [7] describes deep-copy mechanisms in Item 11 and copy assignment in Items 15–17.

4.9   Constant Methods

We have already encountered several examples of constant member functions previously. For example, the `toggle()` function in the LED program of Sect. 1.1 and the `squared_euclidean_distance()` member of the `point` structure in Sect. 3.5 are both constant methods.

Constant member functions have read-only character regarding the member variables of a class. As such, they can not modify the value of any class member variable. If there are good reasons to do so, however, a constant member function can modify a non-constant variable if that variable is qualified with the **mutable** keyword.

We will now examine an example of a richer class that has both constant as well as non-constant member functions. Consider a `communication` class designed to send and receive single-byte data frames.

```
extern "C"
void com_recv_isr() __attribute__((interrupt));

class communication
{
```

```cpp
public:
  communication() : recv_buf(0U),
                    has_recv(false) { }
  ~communication() { }

  bool send_byte(const std::uint8_t by) const
  {
    *reinterpret_cast<volatile std::uint8_t*>(tbuf)
      = by;
  }

  bool recv_ready() const { return has_recv; }

  std::uint8_t recv_byte()
  {
    if(has_recv)
    {
      has_recv = false;
      return recv_buf;
    }

    return 0U;
  }

private:
  static constexpr std::uint8_t tbuf = 0xAAU;
  static constexpr std::uint8_t rbuf = 0xAEU;

  std::uint8_t recv_buf;
  bool has_recv;

  communication(const communication&) = delete;
  const communication& operator=(const communication&)
    = delete;

  friend
  void com_recv_isr() __attribute__((interrupt));
};
```

The communication class is simple and versatile. It is designed for low-level asynchronous communication with a microcontroller peripheral interface. With slight modification, the communication class can be used with physical layers such as SPI™, CAN [6], etc. The serial SPI™ driver class in Sect. 9.5, for example, is based on the communication class shown above.

For now, do not worry about the *friend* function com_recv_isr() nor about its interrupt __attributes__(). Class friends are described in greater detail in Sect. 4.11, and additional information on interrupts and GCC's language extensions for them is provided in Sect. 9.2.[2]

Byte transmission is carried out with the send_byte() member using direct memory access to write a to-be-transmitted byte to communication's transmit buffer tbuf. As such, send_byte() does not need to modify any class-internal data and can be declared as **const**. In particular,

```
class communication
{
public:
  // ...

  bool send_byte(const std::uint8_t by) const
  {
    *reinterpret_cast<volatile std::uint8_t*>(tbuf)
      = by;
  }
};
```

A client using a constant instance of class can only call constant members of the class. For instance,

```
bool wakeup(const communication& com)
{
  // OK. Call a const member of a const reference.
  return com.send_byte(0x12U);
}
```

In this code, wakeup() uses a constant communication reference, in other words **const** communication&, to send the wake-up pattern. The wake-up is sent with a call to the constant send_byte() member. This compiles without error.

Consider the implementation of a communication login that sends the wake-up pattern 0x12 and expects to receive the login response 0x34. In particular,

```
bool login(const communication& com)
{
  // OK. Call the const send_byte on a const reference.
```

---

[2]In the example here, however, simplified interrupt attributes have been used for the sake of clarity.

```
const bool wakeup_is_ok = com.send_byte(0x12U);

if(wakeup_is_ok)
{
  // Compiler error!
  return (com.recv_byte() == 0x34U);
}
else
{
  return false;
}
}
```

In `login()`, the call of the constant `send_byte()` member on the constant communication class reference compiles without error. The attempted call of the non-constant `recv_byte()` member, however, does not. The compiler issues an error because calling a non-constant member on a constant object is not allowed.

In order to call `recv_byte()`, the reference to `communication` must be made non-constant in the input parameter to the `login()` function. In other words,

```
bool login(communication& com)
{
  // OK.
  const bool wakeup_is_ok = com.send_byte(0x12U);

  if(wakeup_is_ok)
  {
    // OK.
    return (com.recv_byte() == 0x34U);
  }
  else
  {
    return false;
  }
}
```

Many development guidelines recommend making member functions constant whenever it makes sense to do so. This provides additional intuitive insight into how a class and its interface are intended to be used. This is a part of what is generally known as *const-correctness* in the literature.

There are no added runtime or storage costs associated with qualifying member functions as **const**. So the microcontroller programmer can freely use constant methods to improve program clarity without introducing undue resource consumption.

4.10 Static Constant Integral Members

The communication class has two static constant integral data members, tbuf
and rbuf. We first encountered static constant integral members of a class in
Sect. 3.8. Similar to symbols defined with a preprocessor #define, static constant
integral members of class types are compile-time constants.

For effective C++ design, it is essential to understand that static constant integral
members have distinct advantages over preprocessor #defines. For example,
static constant integral members have a clearly defined type and name. They may,
thus, potentially have compiler symbol information. Symbols that have been defined
with a preprocessor #define, on the other hand, are used exclusively by the preprocessor and lack these. Type and symbol information can be useful with a debugger or when examining program contents in a linker *map file* (Section also 6.5).

At the same time, static constant integral class members are guaranteed to be
known at compile time. Using them often eliminates the code overhead associated
with runtime address load or move operations by taking advantage of constant
folding (Sect. 2.6). For further discussions of static constant integral members
versus preprocessor #defines, see Item 1 in Meyers [7].

4.11 Class Friends

Byte reception in the communication class of the previous section uses the
member function recv_byte(). This receive function does not directly retrieve
the byte by reading the UART's hardware buffer register. Instead, recv_byte()
reads the *software* receive buffer, recv_buf. It thereby also checks and clears the
has_recv-flag. In this way, communication is designed for asynchronous byte
reception.

To provide a mechanism for asynchronous receive, communication uses a
friend subroutine called com_recv_isr(). As perhaps expected, the "isr"-part
of the friend subroutine's name is, in fact, intended to indicate that this an interrupt
service routine.

```
extern "C"
void com_recv_isr() __attribute__((interrupt));

class communication
{
  // ...

  friend
  void com_recv_isr() __attribute__((interrupt));
};
```

A friend of a class is allowed to access any class member variable or method regardless of its access level, public, protected or private. Class friends can be either global or local functions, member functions or even other class types. Note that friend functions do not necessarily need to have C-linkage (qualified with **extern** "C"). This is a characteristic of the particular example at hand which uses a friend function that just so happens to be an interrupt service routine.

A possible implementation of com_recv_isr() is shown below.

```
extern "C"
void com_recv_isr() __attribute__((interrupt));

communication com;

// Communication's friend and also an ISR.
void com_recv_isr()
{
  // Asynchronous byte reception can use the
  // private members of com.

  com.recv_buf =
    *reinterpret_cast<volatile std::uint8_t*>
    (communication::rbuf);

  com.has_recv = true;
}
```

The communication object com is a static instance of the communication class with global scope. When an asynchronous hardware receive interrupt occurs, the microcontroller calls com_recv_isr(). This interrupt service routine subsequently reads the hardware receive buffer (communication::rbuf) and fills com's receive buffer with the received byte. The com_recv_isr() interrupt also activates the has_recv-flag. This announces the new reception to a polling listener. In this way, com_recv_isr() executes asynchronous byte-reception. Notice in all this how the interrupt service routine—a friend of the communication class—can access communication's private members.

Another part of the program such as a cyclical task can poll com, querying its Boolean member function recv_ready() to find out if a new byte has been received. Upon reception of a new byte, recv_ready() returns **true**. The new byte in the receive queue can be retrieved with the recv_byte subroutine. For example,

```
extern communication com;

void task_poll_the_com()
```

```
{
  if(com.recv_ready())
  {
    const std::uint8_t the_byte = com.recv_byte();

    // Do something with the_byte.
    // ...
  }
}
```

Some developers avoid using class friends, arguing they break data hiding
and fragment encapsulation. This is not necessarily the case. Class friends can
actually improve data encapsulation in some cases by eliminating set()-and-
get() interfaces that may weaken class boundaries by exposing internal class
details. This tends to ensure that private members remain *private*. See FAQ 14.2
at Parashift [1] for a further discussion of this.

It can be wise to use class friends, but sparingly, and only if the use of friendship
is justified by tangible design improvement beyond mere convenience. For example,
interrupt service routines require static C-linkage, making them difficult to be
encapsulated in a class while simultaneously included in the interrupt vector table
(Sect. 9.2). When accessing a global object such as com within an interrupt service
routine, class friendship can provide just the right mechanism to retain encapsulation
while adhering to the constraints of interrupt programming.

4.12   Virtual Is Unavailable in the Base Class Constructor

The virtual function mechanism for a given class is neither available in its own class
constructor nor in any base class constructor because the object is not fully formed
yet. Any attempt to use the virtual function mechanism within a base class constructor will result in undefined behavior. In the code below, communication_base
is a base class for communication and communication_serial is a specialized
class derived from it. In particular,

```
class communication_serial : public communication_base
{
public:
  communication_serial(const std::uint16_t c,
                        const std::uint8_t  b)
    : channel(c),
      baud(b) { }

  virtual ~communication_serial() { }
```

```
virtual void init()
{
  // Initialize this communication_serial class.
  // ...
}

private:
  const std::uint8_t channel;
  const std::uint16_t baud;
};
```

The candidate base class communication_base is shown below. It makes erroneous, undefined use of the virtual function mechanism in the base class constructor.

```
class communication_base
{
public:
  virtual ~communication_base() { }

  // A virtual initialization function.
  virtual void init() { }

protected:
  communication_base()
  {
    // Undefined use of the virtual mechanism!
    init();
  }
};
```

Here, the constructor of communication_base attempts to use the virtual function mechanism to call init(). Unfortunately, this code might not do what its author intended. The code is meant to use the virtual function mechanism to call the init() function of the derived class in the base class constructor. The virtual function mechanism is, however, unavailable in the base class constructor. Therefore, the communication_serial object might be created using the empty init() function of communication_base.

The compiler might not even issue a warning for attempting to use the virtual mechanism in a base class constructor because it may be incapable to differentiate an inadvertent *to-be-warned* virtual function call from an intended *it's-my-own-member* call.

In order to properly initialize communication_serial, its init() function needs to be explicitly called *after* the constructors are finished. In particular,
we will redesign communication_base such that its constructor no longer calls
init().

```
class communication_base
{
public:
  // ...

protected:
  // Remove initialization from the base class ctor.
  communication_base() { }
};

class communication_serial : public communication_base
{
  // ...
};
```

Now the constructor of the communication_base class no longer attempts
to call the virtual init() function. Clients of the communication_serial
class need to explicitly call the init() method *after* the object has been created.
For example,

```
void do_something()
{
  // Create com_serial on channel 1 with 9600bps.
  communication_serial com_serial(1U, 9600U);

  // Explicitly initialize com_serial.
  // It is fully formed.
  com_serial.init();

  // Use com_serial.
  // ...
}
```

Understandably, it can be all too easy to forget to explicitly call the init()-
like functions of a class needing explicit initialization after creation. One possible
remedy for this problem uses an abstract interface (often called a *factory*) to

dynamically create objects and simultaneously ensure that they are explicitly initialized when fully formed, but before being used.[3]

Through empirical investigations or trial-and-error, one may find compilers for which, by chance, the virtual function mechanism seems to be available in the base class constructor. Relying on this behavior, however, is unreliable and can be confusing because the code might work with one compiler yet be broken by another.

Always remember that the C++ language specification is clear on this matter. The virtual function mechanism is not available in the base class constructor. Potential confusion can be spared by remembering and adhering to this rule. See Item 23.5 at Parashift [1] for more information on the unavailability of the virtual function mechanism in the base class constructor.

References

1. M. Cline, *Parashift C++ FAQ* (2012), http://www.parashift.com/c++-faq
2. J.O. Coplien, *Advanced C++ Programming Styles and Idioms* (Addison Wesley, Reading, 1992)
3. B. Dawes, D. Abrahams, *Boost C++ Libraries* (2012), http://www.boost.org
4. B. Eckel, *Thinking in C++ Volume 1: Introduction to Standard C++*, 2nd edn. (Pearson Prentice Hall, Upper Saddle River, 2000)
5. E. Gamma, R. Helm, R. Johnson, J. Vlissides, *Design Patterns: Elements of Reusable Object-Oriented Software* (Addison Wesley, Reading, 1994)
6. ISO, *ISO 11898–1:2003: Road vehicles—Controller area network (CAN)—Part 1: Data Link Layer and Physical Signaling* (International Organization for Standardization, Geneva, 2003)
7. S. Meyers, *Effective C++: 55 Specific Ways to Improve Your Programs and Designs*, 3rd edn. (Addison Wesley, Reading, 2005)
8. Programming Research Group, *High-Integrity C++ Coding Standard Manual* (2007), http://www.codingstandard.com/HICPPCM/index.html

---

[3]Factories are described in good design books such as [5]. In addition, Sect. 5.9 in this book uses a simple factory to introduce variadic templates.

Chapter 5
C++ Templates for Microcontrollers

C++ templates use the same source code for different types. This can improve code flexibility and make programs easier to maintain because code can be written and tested once, yet used with different types. Templates can also be used in generic programming that treats different types with the same semantics. This chapter introduces templates and static polymorphism, the STL, template metaprogramming and some generic programming methods, and shows how these can be used effectively for microcontrollers.

5.1 Template Functions

Consider the simple template function below.

```
template<typename T>
T add(const T& a, const T& b)
{
  return a + b;
}
```

The template function add() returns the sum of (a + b), where the types of a, b and add()'s return value are the *template parameter* T. A template parameter can be considered a placeholder for a not-yet-specified type. Template parameters can be class types, built-in types, constant integral or pointer values, but not floating-point values. See Sect. 4.3 in Vandevoorde and Josuttis [3].

When a template is used in code, the compiler *instantiates* it for a known type by filling in the template code corresponding to its template parameters at compiler time. This is the same vocabulary that is used for instances of a class types in object-oriented programming. The context should be considered when discerning the two.

C.M. Kormanyos, *Real-Time C++*, DOI 10.1007/978-3-642-34688-0_5,
© Springer-Verlag Berlin Heidelberg 2013

The code below, for example, uses add() twice, one time to add two integer variables and a second time to add two variables of type std::string, the standard library's string class.

```
int n = add(1, 2); // 3

std::string s = add(std::string("abc"),
                    std::string("xyz")); // "abcxyz".
```

In the calls to add() above, the template parameter is not explicitly given. The compiler can automatically *deduce* the types of template parameters if it has sufficient information to do so from the context of usage. Even if the template parameters could be deduced, though, they can still be optionally provided. Template parameters are provided in a comma-separated template parameter list in angled brackets. For example,

```
const int c = add<int>(a, b);
```

The template parameters must be compatible with the functionality of the templated code. For example, in order to be used with add(), a given template parameter must support addition (in other words **operator+**).

The compiler does not automatically perform type conversion for templates. So if the function's parameters do not exactly match those of the template, then the template parameters must be explicitly provided. For example,

```
double d1 = add(1.1, 2.2);        // OK, 3.3, double
double d2 = add(1.1, 2);          // Not OK, ambiguous
double d3 = add<double>(1.1, 2);  // OK, 3.1, double
```

If multiple types are needed, template functions can have more than one template parameter. For instance,

```
template<typename T1,
         typename T2>
T1 add(const T1& a, const T2& b)
{
  return a + T1(b);
}

double d = add(1.1, 2); // OK, 3.1, double
```

5.2   Template Scalability, Code Re-use and Efficiency

Templates are scalable. For instance, we will now consider a scalable template function that may be useful in microcontroller programming. It is based on the ubiquitous "MAKE_WORD()" preprocessor macro. The MAKE_WORD() macro is normally used to *make* a 16–bit unsigned integer from two constituent 8–bit unsigned bytes. One possible implementation of MAKE_WORD() using a C-style preprocessor macro with **#define** is shown below.

```
#define MAKE_WORD(lo, hi) \
          (uint16_t) (((uint16_t) (hi) << 8) | (lo))
```

We will now replace the C-style MAKE_WORD() preprocessor macro with a more generic template function called make_large(). In particular,

```
template<typename ularge_type,
         typename ushort_type>
ularge_type make_large(const ushort_type& lo,
                       const ushort_type& hi)
{
  constexpr int ushort_digits
    = std::numeric_limits<ushort_type>::digits;

  constexpr int ularge_digits
    = std::numeric_limits<ularge_type>::digits;

  // Ensure proper width of the large type.
  static_assert(ularge_digits == (2 * ushort_digits),
               "error: ularge_type must be twice
                as wide as ushort_type");

  // Shift the high part to the left.
  const ularge_type uh
    = static_cast<ularge_type>(hi) << ushort_digits;

  // Return the composite result.
  return static_cast<ularge_type>(uh | lo);
}
```

The make_large() template function returns the composite value of a larger unsigned type ularge_type made from two constituents of a smaller unsigned type ushort_type. Here, ularge_type is twice as wide as ushort_type. The high-part of the composite value is first shifted left by an amount corresponding to the width of the smaller unsigned type `ushort_type`. Afterwards, the low-part is `OR`-ed with the shifted high-part to generate the result.

The standard library's `std::numeric_limits` template is used to obtain the number of binary digits in the large and short types (Sect. A.5). This template function also uses **static_assert**() to ensure that the `ularge_type` has exactly twice as many binary digits as the `ushort_type`. It can be wise to build these types of checks into template utilities to prevent error caused by instantiation with non-compatible types. Further security could be included by adding compile-time assertions that verify that `ularge_type` and `ushort_type` are both unsigned integer types.

Using `make_large()` in code is simple. For example,

```
std::uint8_t   lo8 = 0x34U;
std::uint8_t   hi8 = 0x12U;
std::uint16_t u16
  = make_large<std::uint16_t>(lo8, hi8);

std::uint16_t lo16 = 0x5678U;
std::uint16_t hi16 = 0x1234U;
std::uint32_t u32
  = make_large<std::uint32_t>(lo16, hi16);

std::uint32_t lo32 = 0x9ABCDEF0UL;
std::uint32_t hi32 = 0x12345678UL;
std::uint64_t u64
  = make_large<std::uint64_t>(lo32, hi32);
```

This code uses `make_large()` to make three results of widths 16, 32 and 64-bit, respectively. The results are made from their corresponding half-width constituents. This shows how templates are *scalable*. Notice how `make_large()` automatically scales its width at compile time to different integer types.

One of the great features of templates is code re-use. To provide the same scalability with preprocessor macros, three individual ones would be needed. In particular, we would need equivalent preprocessor macros such as MAKE_WORD() for 16–bit results, MAKE_DWORD() for 32–bit results and MAKE_QWORD() for 64–bit results. The `make_large()` template is superior to multiple preprocessor macros because it only needs to be implemented once and maintained in one place.

A generic template, tested and written in a type-safe fashion, is a tool that can be used, re-used and readily ported to other platforms without needing redesign. Furthermore, preprocessor macros can be plagued by non-safe side-effects such as unwanted parameter modification, etc. C++ Templates are freed from the problems of C-style macros and generally improve code portability and robustness.

Templates are not necessarily expanded inline by default because template inlining is relegated to the compiler's internal optimization characteristics. The

inline keyword can be used in order to *recommend* to the compiler to treat a template function as inline. The compiler can, however, still optionally choose to disregard the **inline** keyword based on its optimization settings, and the length and complexity of a given template. See Sect. 6.1 for further information on optimization.

Templates facilitate efficiency because they make all of their code and template parameters known to the compiler at compile time. Templates can, however, also incur additional code costs. Each time the compiler encounters a template subroutine or object, it must create new code for each individual instance. This phenomenon can potentially lead to excessive *code bloat* if left unchecked. For additional discussion on code bloat and how to avoid it, see Eckel [1], Chap. 5, section "Preventing template code bloat". The microcontroller C++ programmer must be aware of this trade-off and wisely find the right mixture of templates and non-templates when designing code. When used properly, templates can be highly effective for optimized programming. The benefits of improved performance and scalability often far outweigh any potential costs.

5.3 Template Member Functions

Member functions of class types can be templates. For example, consider a simplified version of the communication class from Sect. 4.9.

```cpp
class communication
{
public:
  virtual ~communication() { }

  virtual bool send(const std::uint8_t b) const;
  {
    // ...
  }

  std::uint8_t recv() const { return recv_buffer; }

protected:
  communication();

private:
  std::uint8_t recv_buffer;
};
```

Say we would like to add the capability of sending larger chunks of data with the communication class. For example, in addition to 8–bit unsigned bytes (std::uint8_t), we would also like to send 16–bit or 32–bit unsigned integers over the communication interface. In order to do this, we could add a new templated send_type() member function. For example,

```cpp
class communication
{
public:
  // ...

  // Add a templated send_type function.
  template<typename unsigned_type>
  bool send_type(const unsigned_type& u) const
  {
    constexpr bool type_is_signed
      = std::numeric_limits<unsigned_type>::is_signed;

    // Ensure that unsigned_type is unsigned.
    static_assert(type_is_signed == false,
                  "error: unsigned_type must be
                  unsigned");

    const std::size_t count =
      std::numeric_limits<unsigned_type>::digits / 8;

    std::size_t i;

    for(i = 0U; i < count; i++)
    {
      const std::uint8_t by = u >> (i * 8U);

      if(!send(by))
      {
        break;
      }
    }

    return (i == count);
  }
};
```

In this listing, the templated Boolean member function send_type() has been added to the communication class. In this code, the type of unsigned_type

is intended to be a right-shift-capable unsigned integral type. Similar to the send()
function, send_type() performs asynchronous data transmission. However,
instead of transmitting a single byte, send_type() transmits the number of bytes
contained in its template parameter type T. For example, send_type() sends
1 byte if unsigned_type is std::uint8_t, 2 bytes for std::uint16_t,
4 bytes for std::uint32_t and 8 bytes for std::uint64_t.

Calling templated class member functions is straightforward. In fact, templated
class methods can be called just like non-templated ones using the usual member
selection operators (.) and (->). For example, we will now use the modified
communication class to simulate communication with an external target system.

```cpp
class communication
{
  // ...
};

namespace login
{
  constexpr std::uint32_t key   = 0x12345678UL;
  constexpr std::uint8_t  ack   = 0x11U;
  constexpr std::uint16_t start = 0xAA55U;
};

bool start_session(const communication& com)
{
  // Send the 32-bit login key.
  const bool key_ok = com.send_type(login::key);

  if(key_ok)
  {
    // Evaluate the login acknowledgment.
    const bool ack_ok = (com.recv() == login::ack);

    // Start the session with the 16-bit key.
    return (ack_ok && com.send_type(login::start));
  }
  else
  {
    return false;
  }
}
```

The start_session() subroutine above depicts a made-up sequence for
starting a communication session with an off-chip target system. The new templated

send_type() member function added to the communication class is used
twice in this sequence, once to send the 32–bit login::key and a second time to
send the 16–bit login::start. The subroutine returns **true** if the login, target
acknowledgment and session start are all successful.[1]

As with non-class template subroutines, the compiler is capable of deducing the
template parameters of templated class methods. Of course, sufficient information
still needs to be available to the compiler for automatic template deduction via the
type(s) of the input argument(s).

Templated member functions can improve coding quality and clarity of design
when used sensibly. For example, the templated send_type() member function
adds flexibility and scalability to communication's send mechanisms. In addition, the templated send_type() function only needs to be implemented and
debugged once. Furthermore, it works for various types. This eliminates potential
sources of error and reduces coding complexity when using communication to
send multi-byte data.

5.4   Template Class Types

Class types can also be templated. This is convenient for making re-usable or
scalable objects. For example, a coordinate point in two-dimensional Cartesian
space $\mathbb{R}^2$ can be implemented as a scalable template. In particular,

```
template<typename x_type,
         typename y_type>
class point
{
public:
  x_type x;
  y_type y;

  point(const x_type& x_ = x_type(),
        const y_type& y_ = y_type()) : x(x_),
                                       y(y_) { }
};

point<std::uint16_t, std::uint16_t> pt16_16 { 1U, 2U };
point<std::uint8_t,  std::uint8_t>  pt08_08 { 2U, 4U };
point<std::uint8_t,  std::uint16_t> pt08_16 { 3U, 6U };
```

---

[1]Notice, as an aside, how a **const** communication& is used as the input parameter to the
start_session() subroutine. Remember from Sect. 4.3 how this technique can also use
dynamic polymorphism if communication is a base class.

5.5 Template Default Parameters

Template functions and class types support default template parameters. For example,

```
template<typename x_type = std::uint16_t,
         typename y_type = x_type>
class point
{
  // ...
};

// An (x16, y16) point.
point<> pt16_16 { 1234U, 5678U };

// An (x8, y8) point.
point<std::uint8_t> pt08_08 { 12U, 34U };

// An (x8, y16) point.
point<std::uint8_t,
      std::uint16_t> pt08_16 { 34U, 5678U };
```

A default template parameter type can be set to the symbolic typename of one of the previously supplied template parameters. For example, the default type of the template parameter y_type above is x_type.

When writing templates with default template parameters, it is not necessary to supply defaults for each template parameter. Template default parameters begin with the last template parameter and work sequentially toward the beginning of the template parameter list.

```
template<typename x_type = std::uint8_t,  // OK.
         typename y_type = std::uint16_t> // OK
class point
{
  // ...
};

template<typename x_type,
         typename y_type = std::uint16_t> // OK
class point
{
  // ...
};
```

```
template<typename x_type = std::uint16_t, // Not OK
         typename y_type>
class point
{
  // ...
};
```

5.6   Template Specialization

Templates can be specialized for a particular type. This creates a unique *template specialization* for this type. When writing a template specialization, the to-be-specialized parameter is removed from original template parameter list and added to a second comma-separated template parameter list following the symbol name.

In particular, suppose that the project design rules forbid the use of floating-point types. In order to enforce this design rule, we might explicitly forbid using floating-point types with the add template by making specialized versions of it with loud errors for **float**, **double** and **long double**. For example,

```
// The original add template function.
template<typename T>
T add(const T& a, const T& b)
{
  return a + b;
}

// Make template specializations of add with
// loud errors for float, double and long double.

template<>
T add<float>(const float&, const float&)
{
  // Make a very loud compiler error!
  static_assert<false,
              "error: float not allowed!">

  return 0.0F;
}

template<>
T add<double>(const double&, const double&)
{
  // Make a very loud compiler error!
```

```
static_assert<false,
              "error: double not allowed!">

  return 0.0;
}

template<>
T add<long double>(const long double&,
                   const long double&)
{
  // Make a very loud compiler error!
  static_assert<false,
                "error: long double not allowed!">

  return 0.0L;
}
```

Template specialization can be applied to templates with multiple parameters and to specialize different parameters. When a subset of template parameters is specialized, it is called a *partial* template specialization. For example, we will now make a partial template specialization of the point class whose *x*-coordinate members are of type std::uint8_t. In particular,

```
// The original point template class.
template<typename x_type,
         typename y_type>
class point { ... };

// A partial specialization of the point
// class with x-axis having type std::uint8_t.

template<typename y_type>
class point<std::uint8_t, y_type>
{
public:
  std::uint8_t x;
  y_type       y;

  point(const std::uint8_t& x_ = x_type(),
        const y_type&       y_ = y_type()) : x(x_),
                                             y(y_)
  {
  }
};
```

5.7   Static Polymorphism

Templates provide a mechanism for static polymorphism, in other words polymorphic behavior determined at compile time. This is distinctly different from the
dynamic (runtime) polymorphism described in Sect. 4.4.

Consider once again the two LED classes in the class hierarchy of Sect. 4.1,
led_port and led_pwm. We will now take a look at static polymorphism using
these two LED classes. We will first slightly modify these classes to be better suited
for static polymorphism instead of dynamic polymorphism. In particular, we will
remove the classes from a class hierarchy and eliminate the virtual functions.

```cpp
class led_port // No base class.
{
public:
  led_port(const port_type p,
           const bval_type b);

  void toggle() // Not virtual.
  {
    // ...
  }

  // ...
};

class led_pwm // No base class.
{
public:
  led_pwm(pwm* p);

  void toggle() // Not virtual.
  {
    // ...
  }

  // ...
};
```

These new LED classes are no longer related to each other through a class
hierarchy. Both of these new LED classes do, however, now have a non-virtual
toggle() function. Therefore, static polymorphism can be used to create a
generic toggle mechanism for them. For example,

```
template<typename led_type>
void led_toggler(led_type& led)
{
  // Toggle with static polymorphism.
  led.toggle();
}
```

The `led_toggler()` subroutine accepts a reference to an `led_type`. So any `led_type` object that has a `toggle()` member can be successfully toggled with `led_toggler()`. Instead of using the virtual function mechanism to select the right toggle function at runtime, the compiler generates the appropriate call of each object's `toggle()` member at compile time. This is static polymorphism.

As a final example of static polymorphism, we will redo the toggle code of the LEDs L0...L3 from Sect. 4.2. This time we will use static polymorphism instead of dynamic polymorphism.

```
namespace
{
  // Two LEDs connected P2.0-P2.1
  led_port led0 { mcal::reg::port2, 1U };
  led_port led1 { mcal::reg::port2, 2U };

  // Two PWMs on channels T0 and T1.
  pwm pwm0 { 0 };
  pwm pwm1 { 1 };

  // Two LEDs connected to pwm0 and pwm1.
  led_pwm led2 { &pwm0 };
  led_pwm led3 { &pwm1 };
}

void toggle_all_leds()
{
  led_toggler(L0); // Uses led_port::toggle().
  led_toggler(L1); // Uses led_port::toggle().

  led_toggler(L2); // Uses led_pwm::toggle().
  led_toggler(L3); // Uses led_pwm::toggle().
}
```

Static polymorphism removes the runtime overhead caused by the virtual function mechanism. As such, static polymorphism *can* improve runtime performance. At the same time, though, a given implementation based on static polymorphism *might* have significantly more code than a comparable implementation based on dynamic polymorphism because of multiple instantiation. On the other hand, static polymorphism could just as well result in improved performance *and* reduced code due the potentially improved optimization made possible by templates. This can also be observed in Table 2.1 of Sect. 2.6.

The microcontroller programmer should be cognizant of the existence of static polymorphism and dynamic polymorphism and be aware of potential advantages or costs resulting from their use. When designing code, one should try to identify situations in which each one (or a mixture of the two) can produce the most effective and reliable results.

5.8   Using the STL with Microcontrollers

The Standard Template Library (STL) is an innovative collection of containers, iterators, algorithms, etc. The STL provides a remarkably complete and powerful set of generic tools and is highly regarded as an example of generic programming in C++. See Sect. 14.5, "Generic Programming" in [3].

The STL is part of the C++ standard library. This section provides only a brief introduction to the richness of the STL. Consult [2] and also Appendix A for further details on the STL.

The code below uses the STL's templated `std::vector` container in combination with the `std::for_each()` algorithm.

```cpp
#include <algorithm>
#include <vector>

void do_something_with_the_stl()
{
  // Create v with the decimal values (1, 2, 3).
  // Initialize with a convenient initializer_list.

  std::vector<char> v { 1, 2, 3 };

  // Use an algorithm with a lambda function.
  // Convert from decimal int to ASCII char.

  std::for_each(v.begin(),
                v.end(),
                [](char& c) { c += 0x30; });
}
```

In this example, the three characters in the vector v with decimal values (1, 2, 3) are converted to ASCII characters with the values ('1', '2', '3'). The conversion from decimal to ASCII is carried out with a so-called *lambda expression* as the third input parameter to std::for_each(). The vector v is constructed and initialized at the same time using a convenient std::initializer_list in combination with uniform initialization syntax. The initializer list is also an STL container. See Sect. A.2 for more information on uniform initialization syntax, Sect. A.9 for lambda expressions and Sect. A.10 for initializer lists.

Sometimes more than one algorithm is available for a particular programming task. The conversion of the characters in v from decimal to ASCII could, for example, just as well be accomplished with std::transform().

```
#include <algorithm>
#include <vector>

void do_something_with_the_stl()
{
  std::vector<char> v { 1, 2, 3 };

  std::transform(v.begin(),
                 v.end(),
                 v.begin(),
                 [](char& c) { c += 0x30; });
}
```

This kind of conversion operation—and many others like it—often arise in real-time C++ software. Although the conversion from decimal to ASCII is somewhat trivial, these examples do provide a glimpse into the power and flexibility of the STL.

The code of the STL can be found in the include path where the compiler's STL headers are stored.[2] Those curious about the implementation details of the compiler's STL, can simply investigate the source code.

The std::for_each() algorithm, for example, could be implemented in the STL in a way similar to the code shown below.

```
namespace std
{
  template<typename iterator_type,
           typename function_type>
  function_type for_each(iterator_type first,
                         iterator_type last,
```

---

[2]It might be difficult to read the code, but it's there!

```
                                 function_type function)
{
  while(first != last)
  {
    function(*first);
    ++first;
  }

  return function;
}
}
```

Using the STL can simplify programming, reduce error and improve efficiency and portability in microcontroller programming. Instead of arduously developing and testing hand-written containers and loops, the standardized components of the STL can be used *out-of-the-box*. With the consistent use of the standardized containers, iterators, algorithms, etc. of the STL, code will adopt a recognizable *look and feel* with easy-to-understand style.

One might also want to glance ahead to Sects. 10.3 and 10.5 which describe methods for outfitting STL containers with custom dynamic memory management mechanisms appropriate for microcontrollers. These techniques allow us to fit surprisingly many parts of the STL into the strictly limited memories of even the most tiny embedded controllers.

5.9   Variadic Templates

Variadic templates are template functions or class types that have a variable number of template parameters. Variadic templates were included in C++11.

Consider a simple software factory.

```
template<typename type_to_make>
type_to_make* factory(void* mem)
{
  // Construct a new pointer of kind type_to_make
  // with the placement-new operator.

  type_to_make* p = new(mem) type_to_make;

  return p;
}
```

This `factory()` makes products of kind `type_to_make`. The placement-**new**() operator, described in Sect. 10.2, is used to create the product in a caller-supplied memory pool.

We will now make *something* with this `factory()`. For example,

```
class something
{
public:
  something() { }
};

extern void* pool;

something* ps = factory<something>(pool);
```

Here, `ps` is created in the memory `pool`. The newly created `ps` is just like any other pointer. It can be used accordingly and deleted when no longer needed.

Consider, next, another class called `something_else`.

```
class something_else
{
public:
  something_else(const int M, const int N)  : m(M),
                                              n(N) { }

  virtual ~something_else() { }

private:
  int m;
  int n;
};
```

Imagine that we would like to create a pointer to `something_else`. Unlike the constructor of the `something` class, the constructor of `something_else` supports has up to two input parameters. In this case, our `factory()` is not flexible enough to create `something_else` because it can only create things with parameter-less constructors.

In order to make a flexible `factory()`, then, we can use a variadic template. For example,

```
template<typename type_to_make,
         typename ...parameters>
type_to_make* factory(void* mem,
```

```
                          parameters... params)
{
  // Construct a new pointer of kind type_to_make
  // with the placement-new operator
  // and a parameter pack argument.

  type_to_make* p = new(mem) type_to_make(params...);

  return p;
}
```

Here, the variadic template parameter `parameters` can contain any number of all kinds of things, including built-in types, class types, etc. Notice that the **operator**... is used in two different ways. The **operator**... is used on the left side to declare a parameter pack in the template parameter list and on the right side to unpack the parameter pack into separate arguments in the function call. The parameter pack will be unpacked at compile time. In this case, C++ trades compilation effort for improved runtime efficiency, which is usually the right trade-off for real-time C++.

With this new, more flexible version of our `factory()`, we can successfully create objects of any class types having any kinds and numbers of constructor parameters. An instance of `something_else`, for example, can readily be made with the new `factory()`. In particular,

```
class something_else
{
  // ...
};

extern void* pool;

something_else* p_else
  = factory<something_else>(pool, 12, 34);
```

Variadic templates add a new dimension of flexibility to template programming. They can be used to elegantly solve a class of problems that arise when multiple varying types need to be handled by a generic mechanism.

5.10   Template Metaprogramming

Template metaprogramming uses templates at compile time to do work that may otherwise need to be done during runtime. Template metaprogramming can be useful for sophisticated optimizations such as compile-time generation of constant values and loop unrolling.

The archetypal introductory template metaprogram computes the value of the unsigned integer factorial function at compile time. A possible implementation of a metaprogram for computing $N!$ is shown below.

```
template<const std::uint32_t N>
struct factorial
{
  // Multiply N * (N - 1) with template recursion.
  static constexpr std::uint32_t value
    = N * factorial<N - 1>::value;
};

template<>
struct factorial<0U>
{
  // Zero'th specialization terminates the recursion.
  static constexpr std::uint32_t value = 1;
};
```

When the compiler instantiates `factorial<N>::value` for a given value of N, it recursively multiplies N with `factorial<N - 1>::value`. Template recursion terminates with the template specialization of `factorial<0U>::value`. The compiler produces no intermediate code and the result of the factorial is generated as a compile-time constant.

Consider, for example, the computation of 5! below.

```
constexpr std::uint32_t fact5 = factorial<5>::value;
```

Here, the `factorial` template is used to calculate 5!, the result of which is $5 \times 4 \times 3 \times 2 \times 1 = 120$. The result is generated by the compiler and directly injected into the code as a compile-time constant value. This example, although somewhat trivial, shows how template metaprogramming uses recursive templates for radical compile-time optimization.

A less trivial metaprogram computes the inner product of two equally sized ranges of adjacent iterator types. Consider the `inner_product` structure below.

```cpp
template<const std::size_t N,
         const std::size_t M = 0U>
struct inner_product
{
  template<typename iterator_left,
           typename iterator_right,
           typename result_type>
  static result_type sum(iterator_left u,
                         iterator_right v,
                         const result_type& init)
  {
    // Add (u[M] * v[M]) recursively.
    const result_type uvm
      = *(u + M) * result_type(*(v + M));

    return uvm
      + inner_product<N, M + 1U>::sum(u, v, init);
  }
};

template<const std::size_t N>
struct inner_product<N, N>
{
  template<typename iterator_left,
           typename iterator_right,
           typename result_type>
  static result_type sum(iterator_left,
                         iterator_right,
                         const result_type&)
  {
    // N'th specialization terminates the recursion.
    return result_type(0);
  }
};
```

The inner_product structure computes the inner product of the elements in the range [M, N-1). The template parameters M and N are used to represent the start index and total length of the inner product, respectively. The Mth value of the sum is recursively passed to the (M + 1)th index in the inner product. Template recursion stops when the index parameter M reaches the upper bound of the inner product N. The inner_product template can be used with C-style arrays, std::array, std::vector, etc. (Sect. 5.8).

The template parameter `result_type` provides for optional scalability of the result. Notice that the start index M does not necessarily need to begin with zero. The inner product can start with an index higher than zero by appropriately setting M in the calling code.

The following code uses the `inner_product` metaprogram to compute the inner product of two `std::arrays`, u and v, where each array has three elements.

```
constexpr std::array<unsigned, 3U> u
{
  { 1U, 2U, 3U }
};

constexpr std::array<unsigned, 3U> v
{
  { 4U, 5U, 6U }
};

constexpr unsigned w
  = inner_product<3U>::sum(u.begin(),
                           v.begin(),
                           0U);
// The result is 32.
```

In this example, the values in both arrays u and v as well as the index parameters are known at compile time. Therefore, the compiler can fully compute the constant value of the inner product when setting w. This metaprogramming technique can be useful in areas involving coordinates or linear algebra such as graphics, vehicle dynamic detection, navigation, etc.

5.11 Tuples and Generic Metaprogramming

One of the most versatile templates added to the standard library with C++11 is `std::tuple`. The `std::tuple` template is a generalization of `std::pair` to triple, quadruple, quin-*tuple*, sex-*tuple*, etc. See Sect. A.13 for more information on tuples.

Unlike templated STL containers such as `std::vector`, a tuple can contain different kinds of objects. For example,

```
#include <tuple>

class apple
{
```

```
  // ...
};

class car
{
  // ...
};

class tiger
{
  // ...
};

std::tuple<apple, car, tiger> things;
```

Grouping objects of different types together can be useful if they need to be organized and manipulated as a cohesive collection. For example, the things tuple above can be passed by reference to a subroutine or included in a class as a member variable. In this way, tuples can improve program organization.

Another advantage of tuples is their ability to be manipulated with templates and metaprogramming. For example, imagine that all of the seemingly unrelated objects in the things tuple, the apple, car and tiger, have a same-named public member function called setup(). In other words, the apple class has apple::setup(), the car class has car::setup() and the tiger class has tiger::setup(). In this made-up example, the setup() member functions are responsible for setting up the internals of their respective class, such as the apple's ripeness, the car's fuel-level or the tiger's state of health. For instance,

```
class apple
{
public:
  apple() { }

  void setup() { /* ... */ }
};

class car
{
public:
  car() { }

  void setup() { /* ... */ }
};
```

```
class tiger
{
public:
  tiger() { }

  void setup() { /* ... */ }
};
```

We will now take our `things` tuple and explicitly `setup()` each element in it using the STL's templated `std::get()` facility. In particular,

```
std::tuple<apple, car, tiger> things;

void do_something()
{
  std::get<0>(things).setup();
  std::get<1>(things).setup();
  std::get<2>(things).setup();
}
```

Here, `std::get()` is used to *get* a reference to each object in the `things` tuple by index. Since each one of the objects in `things` has a `setup()` function, it can be called with the regular member selection operator (.) for references.

This situation lends itself well to generic metaprogramming. In particular, we could easily modify the inner product example from the last section to run through the indexes in a tuple and call each object's `setup()` function.

```
template<const unsigned N,
         const unsigned M = 0U>
struct tuple_setup_each
{
  template<typename tuple_type>
  static void setup(tuple_type& t)
  {
    // Setup the M'th object and the next higher one.
    std::get<M>(t).setup();
    tuple_setup_each<N, M + 1U>::setup(t);
  }
};

template<const unsigned N>
struct tuple_setup_each<N, N>
{
```

```
template<typename tuple_type>
static void setup(tuple_type&) { }
};
```

With the `tuple_setup_each` metaprogram, it's almost trivial to `setup()` the objects in the `things` tuple. In particular,

```
std::tuple<apple, car, tiger> things;

void do_something()
{
  // Setup the things.
  tuple_setup_each<3U>::setup(things);
}
```

The `tuple_setup_each` metaprogram recursively generates setup code for each object in the `things` tuple via its `setup()` member.

This code can be made more generic by employing the `std::tuple_size` facility, which returns the number of objects in a tuple-type as a compile-time constant. We will now slightly modify the code accordingly.

```
// Use a convenient type definition for the tuple_type.
typedef std::tuple<apple, car, tiger> tuple_type;

tuple_type things;

// Use tuple_size to get the size of the things.
constexpr unsigned size
  = std::tuple_size<tuple_type>::value;

void do_something()
{
  // Setup the things.
  tuple_setup_each<size>::setup(things);
}
```

This metaprogramming technique can setup the things in any tuple with any number of elements, as long as the type of each element in the tuple has a `setup()` function. Generic metaprogramming with tuples can be useful when objects with a partially or wholly common interface are to be treated with the same semantics.

References

1. B. Eckel, *Thinking in C++ Volume 2: Practical Programming* (Pearson Prentice Hall, Upper Saddle River, 2004)
2. N.M. Josuttis, *The C++ Standard Library: A Tutorial and Reference*, 2nd edn. (Addison Wesley, Reading, 2011)
3. D. Vandevoorde, N.M. Josuttis, *C++ Templates: The Complete Guide* (Addison Wesley, Reading, 2003)

Chapter 6
Optimized C++ Programming for Microcontrollers

Embedded systems software, possibly even more than other kinds of software, is time critical and has cost-sensitive size constraints. Literally every *bit* of the microcontroller software costs precious code space and cycles. Even the most minute software weakness can lead to system-debilitating resource problems. Writing efficient C++ code for microcontrollers mandates command of the language and solid development practices. This chapter aids this endeavor by providing a selection of helpful tips for optimized C++ microcontroller programming.

6.1 Use Compiler Optimization Settings

Compiler optimization settings allow for flexible tuning of the compiler's code generation. It is possible to optimize with emphasis on space, speed or a combination thereof. GNU compilers have a particularly rich set of command line optimization settings. See van Hagen [1] Chap. 5 and Appendix A for further information on optimization settings in GCC.

When researching microcontroller optimization techniques for this book, for example, a computationally intensive code sequence rich in 32–bit operations implementing an MD5 message-digest algorithm has been benchmarked. The original MD5 code was based on the reference implementation of RFC 1321 [2, 3], herein identified as the "RSA Data Security, Inc. MD5 Message-Digest Algorithm". The RSA code was re-factored in [4]. For the investigation here, the code was further modified and optimized for the microcontroller port. The resulting MD5 code is included in the reference project of the companion code.

After being prepared for efficient use with microcontrollers, the MD5 code was compiled two times for our target with the 8–bit microcontroller, the first time optimized for speed and the second time optimized for space.

C.M. Kormanyos, *Real-Time C++*, DOI 10.1007/978-3-642-34688-0_6,
© Springer-Verlag Berlin Heidelberg 2013

Table 6.1 The code size and runtime for an MD5 algorithm on our target with the 8–bit microcontroller with optimization tuned for space and speed are listed

Optimization goal	Code size MD5 (byte)	Runtime MD5("creativity") (μs)
Space	9,588	1,690
Speed	11,276	1,400

When building the MD5 program for speed, the optimization settings shown below have been used.

```
-O3 -finline-functions -finline-limit=64
```

The optimization settings shown below have been used when optimizing the MD5 program for space.

```
-Os -fno-inline-functions
```

Table 6.1 shows the benchmark results for computing the MD5 of the ten 8–bit ASCII unsigned characters in "creativity" (in other words, 0x63, 0x72, 0x65, 0x61, 0x74, 0x69, 0x76, 0x69, 0x74, 0x79). Both the space-optimized version as well as the speed-optimized version of the executable obtain the correct result for the MD5.[1] In particular,

$$\text{MD5 ("creativity")} =$$

$$\text{0x4F1D1909B527806E7633504AB7BF789F.} \quad (6.1)$$

The space-optimized algorithm has a code size about 15 % smaller than the one optimized for speed, whereas the speed-optimized version runs approximately 20 % faster than the space-optimized one. In general, space and speed are opposing optimization goals. Improvements in speed are usually obtained at the cost of larger code size. The benchmark results shown above confirm this tendency.

Differences between speed and space optimization can be strongly pronounced if inline-depth control, loop unrolling and common subexpression elimination are available. In particular, the size and speed of template-intensive code can be strongly influenced by the compiler optimization settings.

It is usually best to carefully study the available compiler optimization settings. If possible, try to understand which optimization features get activated at each optimization level and select the right compiler optimization settings for the project.

---

[1]This is another testament to the quality and language standards adherence capabilities of GCC. GCC correctly compiled this 32–bit computationally intensive MD5 calculation with ease and absolute correctness, even for an 8–bit platform.

6.2 Know the Microcontroller's Performance

The same C++ code running on different microcontrollers can have vastly different performance on each of them. Consider the two microcontrollers used in this book, the 8–bit target running at 16 MHz and the 32–bit target clocked at 24 MHz. These are both excellent microcontrollers offering the industry's highest levels of product quality combined with world-class CPU architectures and peripherals. In addition, both microcontrollers can readily be programmed in C++ with the versatile GCC. The two microcontrollers are, however, in radically different performance classes, and this must be taken into account when assessing their ranges of application.

Table 6.2 compares the code size and runtime for the MD5 algorithm from the previous section on these two microcontrollers. As mentioned above, this MD5 code is computationally intensive and has numerous 32–bit integer operations. Consequently, the program runs significantly faster—about 16 times faster—on the 32–bit microcontroller than on the 8–bit machine. In addition, the code on the 32–bit target requires merely 1/3 of the program space taken up by the corresponding code on the 8–bit target.

The reasons for these performance and size differences are easy to understand. Basic operations on 32–bit integers such as add, subtract, multiply and shift make up the core of the MD5 algorithm. These operations require significant software support on the 8–bit microcontroller, whereas they are single opcodes on the 32–bit target. From the perspective of code size, on the other hand, 32–bit opcodes are wider than the 8–bit or 16–bit opcodes in the vocabulary of the 8–bit machine. So 32–bit code *could*, in general, be larger than corresponding 8–bit code.[2] In the case of the MD5 algorithm, however, the improved efficiency of 32–bit operations is so overwhelmingly beneficial for the MD5 that both the code size as well as the runtime are significantly better on the 32–bit machine.

Bigger and faster is not always better. If the application is cost-sensitive and only needs to perform a few functions, then a small 8–bit microcontroller can be the right choice. A big 32–bit microcontroller might be too expensive for the application. If, however, the microcontroller lacks sufficient resources for the requirements of the application, then the CPU may be overloaded and the system could be unreliable or might even fail. In this case, a larger 32–bit CPU may be necessary. In order to guarantee the right efficiency for the application, it is necessary to select a microcontroller with the right performance and size.

A large chunk of portable, computationally intensive microcontroller C++ code such as an MD5 algorithm can be used as part of a benchmark to provide reliable data for proper microcontroller selection. There are additional notes on

---

[2] In fact, it is not uncommon that code compiled for an 8–bit target is more compact than the corresponding code compiled for a 32–bit target. This usually only occurs if the code at hand can, without introducing error, be scaled to the architecture using, among other things, the so-called *native* integer width of the CPU (Sect. 6.10).

Table 6.2 The code size and runtime for an MD5 algorithm on our targets with 8– and 32–bit microcontrollers are listed. The compiler optimization has been tuned for speed

Target system	Code size MD5 (byte)	Runtime MD5(`"creativity"`) (µs)
32–bit target at 24 MHz	3,408	86
8–bit target at 16 MHz	11,276	1,400

microcontroller selection in the checklist of Sect. B.1 and some details on establishing reliable runtime limits in Sect. B.3.

6.3   Know an Algorithm's Complexity

In computer science, the limiting behavior of algorithmic complexity can be characterized by the number of terms N in the algorithm's input size. The so-called *big-O* notation (pronounced *big-oh*) is often used to express the algorithmic complexity as a power of N. For example, counting loops, simple additive checksums such as CRCs and digital filters (Chap. 14) have linear complexity of order N, in other words $O(N)$. Traditional grade-school multiplication of $a \times b$, where both a and b have N constituents, has quadratic complexity of $O(N^2)$.

The runtime of an algorithm may grow rapidly or—for all practical matters— become essentially unbounded as N increases. In such cases, it usually makes sense to find better algorithms for large N. For example, interpolation in an ordered set of points can use either a linear search or a binary search (Sect. 15.4). A linear search has complexity of $O(N)$ because it loops through the points until the interpolation pair is found. A binary search, on the other hand, uses interval-halving methods with logarithmic complexity of $O(\log_2 N)$. If N is 128, then a linear search has a maximum complexity of $\sim$128, while the corresponding binary search with the same N has a complexity of $\sim$7. Many searching and sorting algorithms in the STL use a binary search under-the-hood. These algorithms, therefore, benefit from the efficiency of logarithmic complexity, as opposed to linear complexity.

The speed of multiplication often determines the performance of mathematical calculations because many calculations spend the majority of their time doing multiplications. The efficiency of multiplication can have a particularly strong influence on common integer calculations such as cryptographic hash algorithms or fixed-point computations. When designing code, then, writing multiplication operations in the optimum way can improve performance.

Consider the multiplication of two unsigned 16–bit integers with an unsigned 32–bit integer result. One potentially efficient way to express this multiplication in C++ on an 8–bit CPU architecture is shown below.

```
std::uint16_t a = 55555U;
std::uint16_t b = 61234U;

void do_something()
{
  // 16 x 16 --> 32-bit result = 3,401,854,870.
  std::uint32_t result
    = a * static_cast<std::uint32_t>(b);
}
```

In this example, only one side of the multiplication of $a \times b$ has been casted to std::uint32_t. The compiler can, therefore, optionally choose between the better of $16 \times 16 \rightarrow 32$–bit multiplication and $32 \times 32 \rightarrow 32$–bit multiplication and still get the right answer. For an 8–bit CPU architecture, a good compiler will select $16 \times 16 \rightarrow 32$–bit multiplication with algorithmic complexity $2^N = 2^2 = 4$. Casting both a and b to std::uint32_t would, however, force the compiler to use $32 \times 32 \rightarrow 32$–bit multiplication with complexity $2^N = 2^4 = 16$. The code as written above is portable, yet still allows the compiler to take advantage of the optimization of half-sized multiplication when necessary.

In mathematics, graphics, signal processing, etc., a convolution such as a fast Fourier transform (FFT) is often used to reduce the computational complexity of an algorithm in the transform space. Transformation makes sense if the added runtime effort of the transformation is more than compensated by reduced work in the transform domain. There is often a cut-off point, in other words a particular value of N, above which the transformation reduces an algorithm's runtime and below which it does not.

Hardware accelerators and digital signal processors (DSP) can be integrated in microcontrollers to perform some functions faster than possible in software. They are commonly used for mathematical operations like multiplication and division, transformations such as FFT, cryptographic hash algorithms like MD5, digital filters and other common signal processing tasks. If computationally intensive operations play a central role in the application, preferentially selecting a microcontroller with the appropriate accelerator or DSP can significantly reduce the CPU work load.

In general, one should attempt to understand the algorithmic complexity and input sizes that are expected in the project. Is binary arithmetic coded with ideal operand sizes? Are linear algorithms adequate? Are optimized algorithms such as those in the STL consistently used? Does the application need hardware acceleration or even a dedicated DSP? These are the kinds of design questions should be consider before selecting the chip and the software libraries or beginning software design and implementation.

6.4 Use Assembly Listings

Assembly listings allow us to follow the original high-level C++ source code into the intricate depths of compiler-generated assembly language and machine-level opcodes. Analyses of assembly listings facilitate the process of designing and writing optimized code because assembly listings show the actual code which will run on the target processor in a very low-level form.

In general, the *way* in which C++ code is written strongly influences *how* the compiler generates assembly code and, ultimately, *which* machine-level opcodes are placed in the executable. A basic understanding of assembly file listings makes it possible to guide the implementations of time critical code sequences in a controlled and iterative fashion. In this way, highly optimized results can be achieved.

By studying assembly listings one will, over time, obtain an intuitive *feeling* for efficient coding. Developing this skill is a long-term process. Investigating assembly listings can teach us when and how to use templates and how to develop efficient class objects. Assembly listings can also reveal the benefits and costs of runtime polymorphism, inline functions, templates, using the STL, etc.

With GNU compilers, an assembly listing can be generated with the `objdump` program. The object dump program is available in GCC's binary utilities and also in the bash shell on most *nix-like environments. A sample command using `objdump` is shown below.

```
objdump -j .text -S my_file.o > my_file.lst
```

In this command, `my_file.o` is an object file that has been created with `g++`. The text-based results are piped into `my_file.lst`.

6.5 Use Map Files

Most linkers can generate a *map file*. Map files contain detailed information about the addresses, types and sizes of program components such as program code, static variables and objects, interrupt tables, debug sections, etc.

Map files can be used to verify that the program parts are properly located in memory and also to investigate their resource consumption. This facilitates guided size optimization. Together with assembly listings, it is possible to use map file information to iteratively find the best compromise between space and speed in the code.

With GNU compilers, a map file can be generated by the linker when creating the absolute object file. For example, `app.map` can be created with the following command.

```
g++ a.o b.o c.o -Wl,-Tldef.ld,-Map,app.map -o app.elf
```

In this command, the files a.o, b.o and c.o are object files compiled from the corresponding source codes a.cpp, b.cpp and c.cpp. The file ldef.ld is a linker definition file (Sect. 8.4). The absolute object file app.elf is the output of the linker in ELF binary format. In this particular example, the map file is a by-product of linking the program.

ELF files are in binary format and can be read with the utility program readelf. Again, readelf is a standard tool available in GCC's binary utilities and on most ∗nix-like environments. A sample command using readelf is shown below.

```
readelf --syms app.elf > app.txt
```

Here, app.elf is the absolute object file mentioned above. The text-based results from readelf are piped into app.txt. The command program option --syms stands for *display the symbol table* and is equivalent to the short-hand option -s.

6.6 Understand Name Mangling and De-mangling

Symbol names created by the C++ compiler can be difficult to read in the map file. C++ supports namespaces, function overrides, etc. This means that symbols can potentially have the same name. For example, both integers in the two separate namespaces below are named the_int.

```
namespace this_space
{
    int the_int;
}

namespace another_space
{
    int the_int;
}
```

Same-named symbols such as the_int need to be uniquely identifiable. In order to guarantee non-conflicting symbol names in C++, the compiler needs to make *decorated* internal names for variables and subroutines using additional information based on the partial names of parameters, namespaces, classes, etc. These can be optionally combined with random numbers, letters and selected non-alphanumeric characters such as '&', '_', '?', '!', '@', etc. to create unique names.

In practice, the names that a C++ compiler makes can be so long and difficult to read that the name-decorating process has come to be known as *name mangling*. Name mangling is mandatory for establishing unequivocal symbol names in C++. As an aside, note that name mangling is dreadfully compiler-specific. Mangled names can not be found in the source code. Mangled names are constructed by the compiler for internal use and will only be encountered in map files, assembly listings, debuggers, etc.

Consider the rather uncomplicated subroutine declaration below.

```
os::event_type os::get_event(const os::task_id_type);
```

This is the name of a multitasking scheduler's get_event() function (such as the kind mentioned toward the end of Chap. 11). This function resides in the namespace os. Its sole input parameter is a **typedef**-ed enumeration for task-IDs, also located within the namespace os. GCC creates the mangled name shown below for the subroutine os::get_event().

```
_ZN2os9get_eventENS_17enum_task_id_typeE
```

The essential elements of the original name are recognizable and it is possible to vaguely guess how the name mangling has augmented the original name with namespace and parameter information to create a unique name. Nonetheless, the mangled name is rather hard to read.

With the c++filt program, it is possible to *demangle* the mangled names created by g++. Yes, it really is called name demangling. The sample bash session below illustrates how c++filt can be used to demangle the mangled name of os::get_event().

```
chris@chris-PC ~
$ c++filt _ZN2os9get_eventENS_17enum_task_id_typeE
os::get_event(os::enum_task_id_type)

chris@chris-PC ~
$ exit
```

It can also be convenient to initially produce a list of mangled names with nm, the *names* program, and subsequently demangle them with c++filt. For example, the following command extracts the mangled names from app.elf with nm, subsequently sorts them numerically (by address) and demangles them by piping the sorted list to c++filt.

```
nm --numeric-sort app.elf | c++filt
```

This simple command demangles even the most complicated names from g++, creating a clean, easy to read list of recognizable symbol names. A basic understanding of name mangling and how to de-mangle names with readily available tools can be helpful when interpreting map files.

6.7   Know When to Use Assembly and When Not To

Assembly programming, by its very nature, is non-portable and should be avoided in C++. Nonetheless, there are a few rare situations in microcontroller programming which require assembly. This can be the case either because assembly programming is the only way to accomplish the programming task at hand or because the efficiency can be so radically improved (e.g. for a time critical sequence that runs frequently) that using assembly is justified.

Assembly sequences should be buried within the microcontroller layer of the software architecture in order to shield the system and application layers from non-portability. See Sect. B.2 for information on layered software architecture. For short assembly sequences of just a few lines, it may be preferable to use so-called *inline assembly*, directly integrated into the C++ compiler via language extension. For larger assembly sequences with more than, say, 10 or 20 lines (e.g., for parts of an extended multitasking scheduler), a dedicated assembly file may be more appropriate.

GCC's inline assembly syntax uses microcontroller-specific assembly dialects expressed in the language of GAS, the GNU assembler. Other compilers have similar language extensions with varying syntaxes.

Inline assembly can be convenient for creating short inline functions for things such as global interrupt enable and disable, the *nop* operation, etc. For example,

```cpp
namespace mcal
{
  namespace irq
  {
    // Interrupt enable/disable.
    inline void enable_all()  { asm volatile ("sei"); }
    inline void disable_all() { asm volatile ("cli"); }
  }
}

namespace mcal
{
  namespace cpu
  {
    // The no-operation.
    inline void nop() { asm volatile ("nop"); }
  }
}
```

Calling a C++ function, whether inline or non-inline, that is either partly or completely composed of assembly is done in the same way as calling a *normal* C++ function. For example, the code sample below enables global interrupts in `main()` via call of `mcal::irq::enable_all()`.

```cpp
int main()
{
  // Enable all global interrupts.
  // The enable_all() function uses assembly!
  mcal::irq::enable_all();

  // Initialize the mcal.
  // ...

  // Start multitasking.
  // ...
}
```

6.8   Use Comments Sparingly

Once, I wrote the following line of code:

```cpp
CalculateSpeed(); // Calculate speed.
```

Years after its origination, an amused colleague indicated that the comment does not foster understanding, but detracts from code legibility instead.

Long, redundant comments throttle coding efficiency, obscuring clarity and readability. Comments can also be a source of error. Code evolves over time and comments, once written by a motivated programmer, often disagree with the code at a later stage in its evolution. In fact, a skeptical developer once said, *If the code and the comment disagree, then they are probably both wrong.* Trying to improve poorly written code by adding comments simply sidesteps an underlying quality problem. Commenting clear code is superfluous.

On the other hand, comments that explain non-obvious algorithm details or illuminate the obscure meaning of register bit assignments do *deserve* to be commented in the code. It is important to find the right compromise between legibility and understanding and, above all, strive to write code that is clear, terse and self-explanatory.

6.9 Simplify Code with `typedef`

Using **typedef** can reduce typing effort and, at the same time, make code easier
to read and understand. In Sect. 7.3 ahead, we will define a template class used for
generic access to microcontroller registers. In particular,

```
template<typename addr_type,
         typename reg_type,
         const addr_type addr,
         const reg_type val>
class reg_access
{
public:
  static void      reg_set() { /* ... */ }
  static void      reg_and() { /* ... */ }
  static void      reg_or () { /* ... */ }
  static reg_type  reg_get() { /* ... */ }

  static void      bit_set() { /* ... */ }
  static void      bit_clr() { /* ... */ }
  static void      bit_not() { /* ... */ }
  static bool      bit_get() { /* ... */ }

  static void variable_reg_set(const reg_type)
  {
    // ...
  }
};
```

The versatile `reg_access` template can be used for most common register
manipulations. For example, we can use the `bit_not()` member to toggle
`portb.5`. In other words,

```
// Toggle portb.5.
reg_access<std::uint8_t,
           std::uint8_t,
           mcal::reg::portb,
           5U>::bit_not();
```

That is quite a bit of typing for the modest task of toggling a port bit. It
is, however, possible to reduce the typing effort of the toggle operation with a
typedef. For instance,

```
typedef reg_access<std::uint8_t,
                    std::uint8_t,
                    mcal::reg::portb,
                    5U> port_b5_type;

// Toggle portb.5.
port_b5_type::bit_not();
```

Previously in Sect. 2.6, we defined the `led_template` class and used it to encapsulate an LED on `portb.5`. Combining the `reg_access` template with **typedef**s can simplify the implementation of this class. In particular,

```
template<typename port_type,
         typename bval_type,
         const port_type port,
         const bval_type bval>
class led_template
{
public:
  led_template()
  {
    // Set the port pin value to low.
    port_pin_type::bit_clr();

    // Set the port pin direction to output.
    port_dir_type::bit_set();
  }

  static void toggle()
  {
    // Toggle the LED.
    port_pin_type::bit_not();
  }

private:
  static constexpr port_type pdir = port - 1U;

  // Type definition of the port data register.
  typedef reg_access<std::uint8_t,
                      std::uint8_t,
                      mcal::reg::portb,
                      port> port_pin_type;
```

```
  // Type definition of the port direction register.
  typedef reg_access<std::uint8_t,
                     std::uint8_t,
                     mcal::reg::portb,
                     pdir> port_dir_type;
};
```

Here, the strategic use of templates and **typedef**s makes the functionality of the led_template class more intuitive and easier to understand. Throughout this book, **typedef** is used to simplify code and improve program clarity.

6.10 Use Native Integer Types

Operations with integers have optimum performance if implemented with the so-called *native* integer type, in other words either the **signed** or **unsigned** version of plain **int**. These are the native integer types of the microcontroller. They are, in some sense, indigenous to the CPU architecture insofar as they typically have the same width as CPU registers. The C99 specification calls **signed** and **unsigned** **int** the *natural* integer types.

For example, 32–bit signed and unsigned integers are the native integer types on a 32–bit machine, whereas 8–bit integers are native to an 8–bit architecture.

Consider the loop operation shown in the subroutine checksum() below.

```
std::uint8_t checksum(const std::uint8_t* p,
                      const std::uint8_t len)
{
  std::uint8_t sum = 0U;

  for(std::uint8_t i = 0U; i < len; i++)
  {
    sum += *p;
    ++p;
  };

  return sum;
}
```

Here, checksum() computes the byte-wise std::uint8_t sum

$$\text{sum} = \sum_{i=0}^{i<\text{len}} p_i, \tag{6.2}$$

where p_i is the zero-based ith element in an `std::uint8_t`-pointer sequence of length `len`, and

$$0 \leq \text{len} < 256. \tag{6.3}$$

We will now compile the `checksum()` subroutine for our target with the 32–bit microcontroller. The compiled subroutine requires 192 bytes of program code, which is excessively large for this simple checksum. Investigations of the assembly listing reveal that the compiler generates code for loading and manipulating 8–bit entities, struggling through numerous zero-clear actions on the three unused bytes in 32–bit registers after loading a value. These operations are inefficient for this 32–bit machine and not actually needed for the checksum algorithm.

Using native integer types improves efficiency. For example, we will now simply change the types of `sum`, `len` and the index `i` from `std::uint8_t` to the compiler's fastest 8–bit unsigned integer type `std::uint_fast8_t`. This is an integer type that is guaranteed to have at least 8–bits (but may optionally have more) and is intended to be the *fastest* one of its kind on its target architecture.[3] We have selected `std::uint_fast8_t` instead of, say, `std::uint_fast32_t` because the resulting code will also be fast on 8– and 16–bit architectures, yet still fulfill the requirements of the checksum operation.

The modified source code is shown below.

```
std::uint8_t checksum(const std::uint8_t* p,
                      const std::uint_fast8_t len)
{
  std::uint_fast8_t sum = 0U;

  for(std::uint_fast8_t i = 0U; i < len; i++)
  {
    sum += *p;
    ++p;
  };

  return sum;
}
```

This minor code change switching from `std::uint8_t` with *exactly* 8 bits to `std::uint_fast8_t` with *at least* 8 bits vastly improves the algorithm's efficiency on the 32–bit target. In particular, the disassembled source code is markedly shorter.

---

[3]Here, the C++ specification leaves the interpretation of *fastest* open to the compiler implementation. In widespread practice, though, the *fast* integer types simply have the same width as CPU registers on the target architecture.

The compiled subroutine using `std::uint_fast8_t` has a size of 24 bytes. Compare 24 bytes with the 192 bytes from the previous listing. Using the fastest 8–bit integer type for the inner loop of the algorithm has improved the space and performance by a factor of ∼8. Yes, that is right, an eightfold improvement. This striking betterment shows that using native integer types can really pay off.

6.11   Use Scaling with Powers of Two

Multiplication and division with powers of two can be replaced by efficient shift operations. For example, division by 4 can be replaced with a right-shift of 2. Multiplication with 32 can be replaced with a left-shift of 5. All good compilers do this automatically, assuming that the right-hand operator is a compile-time constant. One of the simplest and most effective ways to remove costly multiply and divide operations is to scale with powers of two.

Consider a software counter, in other words a prescaler, used to divide a timebase into slower secondary frequencies.

```cpp
namespace { std::uint_fast16_t prescaler; }

void do_something()
{
  ++prescaler;

  do_it_at_01x_period();

  if((prescaler % 2U) == 0U)
  {
    do_it_at_02x_period();

    if((prescaler % 4U) == 0U)
    {
      do_it_at_04x_period();

      if((prescaler % 8U) == 0U)
      {
        do_it_at_08x_period();
      }
    }
  }
}
```

In this example, different software operations are carried out with frequencies of 1, 1/2, 1/4 and 1/8 of the base frequency. The conditional operations are performed with modulus 2^n so the compiler automatically uses shifts instead of costly division for them. If a base–10 prescaler were used instead, it would require division. This would be *much* less efficient. Here, we assume that the `do_it_at...()` functions are frequently-called inline functions, possibly in an ISR, quick enough in call and execution to warrant the prescaler optimization. A further refinement is achieved by nesting the **if**-statements, reducing the average load of conditional-testing, making it non-constant though.

6.12 Replace Multiply with Shift-and-Add

The compiler often replaces potentially slow multiplication operations with fast shift-and-add sequences. Good compilers *know* which is faster, a shift-and-add sequence or its corresponding multiplication operation. For example, a long sequence of shift-and-add algorithms might be slower than a single multiplication with a large integer or an integer having a non-simple prime factorization. Consider multiplication by 23, which needs three shifts and three adds (i.e., $23 = 16 + 4 + 2 + 1$). This is a lot of shift-and-add and it might be slower than the corresponding multiplication operation.

Modern compilers are remarkably aware of these situations and preferentially select the faster of multiply or shift-and-add. Positive integers that are small-valued, even and non-prime lend themselves well to optimization with shift-and-add. Preferentially using them can lead to significant performance improvements. Check the assembly listings (Sect. 6.4) to ensure that the compiler is aware of optimization via shift-and-add, and preferentially use compile-time constants that lend themselves well to shift-and-add.

6.13 Consider Advantageous Hardware Dimensioning

Peripheral hardware can be dimensioned so that it simplifies microcontroller programming. In particular, carefully designed hardware can make it possible to write code for which the compiler can replace costly multiplication and/or division with shift operations. In this way, a few simple hardware design considerations can significantly improve software efficiency.

For example, scaling with 2^n can be directly designed into the microcontroller board. Consider the simple Analog-Digital Converter (ADC) circuit shown in Fig. 6.1. Suppose the ADC has 10–bit resolution and 5 V logic. Conversion results range from 0 ... 1,023 steps for ADC voltage after the voltage divider (V_{ADC}) ranging from 0 ... 5 V.

Fig. 6.1 An ADC circuit is shown

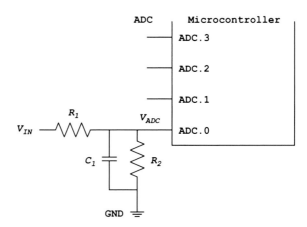

We will now design the ADC circuit for input voltage $V_{IN} \lesssim 25\,\mathrm{V}$ and simultaneously select the voltage divider parameters such that software conversion from ADC raw value to mV can be accomplished with multiplication by 32, which is a left shift by 5.

The maximum ADC result of 1,023 steps should occur when the maximum readable input voltage of $32\,\mathrm{mV} \times 1,023 = 32,736\,\mathrm{mV}$ lies on V_{IN}. This corresponds to the maximum ADC voltage of 5 V (in other words, 5,000 mV) on V_{ADC}. So the voltage divider made from R_1 and R_2 should be dimensioned according to

$$\frac{V_{ADC}}{V_{IN}} = \frac{5,000}{32,736} = \frac{R_2}{R_1 + R_2}, \tag{6.4}$$

which gives

$$R_2 = \left(\frac{5,000}{27,736}\right) \times R_1. \tag{6.5}$$

We will use resistors with 1 % tolerance and limit the worst-case injection current on the ADC pin to $\leq 1/2\,\mathrm{mA}$ for $V_{IN} = 25\,\mathrm{V}$ by selecting the resistor $R_1 = 64.9\,\mathrm{k\Omega}$. This results in $R_2 \approx 11.70\,\mathrm{k\Omega}$, which is very close to the nearest standard 1 % resistor value of 11.8 kΩ. So, the final dimension of the voltage divider is $R_1 = 64.9\,\mathrm{k\Omega}$ and $R_2 = 11.8\,\mathrm{k\Omega}$. We can complete the circuit by selecting $C_1 = 22\,\mathrm{nF}$ such that the low-pass filter has a rise time of $\tau \sim 1.4\,\mathrm{ms}$.

We will now verify the dimension of the ADC circuit. For an input voltage V_{IN} of 16 V, the voltage on V_{ADC} is

$$16\,\mathrm{V} \times \left(\frac{11.8}{64.9 + 11.8}\right) \approx 2.4615\,\mathrm{V}, \tag{6.6}$$

resulting in an integer conversion value of

$$1,023 \times \left(\frac{2.4615}{5.0}\right) = 503. \tag{6.7}$$

To check the result, multiply 503×32 mV, giving $16{,}096$ mV. This result is better than within 1 % of the true value of $16{,}000$ mV. The circuit dimension is quite acceptable. The accuracy of the software conversion is less than but comparable to the total hardware uncertainty, estimated by

$$\sqrt{2\,(0.01)^2 + \left(\frac{2}{1{,}023}\right)^2} \;\lesssim\; 2\,\%,\tag{6.8}$$

originating from two resistors with 1 % tolerance and 2 LSB tolerance (a typical value) for the ADC.

When the software designers write a conversion routine from ADC raw to mV for this circuit, it will be a simple multiplication with 32. For example,

```cpp
inline std::uint16_t raw2mv(const std::uint16_t& raw)
{
  return raw * 32U;
}
```

6.14   Consider ROM-Ability

In microcontroller programming, every resource is limited. In many projects, though, the most rare resource of all can be RAM. This makes it essential to preferentially use objects that can be entirely placed in read-only program memory, so-called "ROM-able" objects. A ROM-able object is entirely constant, in other words bitwise constant, and the compiler can save costly RAM by locating ROM-able objects in program code.

Consider the two version strings shown below.

```cpp
namespace
{
  // A version stored in a constant std::string.
  const std::string version_string1("1.23");

  // A version stored in a constant std::array.
  const std::array<char, 5U> version_string2
  {
    { '1', '.', '2', '3', '\0' }
  };
}
```

In this example, `version_string1` is stored in a constant `std::string` and `version_string2` is stored in a constant `std::array`. Both version strings have roughly equivalent values for the user. They both represent the ASCII character string "1.23". The storage requirements, however, can be quite different for the two version strings. Benchmark examinations of various map files for a few different CPU architectures revealed that `version_string1` must always be stored in RAM, whereby `version_string2` can potentially be stored in read-only program code for some targets. Furthermore, `version_string1` requires the overhead of compiler-generated constructor code for its pre-`main()` initialization.

The instance of `version_string1` is not ROM-able because, among other reasons, it is a complex object involving runtime initialization with a constructor and memory allocation (e.g., with a custom allocator, as described in Sect. 6.16 and Chap. 10). The instance of `version_string2`, on the other hand, is ROM-able because its contents are entirely known at compile time and can be directly placed in program code accordingly—or even used by the compiler *on-the-fly*.

In fact, `std::array`s of constant-valued built-in types fulfill the requirements for **constexpr**. It is, therefore, possible to *force* the compiler to treat the version string as a compile-time entity by using **constexpr** instead of **const**. In particular,

```
namespace
{
  // A version that is compile-time constant.
  constexpr std::array<char, 5U> version_string
  {
    { '1', '.', '2', '3', '\0' }
  };
}
```

It can be even more efficient (and the version string is just as constant) if the data are placed in an initializer list. For example,

```
namespace
{
  // A version that is compile-time constant.
  constexpr std::initializer_list<char> version_string
  {
    '1', '.', '2', '3', '\0'
  };
}
```

When programming with constant-valued objects, consider their ROM-ability and their potential to be treated as compile-time constant. Preferentially employing ROM-able constant objects when possible can save significant RAM in the project.

6.15 Minimize the Interrupt Frame

Interrupts can be called frequently, so it is essential they be programmed efficiently. We will now examine how the code in an interrupt service routine can influence the efficiency of its *interrupt frame*. The interrupt frame is the compiler-generated assembly code at the head and tail of the ISR that brackets the user-written code. The interrupt frame is responsible for context save and restore at interrupt entry and exit. See Sect. 9.2 for more information on interrupts.

The code below establishes the system timebase of the software by incrementing the system_tick in timer interrupt __timer0_cmp_a_isr(). Essentially the same code can be found in the general-purpose-timer (gpt) part of the MCAL in the reference project of the companion code. It is the interrupt service routine for the timer0 compare register A match event.

```
namespace
{
  volatile uint16_t system_tick;
}

// Attributes indicate interrupt service routine.
extern "C"
void __timer0_cmp_a_isr() __attribute__((interrupt));

// This is the interrupt service routine.
// This interrupt occurs when the 8-bit timer0
// counter register reaches the value in the
// compare register a.
void __timer0_cmp_a_isr()
{
  // Increment the system-tick.
  ++system_tick;
}
```

A summarized representation of the assembly code that the GNU compiler creates for the interrupt service routine __timer0_cmp_a_isr() is shown below.

```
extern "C" void __timer0_cmp_a_isr()
{
  ; Save the ISR context.
  ; 7 assembly lines for ISR frame context save.

  ; Increment the system-tick.
  ; ++system_tick;
```

```
;   5 assembly lines for increment.

;   Restore the ISR context.
;   7 assembly lines for ISR frame context restore.
}
```

The interrupt frame is relatively brief. It uses seven assembly lines to *push* a handful of registers in preparation for the interrupt. In the body of the interrupt service routine, the value of the 16–bit system_tick is incremented. This requires only two 8–bit CPU registers. Since just a few registers are used in the ISR, the compiler knows that it does not have to save and restore the entire register context information, just those registers that are actually used in the interrupt service routine itself. All good C and C+++ compilers keep track of the registers used in an interrupt service routine. Consequently, the compiler generates a minimal interrupt frame.

If more complicated code is placed in an ISR, the interrupt frame grows accordingly. The worst situation results from calling a non-inline, external function in an ISR. Consider an alternative way to increment the system-tick using a subroutine call in the interrupt service routine. For instance,

```
extern "C"
void __timer0_cmp_a_isr() __attribute__((interrupt));

extern void increment_system_tick();

void __timer0_cmp_a_isr()
{
    // Increment the system-tick with a subroutine call.
    increment_system_tick();
}
```

This version of the interrupt service routine __timer0_cmp_a_isr() also increments the system-tick. The system_tick variable is, however, not directly incremented. Rather the increment operation takes place in a non-inline, external subroutine called increment_system_tick().

The corresponding interrupt frame generated by the compiler for this version of the interrupt service routine is extensive. The synopsis is shown below.

```
extern "C" void __timer0_cmp_a_isr()
{
    ;   Save the ISR context.
    ;   17 assembly lines for ISR frame context save.

    ;   Increment the system-tick.
```

```
; increment_system_tick();
; call the increment function.

; Restore the ISR context.
; 17 assembly lines for ISR frame context restore.
; Save the ISR context.
}
```

This is certainly a drastic difference caused by changing just one line of code. The sizes of the head and tail in the interrupt frame have grown from 7 to 17 lines in the assembly listing. The increased size of the interrupt frame is, however, mandatory. As far as the compiler knows, there might be complicated operations or secondary subroutine calls in `increment_system_tick()`. The values of every register *might* be changed or modified (i.e., clobbered). Perhaps none or only some registers will really be clobbered. The compiler, however, has no way to determine what happens in the function call because it lacks call-tree analysis capabilities.

Instead of saving and restoring the registers used before and after the call of `increment_system_tick()`, then, the compiler must perform a full context save and restore of *all* the user-registers in the interrupt frame of this version of `__timer0_cmp_a_isr()`. Each register is sequentially *push*-ed onto the stack in the head of the interrupt frame. Each register is subsequently restored via *pop* instruction in reverse order in the tail thereafter.

The difference in performance and size is striking. To do the same tick incrementing, the total work of the interrupt routine has grown significantly. This kind of hidden performance hit can be eliminated by avoiding complicated code in interrupts, especially calls to non-inline external functions. This minimizes the interrupt frame and saves precious cycles.

6.16   Use Custom Memory Management

Small-to-medium size microcontrollers might have a tiny heap for dynamic memory allocation, or even no heap at all. It rarely makes sense, therefore, to allow unconditional use of **new** and **delete**. When using **new** and **delete** during runtime, the heap quickly runs out of memory or becomes fragmented beyond repair, taking on a non-usable form. In addition, the standard implementations of global **new** and **delete** may require undesired linked-in object code from the C++ library.

Developers can forget to **catch**() an std::bad_alloc exception thrown by a potentially failed allocation attempt, Sect. 10.7. This can result in a hard-to-find defect because a non-caught exception or a non-thrown one can be difficult to detect or reproduce during testing.

The problems outlined above can be avoided, and in most cases eliminated altogether, if careful, attentive use is made of user-defined memory management using placement-**new**. STL containers can also take advantage of user-defined memory allocation using custom allocators based on placement-**new**. User-defined allocation provides fine-grained control over dynamic memory resulting in efficient resource use and error reduction. Using placement-**new** and designing custom allocators for STL containers are described in Chap. 10.

6.17   Use the STL Consistently

Use the STL consistently throughout the entire microcontroller software project. In doing so, it is possible to significantly decrease coding complexity while simultaneously improving legibility, portability and performance. Loops previously written with laborious, possibly error-prone attention to detail will become simple, eloquent *one-liners*. For all good compilers, the STL authors have meticulously optimized the STL implementation for the specific characteristics of the compiler at hand. One can be relatively certain that the library developers have used programming idioms that can be optimized particularly well by the compiler. When using anything from the STL, then, one can be relatively sure that these parts of the code will reach the highest level of efficiency that the compiler has to offer.

As a case in point, reconsider the checksum algorithm from Sect. 6.10. We will now investigate the efficiency of the summation if, instead of a manually-written algorithm, `std::accumulate()` from STL's `<numeric>` is used.

```
#include <numeric>

std::uint8_t checksum(const std::uint8_t* p,
                      const std::uint_fast8_t len)
{
  return std::accumulate(p,
                         p + len,
                         std::uint_fast8_t(0U));
}
```

The implementation is a simple one-liner. In addition, it is even more efficient than the second optimized implementation in Sect. 6.10. It is an interesting exercise to use reverse engineering in an effort to find out how the STL might program this particular algorithm with such high efficiency. After a few attempts via trial-and-error, the implementations shown below has been discovered. It has the same efficiency as the STL implementation.

```
std::uint8_t checksum(const std::uint8_t* p,
                      const std::uint_fast8_t len)
{
  std::uint_fast8_t   sum = 0U;
  const std::uint8_t* end = p + len;

  while(p != end)
  {
    sum += *p;
    ++p;
  };

  return sum;
}
```

This, for example, may or may not be how one programs. It is, nonetheless, probably the most efficient way to implement this particular algorithm in C++ for this compiler. When investigating this benchmark, for example, I did *not* innately program in such a way as to reach the compiler's highest efficiency. The STL implementation beat me by two lines of assembly.

A common algorithm rarely needs to be reinvented and programmed from scratch because the algorithm is probably available in the STL. In addition, the STL authors have diligently optimized it and tested it. Using the STL throughout the project, therefore, results in a more legible, efficient and portable body of source code, automatically. In addition, other developers will find it easy to analyze and review source code that uses the STL because the standardized template interface encourages consistent style and reinforces coding clarity.

6.18   Use Lambda Expressions

The example below is based on part of the startup code as described in Sect. 8.3. The code initializes the static ctors before the jump to main(). The code calls the compiler-generated ctors in the range [ctors_begin, ctors_end) using the STL's std::for_each() algorithm.

We will now write this part of the startup code in two ways. The first uses the std::for_each() algorithm in combination with a lambda expression, whereas the second uses a function with static linkage.

The code below is written with a lambda expression.

```
typedef void(*function_type)();

function_type ctors_end[];
function_type ctors_begin[];

void init_ctors()
{
  std::for_each(ctors_begin,
                ctors_end,
                [](const function_type& pf)
                {
                  pf();
                });
}
```

The following code uses a static function.

```
typedef void(*function_type)();

function_type ctors_end[];
function_type ctors_begin[];

namespace
{
  void call_ctor(const function_type& pf) { pf(); }
}

void init_ctors()
{
  std::for_each(ctors_begin, ctors_end, call_ctor);
}
```

Analyses of the assembly listings of the two cases reveal that the version using the algorithm with the lambda expression has higher performance. In my benchmark, the version using the lambda expression had a savings of about 25 % in runtime.

Lambda expressions offer the compiler more opportunities to optimize by making the function, its iterator range and its parameters *visible* to the compiler within a single block of code. In this way, the compiler has access to richer set of register combinations, merge possibilities, etc. and it can do a better optimization. Using lambda expressions consistently throughout an entire project can save significant code and generally improve the performance of the whole software.

6.19   Use Templates and Scalability

Templates expose all of their code, their template parameters, function calls, program loops, etc. to compiler optimization at compile time. This provides the compiler with a wealth of information allowing for many intricate optimizations such as constant folding and loop unrolling. Using templates can result in many (sometimes subtle) improvements in runtime performance.

Always remember, though, that additional template instantiation *could* result in the creation of additional code. Although this does not necessarily have to be the case because added code resulting from templates might be more than offset by size reductions gained from improved compilation efficiency. So, if performance and size really matter, consider template design. Write the code without templates. Write it again with templates. If a mix is better, templates can be combined with non-templates. Analyze the assembly code listings along the way and strike the right balance between using templates and using non-templated classes and subroutines.

As mentioned above in Sect. 6.17, one of the most effective ways in which templates can improve overall performance is simply by using the STL. In many senses, making consistent use of the STL is a kind of *global* project optimization.

Templates provide for *scalability*, allowing the scale and complexity of a particular calculation to be adjusted by changing the template parameters. For example, the timers of Sect. 15.3 are implemented as scalable templates. The best efficiency of these timers can be achieved if the template parameter uses the native unsigned integer type (Sect. 6.10). The digital filter classes of Chap. 14 are also scalable. Section 14.4 shows how to achieve maximum filter performance and functionality by properly scaling the template parameters.

6.20   Use Metaprogramming to Unroll Loops

Template metaprogramming can be used to improve code performance by forcing compile-time loop unrolling. An interesting analysis of this can be found by revisiting the inner product metaprogram in the code samples of Sect. 5.10.

In the original example, both sides of the dot-product, $(\mathbf{u} \cdot \mathbf{v})$ including their ranges were compile time constants, allowing for complete evaluation of the result at compile time. In other situations, however, the values of the container elements might not be known at compile time. For example, if dynamic containers with variable size unknown to the compiler are used or if a lower optimization level is applied, the inner product might *not* be unrolled by compiler optimization alone.

A template metaprogram will *always* force loop unrolling, regardless of the container type or optimization level. Care must be taken, though, to ensure that the range index stays in bounds when unrolling dynamic containers with metaprogramming. Loop unrolling with template metaprogramming is a versatile programming tool that can be employed to improve performance in many different situations.

References

1. W. van Hagen, *The Definitive Guide to GCC* (Apress, Berkeley, 2006)
2. R. Rivest, *The MD5 Message-Digest Algorithm* (1992), http://www.ietf.org/rfc/rfc1321.txt
3. RSA Data Security, Inc., *Reference Implementation of RFC 1321*, herein identified as the "*RSA Data Security, Inc. MD5 Message-Digest Algorithm*" (RSA Data Security, Inc., Bedford, 1991)
4. F. Thilo, *MD5 Converted to a C++ Class* (2012), ftp://ftp.mirrorservice.org/pub/sourceforge/w/project/wj/wjd/src

Part II
Components for Real-Time C++

Chapter 7
Accessing Microcontroller Registers

Microcontroller programming requires efficient techniques for register access. Registers are used to configure the CPU and peripheral hardware devices such as flash access, clocks, I/O ports, timers, communication interfaces (UART, SPI^{TM}, CAN [1]), etc. This chapter describes C++ methods that can be used to manipulate microcontroller registers. The focus of this chapter is placed on template methods that provide for efficient, scalable and nearly portable register access.

7.1 Defining Constant Register Addresses

C programmers often define register addresses with a preprocessor **#define**. For example,

```
// The 8-bit address of portb.
#define REG_PORTB ((uint8_t) 0x25U)
```

The preprocessor symbol `REG_PORTB` represents the 8–bit address of `portb` on our target with the 8–bit microcontroller. We first encountered this register in the LED program of Sect. 1.1. The value of `portb`'s address is `0x25`. The type of the address is `uint8_t`. In addition, the type information is tightly bound to the preprocessor definition with a C-style cast operator. All-in-all, this is a robust register definition in C.

As mentioned in association with the LED program in Sect. 1.10, `portb` can also be manipulated via direct memory access in the C language. For example, the following C code sets the value of `portb` to zero.

```
// Set portb to 0.
*((volatile uint8_t*) REG_PORTB) = 0U;
```

C.M. Kormanyos, *Real-Time C++*, DOI 10.1007/978-3-642-34688-0_7,
© Springer-Verlag Berlin Heidelberg 2013

In C++ it can be convenient to define register addresses with compile-time constant static integral members of a class type (such as a structure) or using the **constexpr** keyword. This technique has already been used a few times in this book and is described in greater detail in Sect. 4.10. In particular,

```cpp
namespace mcal
{
  struct reg
  {
    static constexpr std::uint8_t portb = 0x25U;

    // Additional registers
    // ...
  };
```

Register addresses can alternatively be defined as compile-time constants with **constexpr** possibly in a namespace for naming uniqueness. For example,

```cpp
namespace mcal
{
  namespace reg
  {
    constexpr std::uint8_t portb = 0x25U;

    // Additional registers
    // ...
  }
};
```

The `mcal::reg` structure (or the `mcal::reg` namespace) can be used to define a variety of microcontroller register addresses. Each register address needed in the program can be included as a compile-time constant. In the `mcal::reg` structure above, for example, the 8–bit address of `portb` on our target with the 8–bit microcontroller has a compile-time constant value equal to `0x25`.

Using the `mcal::reg` structure (or alternatively the namespace `mcal::reg`) it is straightforward to set `portb` via direct memory access in C++. For instance,

```cpp
// Set portb to 0.
*reinterpret_cast<volatile std::uint8_t*>
  (mcal::reg::portb) = 0U;
```

As mentioned in Sects. 1.10 and 4.10, compile-time constants are just as efficient as preprocessor **#define**s, but have superior type information. Compile-time constants are well-suited for defining register addresses because they require no storage and are available for constant folding. Register addresses defined as compile-time constants can also be used as parameters in C++ templates. This can be used to create highly optimized template classes that can be mapped to the microcontroller's peripherals resulting in efficient hardware-access code that possesses a high degree of portability. This technique will be shown in the next section and also used for a serial SPI[TM] driver in Sect. 9.5.

7.2   Using Templates for Register Access

Consider the template class below. It is a scalable template class designed for setting the value of a microcontroller register.

```cpp
template<typename addr_type,
         typename reg_type,
         const addr_type addr,
         const reg_type val>
class reg_access
{
public:
  static void reg_set()
  {
    *reinterpret_cast<volatile reg_type*>(addr) = val;
  }
};
```

The reg_access class has four template parameters that specify the characteristics of the microcontroller register. The addr_type parameter defines the type of the register's address. When used with portb on our target with the 8–bit microcontroller, for example, the type of addr_type is std::uint8_t. The reg_type parameter defines the physical width of the register. This is also std::uint8_t for portb on our target with the 8–bit microcontroller.[1] The last two template parameters, addr and val, define the register's address and the value that should be written it. These two parameters must be integral compile-time constants.

The reg_access template has one static method called reg_set(). This function is designed for setting a register at a fixed address with a constant value. For example,

---

[1]Note, however, that a register's width need not necessarily have the same type as its address. One often encounters registers with 8–bit width or 16–bit width on a 32–bit machine, etc.

```
// Set portb to 0.
reg_access<std::uint8_t,
           std::uint8_t,
           mcal::reg::portb,
           0x00U>::reg_set();
```

As in the examples in the previous section, this code also sets the value of the portb register to zero. This is accomplished by calling the reg_set() function. Notice how this code obtains the address of portb from the mcal::reg class.

There are several advantages to implementing register access functions in a templated class such as reg_access. In particular, reg_access offers scalability and portability because it can be used with different register types and microcontroller architectures.

In the code below, for example, a register with a 32–bit address and an 8–bit width is set with an 8–bit value.[2]

```
// Set timer0 mode register tm0ctl0 to zero.
reg_access<std::uint32_t,
           std::uint8_t,
           mcal::reg::tm0ctl0,
           0x00U>::reg_set();
```

In the following code, a register with a 32–bit address and 16–bit width is set with a 16–bit value.

```
// Set timer0 compare register tm0cmp0 to 32,000.
reg_access<std::uint32_t,
           std::uint16_t,
           mcal::reg::tm0cmp0,
           32000U>::reg_set();
```

The reg_set() function of the reg_access class is quite efficient because all the template parameters are compile-time entities. When compiling the sample above, for example, the compiler eliminates the addr and val template parameters via constant folding and *sees* in reg_set() the following statement.

```
*reinterpret_cast<volatile std::uint16_t*>
  (0xFFFFF694UL) = 32000U;
```

---

[2]This example and the following one have been taken from code that I once wrote to initialize timer0 for a well-known 32–bit microcontroller.

Since this code is entirely known at compile time, the compiler can optimize it to the best of its ability. In fact, the compiler could potentially substitute a single opcode for the operation if one is available for the CPU architecture and the compiler is capable of recognizing the opportunity to do so.

7.3   Generic Templates for Register Access

Based on the reg_set() subroutine in the previous section, we can add additional functions such as logic and bit operations to the reg_access class. For example, we will now add to the reg_access class a function for the logical or operator.

```
template<typename addr_type,
         typename reg_type,
         const addr_type addr,
         const reg_type val = 0>
class reg_access
{
public:
  static void reg_set()
  {
    *reinterpret_cast<volatile reg_type*>(addr) = val;
  }

  static void reg_or()
  {
    *reinterpret_cast<volatile reg_type*>(addr) |= val;
  }
};
```

The reg_or() function is similar to the reg_set() function. The only difference is that instead of setting the value with **operator=**(), the logical **or** operator is used. This subroutine can be used for **or**-ing the value of a register at a fixed address with a constant value. In particular,

```
// Set portb.5 to 1.
reg_access<std::uint8_t,
           std::uint8_t,
           mcal::reg::portb,
           0x20U>::reg_or();
```

This code is equivalent to

```
*reinterpret_cast<volatile std::uint8_t*>(0x25) |= 0x20;
```

and it performs a bitwise **or** of portb with the 8–bit value 0x20. This sets
portb.5 on our target with the 8–bit microcontroller to high.

As a final example, we will add a dedicated bit operation to the reg_access
class. For example,

```
template<typename addr_type,
         typename reg_type,
         const addr_type addr,
         const reg_type val = 0>
class reg_access
{
public:
  // ...

  static void bit_not()
  {
    *reinterpret_cast<volatile reg_type*>(addr)
      ^= (1 << val);
  }
};
```

The bit_not() function performs a bitwise exclusive-or (xor) of a register
with a bitmask containing a single bit. Notice that the val parameter here is used
to create the bitmask from 1 shifted left val times.

The bit_not() function has the effect of toggling a bit from low to high and
vice versa. For example,

```
// Toggle portb.5.
reg_access<std::uint8_t,
           std::uint8_t,
           mcal::reg::portb,
           5U>::bit_not();
```

This code is equivalent to

```
*reinterpret_cast<volatile std::uint8_t*>(0x25) ^= 0x20;
```

and it performs a bitwise `xor` of `portb` with 0x20. This toggles `portb.5` on our target with the 8–bit microcontroller from low to high and vice versa. It is the same register manipulation that was introduced in the `toggle()` function of the `led` class in the LED program of Sect. 1.1.

So now the `reg_access` class includes functions for register set, logical `or` and bitwise `xor`. It is straightforward to add even more register functions. For example, the class synopsis of an extended `reg_access` class is shown below.

```cpp
template<typename addr_type,
         typename reg_type,
         const addr_type addr,
         const reg_type val>
class reg_access
{
public:
  static void     reg_set() { /* ... */ }
  static void     reg_and() { /* ... */ }
  static void     reg_or () { /* ... */ }
  static reg_type reg_get() { /* ... */ }

  static void     bit_set() { /* ... */ }
  static void     bit_clr() { /* ... */ }
  static void     bit_not() { /* ... */ }
  static bool     bit_get() { /* ... */ }

  static void variable_reg_set(const reg_type)
  {
    // ...
  }
};
```

This version of the `reg_access` class is contained in the companion code of this book. It has functions for register set, get, various bit operations, etc. In this sense, the `reg_access` class is a scalable, flexible and generic template that can be used for register manipulation on any microcontroller platform, regardless of the address widths and register types.

Register manipulation code can never be truly portable because the addresses and purposes of registers are specific to a given microcontroller. The `reg_access` class, however, makes no use of these kinds of microcontroller-specific details. So as long as the microcontroller-specific details are localized somewhere else (such as in something like the `mcal::reg` structure), the `reg_access` class remains portable—perhaps as portable as possible for microcontroller register access.

7.4 Bit-Mapped Structures

Microcontroller programmers often use C-style structures with bit-fields to represent bits or groups of bits in a register. This is useful for creating a bit-mapped structure that identically matches the bits in a hardware register. For example, an 8–bit port register can be represented with the C-style bit-mapped structure shown below.

```
typedef struct struct_bit8_type
{
  std::uint8_t b0 : 1;
  std::uint8_t b1 : 1;
  std::uint8_t b2 : 1;
  std::uint8_t b3 : 1;
  std::uint8_t b4 : 1;
  std::uint8_t b5 : 1;
  std::uint8_t b6 : 1;
  std::uint8_t b7 : 1;
}
bit8_type;
```

Using the bit8_type structure is straightforward. For example, the code below sets portb.5 to high.

```
reinterpret_cast<volatile bit8_type*>
  (mcal::reg::portb)->b5 = 1U;
```

It can also be convenient to combine a built-in integral type with a bit-mapped register structure in a C-style union. For instance,

```
typedef union union_reg_map_c
{
  std::uint8_t value;
  bit8_type    bits;
}
reg_map_c;
```

In this example, we have combined the 8 bits in the bit8_type structure with an std::uint8_t in the reg_map_c union. This makes it possible to manipulate either the individual bits or the value of the entire register depending on the coding situation. In particular,

```
// Set portb to 0.
reinterpret_cast<volatile reg_map_c*>
  (mcal::reg::portb)->value = 0U;

// Set portb.5 to 1.
reinterpret_cast<volatile reg_map_c*>
  (mcal::reg::portb)->bits.b5 = 1U;
```

In C++, it is possible to take the concept of the `reg_map_c` union and create from it a generic template class for register mapping. For example,

```
template<typename addr_type,
         typename reg_type,
         typename bits_type,
         const addr_type addr>
class reg_map
{
public:
  static reg_type& value()
  {
    return
      *reinterpret_cast<volatile reg_type*>(addr);
  }

  static bits_type& bits()
  {
    return
      *reinterpret_cast<volatile bits_type*>(addr);
  }
};
```

The `reg_map` class has four template parameters similar to the ones in the `reg_access` structure from the previous sections of this chapter. In particular, the `addr_type` parameter specifies the type of the register's address. The `addr` parameter provides the constant value of the register's address. The `reg_type` gives the type of the register. The new `bits_type` template parameter is intended to be a bit-mapped structure representing the bit-mapping of the hardware register.

These template parameters are used by `reg_map`'s two static members functions to provide access the register as a value or a bit-map. The `value()` subroutine returns a non-constant (i.e., modifiable) reference to the value of the register. The `bits()` subroutine returns a non-constant reference to the bit-mapped value of the register.

Imagine we would like to use the reg_map class to access the portb register on our target with the 8–bit microcontroller. In particular,

```
// Set portb to 0.
reg_map<std::uint8_t,
        std::uint8_t,
        bit8_type,
        mcal::reg::portb>::value() = 0U;

// Set portb.5 to 1.
reg_map<std::uint8_t,
        std::uint8_t,
        bit8_type,
        mcal::reg::portb>::bits().b5 = 1U;
```

Bit-mapped structures provide an intuitive and elegant way to identically map a software structure to a hardware register or set of registers. Using bit-mapped structures, however, can result in potentially non-portable code. This is because, according to specification, the type of bit-field members in a structure must be one of **signed** or **unsigned int**. Bit-mapped structures, however, often use other integral types in order to obtain the right structure packing for the hardware.

If bit-mapped structures are to be used, one may want to check how the compiler handles them and ensure that the desired bit-mapping is actually carried out. The code of bit-mapped structures should also be clearly marked with a comment indicating potential non-portability.

Reference

1. ISO, *ISO 11898-1:2003: Road Vehicles—Controller Area Network (CAN)—Part 1: Data Link Layer and Physical Signaling* (International Organization for Standardization, Geneva, 2003)

Chapter 8
The Right Start

The *startup code* is called by the microcontroller hardware after reset and is the first code to execute before calling the main() subroutine. The startup code predominantly consists of initialization code and may include, among other things, CPU-initialization, zero-clear RAM initialization, ROM-to-RAM static initialization and static ctor call initialization. The compiler's default startup code is often tightly bound to the compiler's runtime libraries and may not be available as source code. In addition, even if the source of the startup code is available, it can be hard to understand because it may be written in assembly and cluttered with a multitude of options required for supporting a variety of chip derivatives. This chapter describes how to implement a custom startup code and its initializations written predominantly in C++, from reset to main().

8.1 The Startup Code

It can be preferable to write a custom version of the startup code. This makes it possible to include specialized initialization mechanisms for I/O pins, oscillators, watchdog timers, etc. These might otherwise be postponed to an unduly late time, such as in the main() subroutine. The flowchart of a custom startup code is shown in Fig. 8.1.

We will now examine the main parts of this startup code going step-by-step through a real example. The code below shows the implementation of the startup code for the 32–bit target in the reference project of the companion code.

```
extern "C" void startup()
{
  // Set the stack pointers.
  asm volatile("movs r1, #0");
```

C.M. Kormanyos, *Real-Time C++*, DOI 10.1007/978-3-642-34688-0_8,
© Springer-Verlag Berlin Heidelberg 2013

```cpp
  // Initialize I/O pins, oscillators and watchdog.
  mcal::cpu::init();

  // Initialize statics from ROM to RAM.
  // Zero-clear non-initialized static RAM.
  crt::init_ram();
  mcal::wdg::trigger();

  // Call all ctor initializations.
  crt::init_ctors();
  mcal::wdg::trigger();

  // Jump to main (and never return).
  asm volatile("bl main");

  // Catch an unexpected return from main.
  for(;;)
  {
    // Replace with an even louder error, if desired.
    mcal::wdg::trigger();
  }
}
```

The first part of the startup code initializes the stack pointer. For other architectures, it may also be necessary to initialize other important CPU registers and data pointers needed for rudimentary operations such as bus access, subroutine calls, etc. These kinds of registers are target-specific and need to be carefully studied in the microcontroller handbook. This portion of the startup code usually needs to be written in assembly or, as is the case above, with one or more lines of inline assembly.

The remaining parts of the startup code can often be written in C++. These include low-level hardware initialization (Chap. 9), RAM initialization, static constructor initialization and the jump to main().

This example of the startup code is primarily written in C++ with small hybrid assembly components. This makes it convenient to distribute the important parts of the initialization sequence in procedural subroutines with easy-to-recognize names. With this technique, it is possible to implement the startup codes for different microcontrollers in a similar fashion. This can potentially be a significant improvement over the all-assembly implementations predominantly found for many compilers and most target systems.

Fig. 8.1 The flowchart of a customized startup code is shown

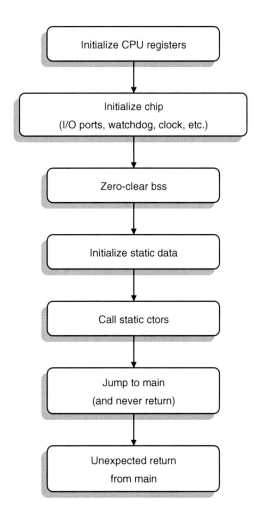

8.2 Initializing RAM

There are usually at least two kinds of RAM that need to be initialized in the startup code. These include both non-initialized static variables as well as the initialized ones. Non-initialized, non-local static variables need to be zero-cleared. Non-local static variables that are initialized must be set with constant values extracted from a so-called ROM-to-RAM table. For example,

```
namespace
{
  std::uint16_t flag;          // Needs zero-clear.
  std::uint8_t version = 3U;   // Needs ROM-to-RAM init.
}
```

In this code, there are two static variables with file-level scope, flag and version. The flag variable is not initialized. As such, it needs to be initialized with the default value of zero. The variable version is initialized with the value 3. Its initialization is carried out with a runtime mechanism that copies into it the initial value of 3.

All non-initialized static variables such as the flag variable shown above need to be zero-cleared. In order to facilitate this, the compiler and linker have located variables of this kind in special linker section. For GNU compilers, this is often called the bss-section.

In order to zero-clear the bss-section, the startup code loops through the bss-section from begin to end and sets its contents to zero. The code below shows a potential implementation of the zero-clear mechanism for the bss-section.

```
// Linker-defined begin and end of the .bss section.
extern std::uintptr_t _bss_begin;
extern std::uintptr_t _bss_end;

void init_bss()
{
  // Clear the bss segment.
  std::fill(&_bss_begin, &_bss_end, 0);
}
```

The init_bss() subroutine uses std::fill() to loop through the bss-section and zero-clear its contents. Notice how the external symbols _bss_begin and _bss_end have been made available to simplify the coding. These symbols have been defined in the *linker script*. We will discuss the linker script and the definitions of these symbols in Sect. 8.4 below.

Initialized static variables such as version shown above need to be initialized with constant values. The compiler and linker have, once again, created two special linker sections to facilitate these kinds of initializations. One linker section contains all the static variables needing initialization. This is often called the data-section. The other linker section contains a table of the actual values used to initialize them. This is referred to as the rodata-section (as in "read-only" data).

In order to initialize the static variables, then, all one needs to do is loop through the data-section and copy to it the contents of the rodata-section. For example,

```
// Linker-defined begin of rodata.
extern std::uintptr_t _rodata_begin;

// Linker-defined begin and end of data.
extern std::uintptr_t _data_begin;
extern std::uintptr_t _data_end;
```

```
void init_data()
{
  // Calculate the size of the data section.
  const std::size_t cnt = (&_data_end - &_data_begin);

  // Copy the rodata section to the data section.
  std::copy(&_rodata_begin,
            &_rodata_begin + cnt,
            &_data_begin);
}
```

The initialization sequence in init_data() uses std::copy() to loop through the rodata-section and copy the ROM-to-RAM initialization contents to the data-section. Again, this mechanism makes use of external symbols that have been defined in the linker script (Sect. 8.4).

8.3   Initializing the Static Constructors

As mentioned in Sect. 1.5, static constructors of class types have compiler-generated constructor code. The same is true for static variables initialized with the return value of a subroutine. For example, recall the constructor call of led_b5:

```
// Create led_b5 on portb.5.
const led led_b5
{
  mcal::reg::portb,
  mcal::reg::bval5
};
```

This code was first introduced in the LED program of Sect. 1.1. It has a static instance of the led class called led_b5. Since led_b5 must be fully formed before it can be used in main(), the compiler has automatically generated a subroutine for its constructor. For example, GCC for our target with the 8–bit microcontroller creates a subroutine named _GLOBAL__I_main() that carries out the initialization of led_b5.

The pseudo-code that the compiler generates for _GLOBAL__I_main() is shown below.

```
000000ba <_GLOBAL__I_main>:
;led(const port_type p, const bval_type b)  : port(p),
;                                             bval(b)
```

```
; 4 assembly lines to initialize port, bval.

;{
;    // Set the port pin to low.
;    *reinterpret_cast<volatile bval_type*>(port)
;    &= static_cast<bval_type>(~bval);

;    ; 1 assembly line to clear the port pin.

;    // Set the port pin to output.
;    *reinterpret_cast<volatile bval_type*>(port - 1u)
;    |= bval;

;    ; 1 assembly line to set the port direction.
;}
```

The original C++ source code from the led class constructor has been included
in this assembly listing in the form of comments. With the source code included,
it is possible to recognize the assembly code sequences generated for both the
constructor initialization list and also for setting the port pin direction to output
and the port pin value to low.

Most C++ programs have numerous objects requiring construction. In general,
the compiler generates a subroutine with construction code for each one of them.
The addresses of these compiler-generated subroutines are stored in a special linker
section. Different compilers use different names for the linker section containing
the constructors. Section names such as ctors, init_array and the like are
used by ports of GCC. Regardless of what the linker section is called, however, it is
essentially just a table of function pointers.

In order to initialize the constructors, then, a mechanism is needed that loops
through the ctors-section and sequentially calls each compiler-generated constructor function. For example,

```
typedef void(*function_type)();

// Linker-defined begin and end of the ctors.
extern function_type* _ctors_begin[];
extern function_type* _ctors_end[];

void init_ctors()
{
  std::for_each(_ctors_begin,
                _ctors_end,
                [](const function_type pf)
```

```
        {
          pf();
        });
}
```

This code was first introduced in Sect. 6.18 as an example providing motivation to use lambda expressions. As mentioned in that section, the code calls the compiler-generated constructors in the range [ctors_begin, ctors_end) with the STL's std::for_each() algorithm. Thereby, each compiler generated constructor code is executed and every static object is fully formed before the jump to main(). Actually, the real code runs through the range of constructors in reverse order using an std::reverse_iterator because GCC stores its static constructors in reverse order. This detail is, however, irrelevant for the example.

8.4   The Connection Between the Linker and Startup

In the previous two sections, we have discussed three initializations that occur before the jump to main(). These include zero-clearing the bss-section, initializing statics in the bss-section and calling all of the static constructors in the ctors-section.

One might wonder how convenient symbols like _bss_begin and _bss_end for the bss-section or _ctors_begin and _ctors_end for the ctors-section come into existence and can be used like normal variables in C++ code. The answer lies in the so-called *linker definition file*, also known as a linker script. The linker definition file defines the addresses where all program components will be located. For example, all normal program code (also known as text) will be located in the text-section. Static variables that need to be zero-cleared will be located in the bss-section, and so on.

The linker definition file needs to be written with intimate knowledge of the microcontroller's memory map in order to ensure that each program component gets located in the right place. Components such as program code, the list of static constructors and the ROM-to-RAM data table should be located in the read-only program memory of the microcontroller. The contents of the bss-section and the data-section need to be placed in static RAM.

GNU compilers use a specific language for the linker definition file. A simplified example of a linker definition file is shown below. For additional information on GNU linker definition files, turn to Barr's book [1].

```
ENTRY(start)

MEMORY
{
```

```
   ROM(rx)   : ORIGIN = 0x08000000, LENGTH = 128K
   RAM(rwx)  : ORIGIN = 0x20000000, LENGTH = 8K
}

SECTIONS
{
  /* Program code, read-only data and static ctors */
  .text :
  {
    . = ALIGN(4);
    KEEP(*(.isr_vector))
    *(.text)
    *(.text.*)
    *(.rodata)
    *(.rodata*)
    _ctors_begin = .;
    KEEP (*(SORT(.init_array.*)))
    KEEP (*(.init_array))
    _ctors_end = .;
  } > ROM

  _rom_data_begin = .;

  /* The ROM-to-RAM initialized data section */
  .data :
  {
    . = ALIGN(4);
    _data_begin = . ;
    *(.data)
    *(.data.*)
    _data_end = . ;
  } > RAM AT > ROM

  /* The uninitialized (zero-cleared) data section */
  .bss :
  {
    . = ALIGN(4);
    _bss_begin = .;
    *(.bss)
    *(.bss*)
    _bss_end = . ;
  } > RAM
}
```

This sketch of a linker definition file shows how the most important linker sections and symbols can be defined in a linker script. It can be difficult to understand the language of the GNU linker. Even without understanding every part of it, though, it is possible to gain an intuitive feeling of how the linker definition file works. There are three main parts in this linker script. The first part uses the ENTRY directive to define the startup routine startup(). This is the routine that was first shown in Sect. 8.1. The second part of the linker definition file uses the MEMORY directive to define two important memory classes, ROM and RAM. The MEMORY directive also defines the addresses and sizes of the ROM and RAM. The third part of the linker definition file uses the SECTIONS directive to define how the various program sections should be located in ROM and RAM.

It is possible to define variables (in other words symbols) in the linker definition file. Symbols defined in this way become available for use in the source code as variables. For example, the bss-section begins at address 0x20000000 in RAM and includes all non-initialized statics. Bracketing the begin and end of the lines describing the bss-section are the symbols _bss_begin and _bss_end. These symbols can actually be used in C++ code, in particular for the C++ loop that initializes the bss-section in init_bss above. Similarly, other symbols such as _ctors_begin, _ctors_end, _data_begin, _data_end, etc. can be defined in the linker script used in their respective C++ initialization loops.

8.5 Understand Static Initialization Rules

Now that we have discussed RAM and static ctor initialization, we will consider some of the storage requirements pertaining to initialization. C++ has several rules governing the initialization of statics. It is essential to understand these rules in order to avoid redundant initialization code and avoid subtle pitfalls such as using an object before it has been initialized.

All statics with file-level or global scope, both built-in types and class types alike, are initialized by the startup code before the jump to main(). In particular, consider non-local statics with one of the built-in integer, character, floating-point or Boolean types. These are initialized by the startup code with the appropriate default values such as 0, '\0', 0.0F, **false**, etc.

The statics in following code, for example, do not need explicit initialization because they are default initialized by the startup code.

```
namespace
{
  std::uint8_t key;  // Default initialized.
  float    val;      // Default initialized.
  bool     flag;     // Default initialized.
}
```

```
struct protocol_frame
{
  static std::uint8_t count;
  protocol_frame() { }
};

// Default initialized.
std::uint8_t protocol_frame::count;
```

If the default value is the desired one, then explicit initialization is not necessary. For example,

```
namespace
{
  std::uint8_t key  = 0;      // Not necessary.
  float        val  = 0.0F;   // Not necessary.
  bool        flag = false;  // Not necessary.
}
```

These static variables do no not need explicit initialization. In fact, extra initialization when the default suffices is redundant. It increases both the code size and the runtime of the pre-main by adding more entries to the initialization sequence.

A static with an initial value that differs from the default value needs to be explicitly initialized. For example,

```
namespace
{
  std::uint8_t version = 3U;     // Explicit init.
  float f             = 4.56F;  // Explicit init.
  bool  flag          = true;   // Explicit init.
}
```

8.6   Avoid Using Uninitialized Objects

Static initialization also has runtime characteristics that should be kept in mind when designing stable software. For example, all non-subroutine-local statics *must* be initialized by the compiler before the call to main(). This is simply a necessity.

Furthermore, a non-subroutine-local static is *guaranteed* to be initialized before any function in its containing file uses it. This rule is simple enough to keep in mind for any given file. Because C++ supports the translation of separate files, though, no rule governs the *order* of initialization of different files. Even though this aspect of the C++ language is well-known, it understandably remains a big source of confusion that can lead to an unpredictable program crash.

We will now examine a case in point. Consider a simple structure called `alpha` and a static instance of it named `instance_of_alpha` residing in `alpha.cpp`. For example,

```cpp
struct alpha
{
  std::uint16_t value;
  alpha(const std::uint16_t a) : value(a) { }
};

// In file alpha.cpp.
alpha instance_of_alpha(3U);
```

Imagine, further, that the `value` member of `instance_of_alpha` is used to initialize an unrelated static unsigned integer called `beta` residing in `beta.cpp`. In particular,

```cpp
// In file beta.cpp.
extern alpha instance_of_alpha; // From alpha.cpp.

// Oops, instance_of_alpha might be uninitialized!
std::uint16_t beta = instance_of_alpha.value;
```

Suppose that the static contents of `beta.cpp` just happen to be initialized *before* those of `alpha.cpp`. In this case, the `instance_of_alpha` object in `alpha.cpp` will be uninitialized when `beta` in `beta.cpp` tries to use it. This subtle, almost hidden, phenomenon can truly wreak havoc in the code of the unwary programmer. It afflicts simple built-in types and class types alike, regardless of an object's complexity. This makes it all too easy to use something *before* it has been initialized.

A well-known design pattern using a so-called *singleton instance* remedies this problem.

```cpp
// In file alpha.cpp.
alpha& safe_reference_to_alpha()
{
  static alpha instance_of_alpha(3U);
  return instance_of_alpha;
}
```

```
// In file b.cpp.
// OK, but mind the overhead.
extern alpha& safe_reference_to_alpha();

// OK, safe_reference_to_alpha() always returns
// an initialized object.
std::uint16_t beta = safe_reference_to_alpha().value;
```

The singleton instance solves this problem because a subroutine-local static will be initialized *one time only*, at the moment first encountered in the subroutine. The solution is simple enough, but it comes at the expense of overhead. In particular, the singleton instance has overhead for the call of the subroutine safe_reference_to_alpha(). This overhead includes both the first-time initialization of the local static object instance_of_alpha as well as the necessity to check its *guard*-variables every time safe_reference_to_alpha() is called.[1] See Item 47 in Meyers [2] for additional details on the singleton instance.

8.7   Jump to main() and Never return

Near the end of the startup code listed in Sect. 8.1, there is line which jumps to main(). In particular,

```
extern "C" void startup()
{
  // ...

  // Jump to main (and never return).
  asm volatile("bl main");

  // ...
}
```

Since the C++ compiler forbids explicit call of the main() subroutine, the jump to main() must be programmed in assembly. This line, of course, must be written in the local assembly dialect of appropriate for the microcontroller being used.

In the startup code presented in this chapter, the program is never expected to return from main(). This is typical for a microcontroller application that

---

[1]Guard-variables are compiler-generated flags used to mark the if a given file-local static has been initialized—a sort of "I am already set" marker preventing multiple initialization. Note also, as an aside, that guard-variables usually have severely mangled names.

starts at power-up and never stops execution, only stopping upon hard power-down (i.e., switching off the microcontroller power). If the application stops with a controlled shutdown, then the return from `main()` must be properly handled and a mechanism for calling the static destructors should be implemented.

Most of the programs in this book are never expected to return from `main()`. An unexpected exit from `main()` is handled with an infinite loop that services the watchdog timer and never breaks. For example,

```cpp
extern "C" void startup()
{
  // ...

  // Catch an unexpected return from main.
  for(;;)
  {
    mcal::wdt::service();
  }
}
```

The strategy used here is to keep the hardware in its last known state and undertake no further actions as a sensible error reaction to an unexpected exit from `main()`. This may or may not be an appropriate reaction for a given microcontroller application. A reset or some other kind of error reaction may be better suited to another application.

8.8   When in `main()`, What Comes Next?

One might be tempted to implement large parts of the application in the `main()` subroutine. It can, however, be considered poor style to do so because this detracts from modularity and clarity of design.

The `main()` function in a typical real-time C++ project, therefore, might consist of just a few lines. For instance,

```cpp
namespace mcal
{
  void init();
}

void scheduler();

int main()
{
```

```
// Initialize the microcontroller layer.
mcal::init();

// Call the multitasking scheduler
// and never return.
scheduler();
}
```

Here, main() is literally a two-liner. After initializing the MCAL (Sect. B.2), the program calls its multitasking scheduler. This scheme for main() is also used in Sect. 11.5.

Control never returns to the main() subroutine, and the application runs indefinitely in a multitasking environment. Ideally the application will be robust, designed with clear modularity, appropriate temporal efficiency and sensible architectural granularity, as described in Appendix B.

References

1. M. Barr, *Programming Embedded Systems with C and GNU Development Tools*, 2nd edn. (O'Reilly, Sebastopol, 2006)
2. S. Meyers, *Effective C++: 55 Specific Ways to Improve Your Programs and Designs*, 3rd edn. (Addison Wesley, Reading, 2005)

Chapter 9
Low-Level Hardware Drivers in C++

Microcontroller applications usually require low-level drivers for peripheral devices such as I/O ports, interrupts, timers, communication interfaces like UART, CAN [2], SPI[TM], etc. This chapter presents several efficient methods for programming peripheral hardware drivers in C++. Low-level drivers are inherently dependent on the microcontroller and its peripherals. Even though the low-level hardware drivers in this chapter are primarily designed for our target with the 8–bit microcontroller, an effort has been made to keep them as portable as possible. In this way, they can be adapted to other microcontrollers.

9.1 An I/O Port Pin Driver Template Class

General purpose I/O ports can be used for a variety of interfaces to on-board and off-board devices. A simple general purpose I/O port can be controlled via three registers, an output *data* register for setting the output value, a *direction* register for selecting input or output, and an *input* data register for reading the input value. Port pins often come grouped in registers that are 8, 16 or 32 bits wide. The general purpose I/O ports on our target with the 8–bit microcontroller, for example, can be controlled with three 8–bit registers, the data register, the direction register and the input register, as shown in Table 9.1.

Table 9.1 The registers of the general purpose I/O ports on our target with the 8–bit microcontroller are summarized

I/O port	Data register	Direction register	Input register
portb	0x25	0x24	0x23
portc	0x28	0x27	0x26
portd	0x2B	0x2A	0x29

C.M. Kormanyos, *Real-Time C++*, DOI 10.1007/978-3-642-34688-0_9,
© Springer-Verlag Berlin Heidelberg 2013

We will now write a template `port_pin` class that encapsulates a port pin in one of the general purpose I/O ports, `portb`, `portc` or `portd`, as summarized in Table 9.1.

```cpp
template<typename addr_type,
         typename reg_type,
         const addr_type port,
         const reg_type bpos>
class port_pin
{
public:
  static void set_direction_output()
  {
    // Set the port pin's direction to output.
    port_dir_type::bit_set();
  }

  static void set_direction_input()
  {
    // Set the port pin's direction to input.
    port_dir_type::bit_clr();
  }

  static void set_pin_high()
  {
    // Set the port output value to high.
    port_pin_type::bit_set();
  }

  static void set_pin_low()
  {
    // Set the port output value to low.
    port_pin_type::bit_clr();
  }

  static bool read_input_value()
  {
    // Read the port input value.
    port_inp_type::bit_get();
  }

  static void toggle()
  {
    // Toggle the port output value.
```

```
    port_pin_type::bit_not();
  }

private:
  static constexpr addr_type pdir = port - 1U;
  static constexpr addr_type pinp = port - 2U;

  // Type definition of the port data register.
  typedef reg_access<addr_type,
                     reg_type,
                     port,
                     bpos> port_pin_type;

  // Type definition of the port direction register.
  typedef reg_access<addr_type,
                     reg_type,
                     pdir,
                     bpos> port_dir_type;

  // Type definition of the port input register.
  typedef reg_access<addr_type,
                     reg_type,
                     pinp,
                     bpos> port_inp_type;
};
```

The port_pin template class is essentially a light-weight wrapper around the reg_access template class previously introduced in Chap. 7. The fixed-bit subroutines of the reg_access class are called in order to manipulate the port pins. The member functions of port_pin class are all declared with the **static** keyword and there is no class constructor because port_pin is designed to be mapped to a specific port pin using a type definition. In other words, objects of type port_pin are not intended to be created.

Using the port_pin template class is straightforward. The code below, for example, maps the port_pin template class to portd.0 and subsequently sets the I/O pin to output with logic level high.

```
void do_something()
{
  // Map portd.0 using a type definition.
  typedef port_pin<std::uint8_t,
                   std::uint8_t,
                   mcal::reg::portd,
                   0U> port_d0_type;
```

```
// Set portd.0 to output with logic level high.
// Set the value before direction to avoid spikes.
port_d0_type::set_pin_high();
port_d0_type::set_direction_output();
}
```

Additional security can be added to the `port_pin` template class if desired. The functions that set the output value, for instance, could first ensure that the port pin direction is actually set to output before setting the logic level.

9.2 Programming Interrupts in C++

Developing low-level drivers in real-time C++ such as a timer counter or a serial UART interface may require the programming of one or more *interrupts*. An interrupt is an asynchronous signal caused by a hardware or software event that indicates that a special interrupt service routine should execute.

Interrupt service routines usually have higher CPU priority than the priority of the `main()` subroutine. Consider, for example, a microcontroller peripheral timer that is programmed to count in the upward direction. This up-counting timer can be configured to generate a hardware interrupt request when the value of the timer counter register reaches the value programmed in its compare register. In this way, a timer can be used to call an interrupt service routine with a fixed period. The resulting interrupt frequency is more precise than that which could be achieved with the CPU priority of the `main()` subroutine.

Programming an interrupt in C++ involves three main steps:

- Writing an interrupt service routine.
- Putting the interrupt service routine in the interrupt vector table.
- Activating the interrupt source and enabling global interrupts.

Among other timers, our target with the 8–bit microcontroller has an 8–bit peripheral timer called `timer0`. The `timer0` has a compare register a. The interrupt service routine shown below is designed to be called when the counter register of `timer0` register reaches the value set in its compare register a. This interrupt service routine has been discussed previously within the context of efficiency in Sect. 6.15.

```
// Attributes for an ISR and C-linkage.
extern "C"
void __timer0_cmp_a_isr() __attribute__((interrupt));

// The timer0 compare-a interrupt service routine.
```

```
void __timer0_cmp_a_isr()
{
  // This interrupt occurs when the counter
  // register reaches the compare-a register.

  // Do something...
}
```

The GNU C++ compiler uses special attributes in the function prototype of an interrupt service routine. These can be seen in the __attribute__ () syntax in the prototype of __timer0_cmp_a_isr(). The __attribute__ () syntax is a language extension specific to the GNU compilers.[1] The pairs of two leading and trailing underscores are intended to make the __attribute__ () language extension uniquely visible.

GCC ports to other microcontrollers use different attribute keys and other compilers use different language extensions for declaring interrupt service routines, making interrupt syntax highly compiler-dependent. Declaring an interrupt service routine in C or C++ always relies on compiler-dependent syntax because it is not specified by ISO/IEC [3, 4], and is considered to be an implementation detail of the compiler.

Interrupt service routines abruptly interrupt normal program flow. The compiler may, therefore, need to create a special subroutine frame consisting of assembly sequences that save and restore the register context at interrupt entry and exit. The __attribute__ () syntax shown above clearly indicates that this function is an interrupt service routine, allowing the compiler to generate the interrupt frame. Assuming that an interrupt service routine can be identified as such via language extensions, the compiler generates the interrupt frame automatically.

Depending on the characteristics of the underlying peripherals and the microcontroller architecture, it may be necessary to actively clear an interrupt request flag in software in the interrupt service routine. It is, on the other hand, just as common for the microcontroller hardware to automatically clear the interrupt request in the interrupt service routine. In __timer0_cmp_a_isr() above, for instance, it is not necessary to explicitly clear an interrupt request flag in software because the microcontroller hardware does it.

Interrupts can be generated for all sorts of hardware and software events, not only for timers. A communication device such as a serial UART, for instance, will usually have at least three unique interrupt sources, one for byte reception, a second for byte transmission and a third for framing error on a failed reception. Typically, these interrupts will be employed when developing a real-time asynchronous serial communication driver.

---

[1]GNU compilers support numerous attributes for functions, variables, objects and types with its __attribute__ () syntax. See [1] and [5] for additional details.

Small microcontrollers usually have a few tens of interrupt sources. Large microcontrollers may have hundreds of interrupt sources or even more. It is customary, then, to store the addresses of the interrupt service routines in what is known as an *interrupt vector table*.

In practice, the interrupt vector table is implemented as an array of function pointers, possibly with added fill bytes, containing the addresses of the interrupt service subroutines. For example, the interrupt vector table for the 8–bit microcontroller in the reference project is shown below.

```cpp
// Declare the interrupt vector table.
extern "C"
const volatile isr_type isr_vectors[26U]
  __attribute__ ((section(".isr_vectors")));

// The interrupt vector table.
extern "C"
const volatile isr_type isr_vectors[26U] =
{
  {{0x0C, 0x94}, startup },        //  1 reset
  {{0x0C, 0x94}, __unused_isr},    //  2 ext0
  {{0x0C, 0x94}, __unused_isr},    //  3 ext1
  {{0x0C, 0x94}, __unused_isr},    //  4 pin0
  {{0x0C, 0x94}, __unused_isr},    //  5 pin1
  {{0x0C, 0x94}, __unused_isr},    //  6 pin2
  {{0x0C, 0x94}, __unused_isr},    //  7 watchdog
  {{0x0C, 0x94}, __unused_isr},    //  8 timer2 cmp a
  {{0x0C, 0x94}, __unused_isr},    //  9 timer2 cmp b
  {{0x0C, 0x94}, __unused_isr},    // 10 timer2 ovf
  {{0x0C, 0x94}, __unused_isr},    // 11 timer1 cap
  {{0x0C, 0x94}, __unused_isr},    // 12 timer1 cmp a
  {{0x0C, 0x94}, __unused_isr},    // 13 timer1 cmp b
  {{0x0C, 0x94}, __unused_isr},    // 14 timer1 ovf
                                   // 15 timer0 cmp a
  {{0x0C, 0x94}, __timer0_cmp_a_isr},
  {{0x0C, 0x94}, __unused_isr},    // 16 timer0 cmp b
  {{0x0C, 0x94}, __unused_isr},    // 17 timer0 ovf
  {{0x0C, 0x94}, __unused_isr},    // 18 spi(TM)
  {{0x0C, 0x94}, __unused_isr},    // 19 usart rx
  {{0x0C, 0x94}, __unused_isr},    // 20 usart err
  {{0x0C, 0x94}, __unused_isr},    // 21 usart rx
  {{0x0C, 0x94}, __unused_isr},    // 22 adc
  {{0x0C, 0x94}, __unused_isr},    // 23 eep Ready
  {{0x0C, 0x94}, __unused_isr},    // 24 comparator
  {{0x0C, 0x94}, __unused_isr},    // 25 two-wire
```

```
  {{0x0C, 0x94}, __unused_isr}     // 26 spm
};
```

The first position in the interrupt vector table is often used by the microcontroller hardware as the entry point of the program. This is where program execution starts after microcontroller reset. In the sample above, for instance, startup() is the program entry point. This is, for example, the same startup() routine that was described in Sect. 8.1. Notice how the timer0 compare register a interrupt service routine __timer0_cmp_a_isr() is entered at the 15th position of the interrupt vector table, which is where it belongs for this particular microcontroller hardware.

The interrupt vector table must usually be mapped to a fixed physical address. The can be accomplished in software using a linker section. As shown above, placing objects in a linker section uses special section attributes, again a language extension particular to GCC. The interrupt vector table uses C-linkage in order to eliminate potential C++ name mangling. This produces a non-mangled name for the interrupt vector table and makes it easier to identify it in the map file, for example, when troubleshooting or verifying the proper location, alignment, contents and length. See Sects. 6.5, 6.6 and 8.4.

It can be good practice to fill unused entries in the interrupt vector table with a user-provided handler for unused interrupts. For example, unused interrupts in the isr_vectors table shown above use the subroutine __unused_isr(). The unused interrupt handler can generate a loud error such as waiting forever in en endless loop, optionally executing a nop-operation or, even louder, toggling a digital I/O port. A potential implementation of an unused interrupt service routine is shown below.

```
extern "C"
void __unused_isr() __attribute__((interrupt));

// The unused interrupt handler.
extern "C"
void __unused_isr()
{
  // Generate a loud error. It could be made
  // even louder by toggling an I/O port.
  for(;;)
  {
    mcal::irq::nop();
  }
}
```

For some microcontrollers, it may also be necessary to add fill bytes to the interrupt vector table. Fill bytes in the interrupt vector table generally have a special hardware purpose such as ensuring proper memory alignment or executing a low-level jump operation. The fill bytes {0x0C, 0x94} shown in the sample interrupt vector table above, for instance, constitute the opcode for a jump operation on our target with the 8–bit microcontroller. These aspects of interrupt programming in C++ are notoriously non-portable. They are specific to a given microcontroller and compiler and usually can not be written in a generic form.

The final step involved in programming an interrupt is enabling the interrupt source. In practice, this is usually done by writing special enable bits in a special function register via direct memory access (Chap. 7). For example,

```
// Enable the timer0 compare match a interrupt.
mcal::reg_access<std::uint8_t,
                 std::uint8_t,
                 mcal::reg::timsk0,
                 0x02U>::reg_set();
```

This line of code enables bit–1 in the timsk0 special function register of our target with the 8–bit microcontroller. This example enables a timer interrupt, and is described in the following section.

9.3 Implementing a System-Tick

A system-tick may be one of the most essential parts of the low-level driver software because it provides the timebase for the entire software project. The multitasking scheduler described in Chap. 11, for instance, uses a timebase that originates from a system-tick. In this section, we will use timer0 on our target with the 8–bit microcontroller counting in the upward direction in compare mode to create a high-resolution 32–bit system-tick with a frequency of 1 MHz.

Since timer0 has counter and compare registers that are 8–bits in width, the 32–bit system-tick needs to be synthesized from a combination of hardware and software. The lower byte of the system-tick comes from the timer0 counter register tcnt0 and the upper 3 bytes are stored in the variable system_tick. This composite representation of the system-tick is shown in Fig. 9.1.

One possible declaration of the system_tick is shown below.

```
namespace
{
  // The one (and only one) 32-bit system-tick.
  volatile std::uint32_t system_tick;
}
```

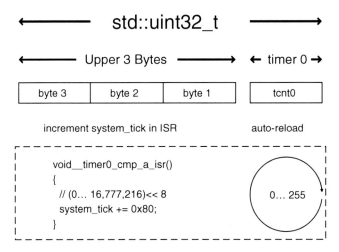

Fig. 9.1 The representation of the 32–bit system-tick is shown. The three upper bytes of the system-tick are stored in the `system_tick` variable. The lower byte of the system-tick comes from `timer0`'s counter register `tcnt0`

The `system_tick` variable is qualified as **volatile**. This tells the compiler that it should avoid aggressive optimization involving `system_tick`. This is necessary because the value of `system_tick` value is changed via incrementation in the interrupt service routine but used elsewhere.

We will now setup `timer0` to generate a periodic interrupt for incrementing the system-tick. The code below initializes `timer0` to count in the upward direction. The frequency of the clock source is set to 2 MHz. The `timer0` compare register a is set to `0xFF = 255` and the compare match interrupt is activated.

```
void mcal::gpt::init()
{
  // Clear the timer0 overflow flag.
  mcal::reg_access<std::uint8_t,
                   std::uint8_t,
                   mcal::reg::tifr0,
                   0x02U>::reg_set();

  // Enable the compare match a interrupt.
  mcal::reg_access<std::uint8_t,
                   std::uint8_t,
                   mcal::reg::timsk0,
                   0x02U>::reg_set();

  // Set ctc mode 2 for timer0 compare match a.
  mcal::reg_access<std::uint8_t,
```

```
                        std::uint8_t,
                        mcal::reg::tccr0a,
                        0x02U>::reg_set();

  // Set the compare match a value to 255.
  mcal::reg_access<std::uint8_t,
                   std::uint8_t,
                   mcal::reg::ocr0a,
                   0xFFU>::reg_set();

  // Set the timer0 source to 16MHz/8 = 2MHz and
  // start counting.
  mcal::reg_access<std::uint8_t,
                   std::uint8_t,
                   mcal::reg::tccr0b,
                   0x03U>::reg_set();
}
```

The `mcal::gpt::init()` routine is designed to be called once, and only once, from the initialization mechanism of the MCAL. The result of the initialization code in `mcal::gpt::init()` is to set the `timer0` frequency to 2 MHz and activate an interrupt at every full cycle of its 8–bit timer period.

When the `timer0` counter register rolls over from 255 to 0, an interrupt for match on compare register a is generated. The corresponding interrupt service routine `__timer0_cmp_a_isr()` is called and it increments the upper 3 bytes of the system-tick. One possible implementation of this mechanism is shown in the code sample below.

```
void __timer0_cmp_a_isr()
{
  // This interrupt occurs every 128us.
  // Increment the 32-bit system-tick by 128.
  system_tick += 0x80U;
}
```

Here, the system-tick is incremented with `0x80` which is 128. The 256 timer ticks required for the compare match interrupt have been divided by 2 because the underlying timer frequency is 2 MHz, which is double the system-tick frequency. In this way, a 32–bit system-tick with a frequency of 1 MHz and a resolution of 1 µs has been created with the 8–bit `timer0` hardware and a small amount of software.

To obtain the entire value of the 32–bit system-tick, the timer counter register `tcnt0` is combined with the upper 3 bytes of the `system_tick` variable using logical `or`. Since the timer counter register is rapidly incremented by the timer

hardware, a consistency check must be included in the routine that reads the
`system_tick` variable.

The interface to the system-tick can be found in the `gpt` namespace of the
MCAL in the reference project of the companion code. Here, `gpt` stands for *general
purpose timer*. The interface to the system-tick uses a procedural subroutine called
`get_time_elapsed()`. In other words,

```
mcal::gpt::value_type mcal::gpt::get_time_elapsed();
```

Complete details on the implementation of the system-tick for both our targets
with the 8–bit microcontroller and the 32–bit microcontroller can be found in the
reference project of the companion code. For the 32–bit target, a 16–bit timer
hardware counter register is combined with a quad-word in software to synthesize a
64–bit system-tick with a frequency of 1 MHz and a resolution of 1 µs.

The standard library time facilities in `<chrono>` require the implementation
of several clocks, one of them being a high-resolution clock. The system-tick
presented in this section is well-suited for providing the underlying timebase for
the `high_resolution_clock` in `<chrono>`. A methodology for using the
system-tick as the timebase for `<chrono>`'s high-resolution clock is presented in
Sect. 16.5.

9.4   A Software PWM Template Class

A pulse-width modulated signal (PWM) is a square wave that usually has a fixed
period and a variable duty cycle. A PWM signal uses a cyclical counter that
increments and is reset at the end of the PWM period. When the counter reaches
the value matching the duty cycle of the PWM, the output switches from high
to low, thereby creating a square wave. PWM signals with duty cycles of 20, 50
and 80 % are shown in Fig. 9.2. PWM signals can be generated with software or
with a peripheral timer. The duty cycle, period and resolution of a PWM signal are
determined by the configuration of the underlying software or timer.

Dedicated PWM units are often integrated in the microcontroller hardware
peripherals. For example, a PWM signal can be created with a peripheral timer
that has a counter, a compare register and a dedicated auto-toggle output pin
associated with the compare event of the timer compare register. A hardware-based
PWM signal can be set up and programmed to run independently without CPU
supervision.

A typical user interface for a PWM signal generator provides public methods
for setting and retrieving the duty cycle. This interface has been used with the `pwm`
class in conjunction with the LED class hierarchy presented previously in Sect. 4.1.
The example here makes a more detailed implementation of a dedicated PWM class
called `pwm_type`.

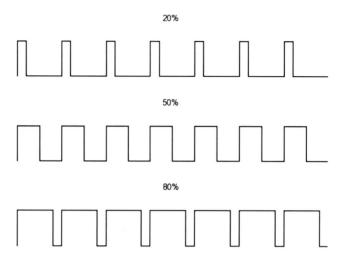

Fig. 9.2 PWM signals with duty cycles of 20, 50 and 80 % are shown

The synopsis of the pwm_type class is shown below.

```
class pwm_type
{
public:
  pwm_type(const std::uint8_t duty = 0U);

  void set_duty(const uint8_t duty);

  std::uint8_t get_duty() const;
};
```

A PWM signal generated with software uses a timebase for the counter and manual manipulation of an I/O pin to toggle the signal. Generating a PWM signal with software may be more CPU-intensive than using a dedicated hardware peripheral. A software PWM signal generator does, however, have a slightly higher degree of flexibility than one in hardware and can also be used even if no dedicated PWM hardware is available.

We will now write a template class designed to encapsulate a software PWM signal generator on a digital I/O port.

```
template<typename addr_type,
         typename reg_type,
         const addr_type addr,
         const reg_type bpos,
         const std::uint8_t resol = 100U>
```

```cpp
class pwm_type
{
public:
  pwm_type(const std::uint8_t duty = 0U)
    : counter(0U),
      duty_cycle(duty),
      shadow(duty)
  {
    // Set the pin to output, low.
    port_pin_type::set_pin_low();
    port_pin_type::set_direction_output();
  }

  void set_duty(const uint8_t duty)
  {
    // Set new duty cycle in the shadow register.
    std::atomic_store(&shadow,
                      std::min(duty, resol));
  }

  std::uint8_t get_duty() const
  {
    // Retrieve the duty cycle.
    return std::atomic_load(&duty_cycle);
  }

  void service()
  {
    // Increment the counter.
    ++counter;

    // Set output according to duty cycle.
    if(counter <= duty_cycle)
    {
      port_pin_type::set_pin_high();
    }
    else
    {
      port_pin_type::set_pin_low();
    }

    if(counter >= resol)
    {
      // Latch in duty cycle from shadow register.
```

```
      duty_cycle = shadow;

      // Reset the counter for a new PWM period.
      counter = 0U;
    }
  }

private:
  std::uint8_t counter;
  volatile std::uint8_t duty_cycle;
  std::uint8_t shadow;

  // Define the type for the PWM port pin.
  typedef port_pin<addr_type,
                   reg_type,
                   addr,
                   bpos> port_pin_type;

  // Make the pwm_type class non-copyable.
  pwm_type(const pwm_type&) = delete;
  const pwm_type& operator=(const pwm_type&) = delete;
};
```

This software encapsulation of a PWM signal driver closely mimics a hardware PWM peripheral timer. When the internal counter is less than the duty cycle, the output pin is set to high. When the internal counter exceeds the duty cycle, the output pin is set to low. In this way, the requested signal is generated on the output pin. The service() member should be called with a fixed tick cycle, such as from a timer interrupt service routine with a period of 50 μs. If there are, say, 100 ticks specified with the resol template parameter and a tick cycle of 50 μs, then the resulting PWM signal will have a frequency of 200 Hz and a resolution of 1 %.

A new duty cycle can be set with the set_duty() member function. It includes a range check and an atomic manipulation of the software shadow register. The new duty cycle is latched in from the shadow register at the end of each full period of the counter. This avoids incomplete PWM periods when setting the duty cycle in a process that is asynchronous to the call of the service() routine.

The example below creates a PWM signal generator on portb.0 with the default initial duty cycle of 0 %. The PWM duty cycle is subsequently set to 20 %. Here, it is assumed that the PWM's service() routine is called with a fixed tick cycle, for instance, in an asynchronous timer interrupt service routine.

Fig. 9.3 SPI™
communication with the
master device connected to a
single slave device is shown

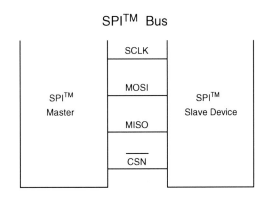

```
// Make a type definition for a PWM signal on portb.0.
typedef pwm_type<std::uint8_t,
                 std::uint8_t,
                 mcal::reg::portb,
                 0U> pwm_b0_type;

// Create pwm0 on portb.0.
pwm_b0_type pwm0;

void do_something()
{
  // Set the duty cycle to 20 percent.
  pwm0.set_duty(20U);
}
```

9.5 A Serial SPI™ Driver Class

SPI™ is a synchronous full-duplex serial communication interface commonly used for microcontroller communication with other devices. SPI™ is a four-wire serial bus. A single bus master device initiates data frame transfer with one or more slave devices using three communication lines and one device-select line per slave device.

An example of an SPI™ bus with the master device connected to one slave device is sketched in Fig. 9.3. Data are clocked out from the bus master to the slave device on the *Master-Out-Slave-In* line (MOSI) and clocked from the slave device into the master on the *Master-In-Slave-Out* line (MISO). The flanks of the serial clock line (SCLK) provide the timebase for bit transfer, which can be quite fast reaching speeds of several mega-bits per second. Depending on the SPI™ dialect, either rising or falling edge can be used for latching the data bits, and the clock can optionally idle to high or low,

The synopsis of a potential SPI™ communication class is shown in the code below. It is designed for a microcontroller bus master. This SPI™ communication class is derived from a `communication` base class similar to the one first introduced in Sect. 4.9.

```cpp
class spi_communication : public communication
{
public:
  spi_communication();
  virtual spi_communication();

  // The virtual communication interface.
  virtual bool send(const std::uint8_t byte_to_send);
  virtual bool send(const data_type& data_to_send);
  virtual bool recv(std::uint8_t& byte_to_recv);
  virtual bool recv(data_type& data_to_recv);
  virtual std::size_t recv_ready() const;
  virtual bool idle() const;

  // Specific channel select for SPI(TM).
  bool select_channel(const std::uint8_t ch);

private:
  // Private class details.
  volatile bool send_is_active;
  circular_buffer<std::uint8_t, 16U> send_buffer;
  circular_buffer<std::uint8_t, 16U> recv_buffer;
  std::uint8_t channel;

  // Friend interrupt service routine for Rx/Tx.
  friend void ::__vector_spi_rx_tx_isr();
};
```

The `spi_communication` class includes members for sending and receiving both 1 byte as well as a specialized container of bytes. Here, the container type is called `data_type` and this can be type defined from a standard container such as `std::vector` or a specialized container. In the reference project, for example, `data_type` is type defined from the custom `circular_buffer` class described in Sect. 15.5.

The `spi_communication` class also supplies the public member functions `recv_ready()` and `idle()`. These are used for querying the number of bytes ready in the receive queue and for checking if the SPI™ bus is idle.

The interface of the `spi_communication` class is intended to be completely independent of the underlying microcontroller registers. Hardware details are hidden in the source file of the class implementation. In this way, the user interface of the spi_communication class is completely portable.

A glance at the private details of the spi_communication class reveals that the send and receive queues use two individual circular buffers (Sect. 15.5). The sizes of these buffers need to be appropriately set for the intended use of the class.

The work of the spi_communication class is predominantly implemented in the send and receive algorithms. The send routine is shown below.

```
bool spi_communication::send(
  const std::uint8_t byte_to_send)
{
  mcal::irq::disable_all();

  // If the SPI(TM) is idle, begin transmission.
  if(!send_is_active)
  {
    // Set the send-active flag.
    send_is_active = true;

    // Set the chip-select-not to low.
    if(channel == 1U)
    {
      mcal::port::port3::set_pin_low();
    }
    else
    {
      mcal::port::port2::set_pin_low();
    }

    // Send the first byte over SPI(TM).
    mcal::reg_access
      <std::uint8_t,
       std::uint8_t,
       mcal::reg::spdr>::reg_set(byte_to_send);

    // Enable the SPI(TM) rx/tx interrupt.
    enable_rx_tx_interrupt();

    mcal::irq::enable_all();
  }
  else
  {
    // A transmission is already in progress.
    // Pack the next byte-to-send in the send-buffer.
```

```
    send_buffer.in(byte_to_send);

    mcal::irq::enable_all();
  }

  return true;
}
```

The send() function uses a standard queuing mechanism. When sending data, the function first checks if the bus is idle by checking the send_is_active flag. If so, data transfer is initiated by writing the first data byte to the transfer register spdr. If a send is already in progress, the byte to send is queued in the circular send buffer. Queued bytes are sent sequentially in a daisy-chained fashion in the SPI^{TM} bus interrupt service routine until the send queue is empty.

This SPI^{TM} bus driver is implemented for two slave devices, and the appropriate chip-select pin is asserted to low prior to the start of data transmission. Enable and disable of both the global interrupts as well as the send and receive interrupts of the SPI^{TM} bus ensure atomic data consistency in the send buffer.

The SPI^{TM} bus interrupt service routine is shown below.

```
void __vector_spi_rx_tx_isr()
{
  // The SPI(TM) interrupt is on end-of-transmission.

  // Receive the byte from the last transmission.
  const std::uint8_t byte_to_recv
    = mcal::reg_access
        <std::uint8_t,
         std::uint8_t,
         mcal::reg::spdr>::reg_get();

  mcal::spi::the_spi.recv_buffer.in(byte_to_recv);

  const bool send_buffer_is_empty
    = mcal::spi::the_spi.send_buffer.empty();

  if(send_buffer_is_empty)
  {
    // The send-buffer is empty and reception from
    // the previous (final) transmission is done.
    // Deactivate the send-active flag.
    mcal::spi::the_spi.send_is_active = false;

    // Reset the chip-select-not to high.
```

```
if (mcal::spi::the_spi.channel == 1U)
{
  mcal::port::port3::set_pin_high();
}
else
{
  mcal::port::port2::set_pin_high();
}

// Disable the SPI(TM) rx/tx interrupt.
disable_rx_tx_interrupt();
}
else
{
  // Send the next byte if there is at least
  // one in the send queue.
  const std::uint8_t byte_to_send
    = mcal::spi::the_spi.send_buffer.out();

  mcal::reg_access
    <std::uint8_t,
     std::uint8_t,
     mcal::reg::spdr>::reg_set(byte_to_send);
}
}
```

The SPI[TM] bus interrupt service routine performs several tasks. It reads the response byte from the receive register and pushes it onto the receive queue. In addition, the interrupt sends the next queued byte in the send buffer. When the last queued byte in the send buffer is fully clocked out of the microcontroller, the chip-select pin is reset to its idle state of high. The SPI[TM] bus interrupt service routine uses a non-global static spi_communication object and is privy to its class internals via friendship with the spi_communication class.

The SPI[TM] bus driver presented here is non-trivial, yet robust, and it has a portable user interface. The implementation of the spi_communication class in its entirety can be found in the reference project of the companion code.

9.6 CPU-Load Monitors

It is good practice to monitor the runtime of all tasks and interrupts in the project during all phases of the development cycle. Adherence to runtime limits can be tested with runtime monitoring mechanisms such as real-time measurements via port pins, software timers or in-circuit emulators.

One of the most rudimentary yet effective means for measuring the runtime of a code sequence is to toggle a digital I/O port to high directly before the sequence begins and to toggle it to low just after the sequence completes. Using this technique, the timing results and the statistical variances thereof can be observed on a digital oscilloscope. Extraneous interrupt load can be eliminated from short timing measurements by disabling all interrupts for the duration of the measurement and enabling them immediately thereafter.[2] Disabling and enabling all interrupts is a CPU-specific operation that can be accomplished by setting and clearing the global interrupt flag or manipulating the CPU priority or other microcontroller-specific means. Most of the real-time measurements in this book have been performed with this kind of technique.

In particular, the code used to measure the runtime of the MD5 checksum algorithm that was used in Sects. 6.1 and 6.2 is shown below.

```cpp
#include <cstdint>
#include <array>
#include <mcal/mcal.h>
#include <math/checksums/md5/md5.h>

std::array<std::uint8_t, 16U> result;

void do_something()
{
  mcal::irq::disable_all(); // Disable all interrupts.

  // Toggle the port pin high (use the LED on PB.5).
  mcal::led::led_b5.toggle();

  // Do the MD5 calculation.
  result = md5("creativity", 10U);

  // Toggle the port pin low (use the LED on PB.5).
  mcal::led::led_b5.toggle();

  mcal::irq::enable_all(); // Enable all interrupts.
}
```

This code simply uses the LED port pin PB.5 as a regular digital I/O pin—one that just so happens to have an LED attached to it. The port pin is toggled to

[2]Note, however, that disabling the interrupts for too long or forgetting to re-enable them in a timely fashion may lead to a system crash with unpredictable results.

high before the MD5 checksum calculation begins and to low after the computation completes. This measurement technique is trivially simple, yet nonetheless highly effective.

References

1. Free Software Foundation, *The GNU Compiler Collection Version 4.6.2* (2012), http://gcc.gnu. org
2. ISO, *ISO 11898–1:2003: Road Vehicles – Controller Area Network (CAN) – Part 1: Data Link Layer and Physical Signaling* (International Organization for Standardization, Geneva, 2003)
3. ISO/IEC, *ISO/IEC 9899:1999: Programming Languages – C* (International Organization for Standardization, Geneva, 1999)
4. ISO/IEC, *ISO/IEC 14882:2011: Information Technology – Programming Languages – C++* (International Organization for Standardization, Geneva, 2011)
5. W. van Hagen, *The Definitive Guide to GCC* (Apress, Berkeley, 2006)

Chapter 10
Custom Memory Management

Effective microcontroller programming in C++ mandates dependable memory management beyond that offered by the language's default mechanisms. Dynamically creating polymorphic objects, using STL containers and mapping hardware devices are some of the countless situations in microcontroller programming that require customized memory management. This chapter describes memory management methods that are robust and reliable enough to perform these tasks while adhering to the strict constraints of limited microcontroller memory resources.

10.1 Dynamic Memory Considerations

Dynamic memory allocation is useful in C++ programming, in particular for creating polymorphic objects. The operators **new** and **delete** can be used for dynamic memory allocation and deallocation in C++.

The **new** operator allocates memory for an object from a storage pool (the heap) and returns a pointer to the object. If successful, **new** initializes the memory using the constructor and returns the non-zero address of the newly allocated initialized object. If insufficient memory is available in the heap, **new** either returns zero or throws an std::bad_alloc exception (depending on the version of **new** being used). Calling **delete** for a memory block allocated with **new** destroys the object by calling its destructor and frees the memory.

The syntax of **new** and **delete** is shown below.

```
class something
{
public:
  something() { }
  ~something() { }
```

```
  void do_my_thing() { }
};

void do_something()
{
  // Allocate ps with the operator new.
  something* ps = new something;

  // Do something with ps.
  ps->do_my_thing();

  // Delete ps when finished with it.
  delete ps;
}
```

As described in Sect. 6.16, the use of **new** and **delete** can be inappropriate for microcontrollers with strictly limited heaps of, say, a few tens or hundreds of bytes. Consider the example above. In a typical microcontroller situation, the subroutine do_something() might be called thousands of times—even millions of times. It might only take a few calls, or at most a few hundred calls of do_something() and similar subroutines to completely fragment a microcontroller's tiny heap beyond repair.

One potential solution to this problem is to overload the global operators **new** and **delete** to provide a memory allocation mechanism for individual classes. This technique can be effective for making selected dedicated class-specific allocators. For an additional description of overloading the global operators **new** and **delete** for a particular class, see Eckel [1], Chap. 13, section "Overloading New and Delete for a Class". Flexible memory management, however, often requires allocation methods that are generic and can be used with any kind of object. So we need to investigate other methods of memory management for microcontroller programming.

10.2   Using Placement-new

Fortunately, **new** is also available in its so-called *placement* version, known as placement-**new**. Placement-**new** allows programmers to explicitly control a dynamically created object's placement in memory (i.e., its physical address).

Placement-**new** is the essential ingredient for generic memory management in microcontroller programming. It allows one to determine *where* (in other words at which address) a given dynamic allocation should be carried out in memory. The caller of placement-**new** is responsible for finding and managing the memory chunks used in calls to placement-**new**. These can be carefully defined memory locations such as the stack in a subroutine call or a local or global static memory pool.

There are several versions of placement-**new**. The form shown below is the most useful one for our purposes in this chapter.

```
void* operator new(size_t, void*) noexcept;
```

This version of placement-**new** creates a pointer to a single object. Placement-**new** does not **throw** any exceptions. The first input parameter to placement-**new** (the one of type size_t) gives the size of the object in bytes. The second input parameter (the one of type **void***) specifies the *place* in memory where the new object should be created.

For example, placement-**new** can be used to place an instance of something in a subroutine-local memory pool on the stack.

```
class something
{
  // ...
};

void do_something()
{
  std::uint8_t pool[sizeof(something)];

  something* ps = new(pool) something;

  // Do something with ps.
  ps->do_my_thing();

  // Do no delete ps when finished with it.

  // The destructor needs to be called manually.
  ~ps();
}
```

In this example, ps is created with placement-**new** rather than the global operator **new**. Instead of using memory from the heap, ps is placed in a memory pool on the stack. Every time do_something() is called, ps is created on the stack. The memory used for storing ps is recycled because the stack is cleared upon subroutine return. Since the heap is not used, there is no risk of fragmenting or overflowing the heap, as might occur when using the global operator **new**.

The code sample above presents an uncommon sight in C++ programming—an explicit call to a class destructor (i.e., the call to ~ps()). Pointers to class types created with placement-**new** require manual destructor call. They should not be deleted with the global operator **delete**. This differs from pointers created with the global operator **new**. These always need a corresponding call to **delete** which recycles the memory and also implicitly calls the destructor. Custom memory management is one of very few programming situations in C++ that requires explicit call of an object's destructor.

10.3   Allocators and STL Containers

STL containers have an additional (sometimes overlooked) template parameter that defines the so-called *allocator type* used for dynamic memory management. For example, the full template definition of std::vector has not only an elem_type parameter for the element-type but also a second alloc_type parameter for the allocator type. In particular,

```
namespace std
{
  template
    <typename elem_type,
      typename alloc_type = allocator<elem_type>>
  class vector
  {
    // ...
  };
}
```

The second template parameter alloc_type is the allocator type. This is the allocator that the given instantiation of std::vector uses to allocate and deallocate elements of type elem_type when dynamically changing the size of the container. If otherwise left unspecified, the value of this allocator type is the STL's templated default allocator class std::allocator instantiated for the type of element in the container.

The key to using STL containers effectively in microcontrollers is to replace the default allocator with a specialized custom allocator. The default allocator uses the global operators **new** and **delete** which, as mentioned previously, can be inappropriate for microcontroller programming. Custom allocators can use memory policies that rely on placement-**new** acting on, for example, a pool of local stack memory or a chunk of re-usable static RAM, etc.

The code below uses std::vector with the default allocator.

```
#include <vector>

// A vector with three 32-bit uints.
std::vector<std::uint32_t> v(3U);
```

The code below is almost the same. However, it uses std::vector with a custom allocator.

```
#include <vector>
#include "my_allocator.h"

std::vector<std::uint32_t,
            my_allocator<std::uint32_t>> v(3U);
```

Here, my_allocator is assumed to have memory allocation and deallocation mechanisms suitable for the microcontroller's memory.

10.4 The Standard Allocator

In order to be used with STL containers, a custom allocator must adhere to the interface of the standard allocator, std::allocator. The partial synopsis of the standard library's default allocator class is shown below.

```
namespace std
{
  template<typename T>
  class allocator
  {
  public:
    typedef std::size_t        size_type;
    typedef std::ptrdiff_t     difference_type;
    typedef T                  value_type;
    typedef value_type*        pointer;
    typedef const value_type*  const_pointer;
    typedef value_type&        reference;
    typedef const value_type&  const_reference;

    allocator() noexcept;
    allocator(const allocator&) noexcept;
    template<class U>
    allocator(const allocator<U>&) noexcept;
```

```
  ~allocator() noexcept;

  template <class U>
  struct rebind { typedef allocator<U> other; };

  size_type max_size() const noexcept;

  pointer address(reference) const;
  const_pointer address(const_reference) const;

  pointer allocate(size_type count,
    typename allocator<void>::const_pointer hint = 0)
    const;

  void construct(pointer p, const value_type&);

  void destroy(pointer);

  void deallocate(pointer, size_type);
  };
}
```

The complete specification of the behavior and requirements of the default allocator can be found in [2], with details in Sect. 20.1.5 (especially Table 32) and Sect. 20.6.9 therein. Consult also Sect. 19.3 of [3] for a detailed description of the data types and operations of `std::allocator`.

10.5 Writing a Specialized `ring_allocator`

In the following, we will write a custom `ring_allocator`. The ring allocator obtains its memory from a static pool that behaves like a ring buffer. Memory is consumed as needed for allocation and automatically recycled in the ring buffer.

The functions needing specialization in a custom allocator are `max_size()`, `allocate()` and `deallocate()` (Sect. 19.2 in [3]). Armed with this list, writing a custom allocator using specialized memory management instead of global **new** and **delete** is straightforward.

We will begin with a base class that predominantly handles the ring allocator's memory management. In particular,

```
class ring_allocator_base
{
public:
```

```
typedef std::size_t size_type;

protected:
  ring_allocator_base() { }

  // The ring_allocator's buffer size.
  static constexpr size_type buffer_size = 64U;

  // The ring_allocator's memory allocation.
  static void* do_allocate(const size_type size);
};
```

The ring_allocator_base class defines the buffer_size. It is 64 bytes in this example. The ring allocator base class also defines a static function called do_allocate(). The do_allocate() function is responsible for the nuts-and-bolts of the memory allocation in the ring buffer. In particular,

```
void*
ring_allocator_base::do_allocate(const size_type size)
{
  // Define a static buffer and memory pointer.
  static std::uint8_t buffer[buffer_size];
  static std::uint8_t* get_ptr = buffer;

  // Does the allocation wraparound the buffer?
  const bool is_wrap =
    ((get_ptr + size) >= (buffer + buffer_size));

  // Get the newly allocated pointer.
  std::uint8_t* p = (is_wrap ? buffer : get_ptr);

  // Increment the pointer for next time.
  get_ptr = p + size;

  return static_cast<void*>(p);
}
```

The do_allocate() subroutine returns a **void**-pointer to the next free chunk of memory in its ring buffer. A local static buffer called buffer and a ring-pointer named get_ptr are defined in the subroutine. The get_ptr variable cycles through the ring buffer, always pointing to the next block of free memory. When the top of the requested memory block exceeds the top of the buffer, get_ptr wraps around to the beginning of the buffer—as with a ring buffer.

Armed with the memory allocation mechanism of the ring allocator base class, it is straightforward to write the derived `ring_allocator` template class. For example,

```
template<typename T>
class ring_allocator : public ring_allocator_base
{
public:
  // ...

  size_type max_size() const noexcept
  {
    // The max. size is based on the buffer size.
    return buffer_size / sizeof(value_type);
  }

  pointer allocate(size_type num,
    ring_allocator<void>::const_pointer = 0)
  {
    // Use the base class ring allocation mechanism.
    void* p = do_allocate(num * sizeof(value_type));
    return static_cast<pointer>(p);
  }

  void deallocate(pointer, size_type)
  {
    // Deallocation does nothing.
  }

  // ...
};
```

This code sample shows possible implementations of the three subroutines needing specialization when creating the custom ring allocator—`max_size()`, `allocate()` and `deallocate()`. The most significant details of these functions include:

- The `max_size()` member. This function evaluates the maximum available memory size based on the `buffer_size`.
- The `allocate()` function. Memory allocation uses the memory management scheme of the `do_allocate()` function in the base class.
- The `deallocate()` function, which is empty. Memory is simply recycled and re-used in the ring buffer without being cleared or otherwise modified. The `deallocate()` function can, therefore, be empty.

The allocate() function of the ring allocator calls do_allocate() as its sole instance for memory allocation. The ring buffer cycles through and eventually wraps around to its start. This means that previously allocated memory is overwritten without taking any particular precautions or even warning the caller for buffer overrun. Users of the ring_allocator, then, need to be acutely aware of this limitation and set the size of the internal buffer accordingly for the intended use of this allocator.

With additional software, an out-of-memory check could optionally be added to the class if needed, possibly in conjunction with the exception mechanism for properly handling an out-of-memory exception. See Sect. 10.7 for further details on this.

Memory alignment is not taken into consideration in the allocation mechanism of the ring_allocator. If memory alignment on, say, 4–byte or 8–byte boundaries is necessary, a simple modulus check needs to be added to the size passed to the allocation routine. A second template parameter used for memory alignment is included in the custom allocators that can be found in the reference project of the companion code.

10.6 Using ring_allocator and Other Allocators

The ring_allocator has been designed to be particularly effective when used with subroutine-local STL containers. Consider, for instance, a subroutine that prepares a made-up login response.

```
// Type definition for the ring allocator of uint8_t.
typedef ring_allocator<std::uint8_t> alloc_type;

// Type definition of a vector using alloc_type.
typedef
std::vector<std::uint8_t, alloc_type> response_type;

// Create the login response in a vector.
void login_response(response_type& rsp)
{
  // Reserve memory in the vector.
  // This uses the ring allocator.
  rsp.reserve(5U);

  // Fill the login data in the response vector.
  rsp.push_back(0x55U); // The login-OK key.
  rsp.push_back(0x31U); // Data rsp[1] = '1'.
  rsp.push_back(0x32U); // Data rsp[2] = '2'.
  rsp.push_back(0x33U); // Data rsp[3] = '3'.
```

```
  // Make a byte checksum of the response payload.
  const std::uint8_t checksum =
    std::accumulate(rsp.begin(),
                    rsp.end()
                    std::uint8_t(0U));

  // Append the checksum to the login response.
  rsp.push_back(checksum);
}
```

The `login_response()` subroutine prepares a communication frame responsible for responding to a login request. These bytes represent a fictional login handshake frame consisting of a key-byte (`0x55`), a response with three data bytes (`'1'`, `'2'`, `'3'`) and a byte-wise checksum over the previous 4 bytes in the frame.

The data bytes in the login response are stored in an `std::vector` that uses the custom `ring_allocator`. The significance of this for the real-time C++ programmer is that the `login_response()` subroutine can be called time and time again—thousands of times, millions of times, etc.—without causing any memory fragmentation whatsoever. Memory for the login response is merely taken from the internal pool of the ring allocator and the modest memory consumption of the login response does not overflow the capacity of the allocator's buffer.

The `ring_allocator` is an efficient, bare-bones allocator. Its allocation routine is fast and the overhead of deallocation is entirely eliminated because its memory is simply recycled through the ring buffer. As mentioned above, though, care must be taken when using `ring_allocator` (or something similar) to ensure that the allocator's buffer is large enough to prevent buffer overrun for the use-cases at hand.

Other kinds of custom allocators can also be written for various situations that commonly arise in microcontroller programming. One may, for example, consider writing a `static_allocator` that has a one-shot, non-recyclable memory pool. This could be useful for static constant STL container objects such as version strings, lookup tables, etc. that are created once and remain unchanged for the duration of the program. Another example of a well-known custom allocator is one that holds a pointer to a buffer called an *arena*. This kind of arena pool can be used to create a stack-based allocator. In addition, it is possible to wrap a constant address in, say, a `mapped_allocator`. This can be used to overlay a memory-mapped vector onto a memory-aligned set of hardware registers such as a DMA in a microcontroller peripheral device.

Custom allocators make it possible to embed the power of STL containers and algorithms working on them in remarkably tiny microcontrollers—safely and efficiently in an environment that is bounded by strict memory limitations. Using custom STL allocators that are tailored to the needs of the application can potentially add a new dimension of elegance and ease to microcontroller programming.

10.7 Recognizing and Handling Memory Limitations

Because we are not using C++ exceptions in this book, the `ring_allocator` described in the previous section does not include checks for out-of-memory or for excessive block size. A standards adherent custom allocator should, however, include checks for both an out-of-memory error as well as an excessive length error. STL authors will, therefore, typically support C++ exceptions when requesting memory from an allocator.

An ideal allocator should throw an `std::bad_alloc` exception if the allocator is out of memory. In addition, it should throw an `std::length_error` exception if the requested block size exceeds the size returned from `max_size()`. The code below depicts a possible implementation of the `reserve()` method that includes support for `std::length_error`.

```cpp
#include <memory>
#include <exception>

template<typename T,
         typename alloc = std::allocator<T>>
class vector
{
public:
  // ...

  void reserve(size_type count);
  {
    // Calculate the requested block-size.
    const size_type size = count * sizeof(value_type);

    // Obtain the maximum size available.
    const size_type the_max
      = allocator_type().max_size();

    // Is the maximum size exceeded?
    if(size > the_max)
    {
      // Throw a length error exception.
      throw std::length_error();
    }
```

```
    // Reserve the requested count.
    // ...
  }

  // ...
};
```

Before allocating any memory, the reserve() method queries the allocator's max_size() to find out if the requested memory size exceeds the available size. If the allocator's max_size() will be exceeded by the requested allocation, then there is insufficient memory and an std::length_error exception is thrown.

Developers can check for exceptions using a **try-catch** clause. We will now modify the login_response() subroutine from the previous section to catch a length error exception that may potentially be thrown when attempting to reserve the response vector.

```
// Type definition for the ring allocator of uint8_t.
typedef ring_allocator<std::uint8_t> alloc_type;

// Type definition of a vector using the alloc_type.
typedef
std::vector<std::uint8_t,
            alloc_type> response_type;

// Create the login response in a vector.
void login_response(response_type& rsp)
{
  // Try to reserve 5 bytes in the vector.
  try
  {
    rsp.reserve(5U);
  }
  catch(const std::length_error& e)
  {
    // Catch a length error exception.

    // Implement an error reaction.
    // ...
  }

  // ...
}
```

C++ exception handling can potentially improve the reliability of embedded real-time software. C++ exception handling may, however, increase the code size of the project by several tens of kilobytes, depending on the characteristics of the compiler implementation of exception handling. Enabling and using C++ exceptions should, therefore, only be undertaken if sufficient resources are available.

References

1. B. Eckel, *Thinking in C++ Volume 1: Introduction to Standard C++*, 2nd edn. (Pearson Prentice Hall, Upper Saddle River, 2000)
2. ISO/IEC, *ISO/IEC 14882:2011: Information Technology—Programming Languages—C++* (International Organization for Standardization, Geneva, 2011)
3. N.M. Josuttis, *The C++ Standard Library: A Tutorial and Reference*, 2nd edn. (Addison Wesley, Reading, 2011)

Chapter 11
C++ Multitasking

A multitasking scheduler is an indispensable tool for providing temporal and functional software distribution. In this chapter, we design a cooperative C++ multitasking scheduler that performs a top-down call of its tasks using time slices and a basic priority mechanism. This multitasking scheduler is compact and portable and can be used for a wide variety of projects ranging from small to large. Toward the end of this chapter, we will discuss additional multitasking features such as extended scheduling with yield and sleep functions and the C++ thread support library.

11.1 Multitasking Schedulers

The basic operation of a multitasking scheduler is depicted in Fig. 11.1. In general, a multitasking scheduler runs, possibly indefinitely, in a loop and uses a *scheduling algorithm* to identify and call *ready* tasks. Here, ready is the state of needing to be called. The scheduler's ready-check usually involves timing and possibly event or alarm conditions. In this way, a multitasking scheduler distributes software functionality among various modules and time slices.

Consider the multitasking scheduler shown below. This basic multitasking scheduler is designed to schedule three tasks, task_a(), task_b() and task_c().

```
#include <array>
#include <algorithm>

void task_a() { /* ... */ }
void task_b() { /* ... */ }
void task_c() { /* ... */ }
```

C.M. Kormanyos, *Real-Time C++*, DOI 10.1007/978-3-642-34688-0_11,
© Springer-Verlag Berlin Heidelberg 2013

```cpp
typedef void(*function_type)();
typedef std::array<function_type, 3U> task_list_type;

const task_list_type task_list
{
  { task_a, task_b, task_c };
}

void scheduler()
{
  for(;;)
  {
    std::for_each(task_list.begin(),
                  task_list.end(),
                  [](const function_type& func)
                  {
                    func();
                  });
  }
}
```

Every multitasking scheduler uses some form of scheduling algorithm to search for ready tasks. In the case of the `scheduler()` above, for example, the searching algorithm is trivially simple. It uses neither timing nor priority nor any other kinds of events or alarms. Since each task is ready to be called at any given time, the ready condition for a given task is simply unconditional-**true**. Accordingly, each task is called via lambda expression in the `std::for_each()` algorithm of the multitasking scheduler as soon as its corresponding iterator in the `task_list` is reached. The outer `for(;;)`-loop causes the multitasking scheduler to run indefinitely.

This multitasking scheduler is extraordinarily simple, requiring only a few tens of bytes of program code and no RAM whatsoever. It sequentially calls the tasks in its `task_list`, indefinitely without pause, break or return.

Even though the rudimentary temporal distribution of this multitasking scheduler may be inadequate for most practical situations, this example does, nonetheless, clearly exhibit the general concept of a multitasking scheduler. In the upcoming sections, we will add timing and a more sophisticated scheduling mechanism to this multitasking scheduler.

11.2 Task Timing

We will now discuss timing aspects for our multitasking scheduler. Imagine that the multitasking scheduler should call `task_a()`, `task_b()` and `task_c()` at even multiples of 2, 8 and 16 ms, respectively.

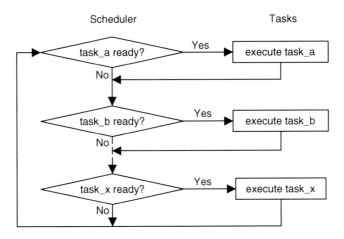

Fig. 11.1 A multitasking scheduler and its tasks, task_a, task_b, ... task_x, are sketched

With this call scheduling, there are time points at which two or more tasks need to be called back-to-back. For example, at even multiples of 8 ms, both task_a() as well as task_b() need to be called. At even multiples of 16 ms, all three tasks need to be called. This could lead to a timing crunch.

In order to avoid timing bottlenecks or at least lessen their impact, call offsets can be added to the call cycle timing of the scheduler. Small-valued prime numbers are well-suited for schedule offsets. For example, we will select for task_b() an offset of 7 ms and for task_c(), an offset of 13 ms, while task_a() retains its 0 ms offset.

The first few scheduled task call times using these offsets are shown in Table 11.1. The bottleneck situation has been effectively removed. As can be seen in the table, task_a() is always called at system-tick values which are multiples of two—and these are always even-numbered. Both task_b() as well as task_c(), however, are always called at odd-numbered values of the system-tick. Therefore, the call of task_a() is never scheduled simultaneously with the calls of either task_b() or task_c(). Furthermore, simultaneous scheduling of task_b() and task_c() has been eliminated because the call cycles of these two tasks no longer intersect.

11.3 The Task Control Block

A class which encapsulates the scheduling characteristics of a task is often called a *task control block*, sometimes also known as a TCB. Typical things in a task control block may include:

- The task to be scheduled
- The timing characteristics of the task's scheduling

Table 11.1 The call schedules for `task_a()`, `task_b()` and `task_c()` with call cycles of (2, 8, 16) ms and call offsets of (0, 7, 13) ms are shown

System-Tick (ms)	Call `task_a()`	Call `task_b()`	Call `task_c()`
0	•		
1		•	
2	•		
3			•
4	•		
5			
6	•		
7			
8	•		
9		•	
10	•		
11			
12	•		
13			
14	•		
15			
16	•		
17		•	
18	•		
19			•

- A scheduling function that checks for task-ready
- A task execution mechanism
- Optional event or alarm information

For example, the scheduling characteristics of `task_a`, `task_b` and `task_c` can be represented with the task control block shown below.

```
class task_control_block
{
public:
  typedef void (*function_type)();

  typedef timer<mcal::gpt::value_type> timer_type;
  typedef timer_type::tick_type tick_type;

  task_control_block(const function_type f,
                     const tick_type c,
                     const tick_type o = 0U)
    : function(f),
      cycle(c),
      time(o) { }
```

```
bool execute();

private:
  const function_type function;
  const tick_type cycle;
  timer_type time;
};
```

The `task_control_block` class has three member variables, `function`, `cycle` and `time`. The variable `function` is a constant pointer to a **void** function with static linkage. This is the function that is encapsulated in the task control block, in other words it is the task that is to be called by the scheduler. The variables `cycle` and `time` contain the task cycle in milliseconds and its interval timer. The interval timer uses the `timer` utility described later in Sect. 15.3.

The `time` member of the task control block is initialized with the offset of the task. The type of the `time` member is `timer_type`, a class-local type that is scaled to the width of the system-tick, Sect. 9.3. A less wide timer type could optionally be used to optimize the RAM storage requirements of the task control block. This, however, assumes that the necessary intervals can still be represented by this type.

The member function `execute()` checks if a task is ready and, if so, calls it. In particular,

```
bool task_control_block::execute()
{
  // Check if the task is ready via timeout.
  if(time.timeout())
  {
    // Increment the task's interval timer
    // with the task cycle.
    time.start_interval(cycle);

    // Call the task.
    function();

    return true;
  }
  else
  {
    return false;
  }
}
```

After a ready task is called, its interval timer is incremented with the task `cycle` and the `execute()` function returns **true**. Otherwise, `execute()` leaves the state of the task unchanged and returns **false**. Since `execute()` returns a Boolean result, it can be used with a predicate-based searching algorithm, as will be shown below.

11.4   The Task List

The `task_list` is a list of `task_control_block` objects that define the task and timing characteristics of the application. For our system with `task_a()`, `task_b()` and `task_c()` and the timing characteristics shown in Table 11.1, a potential `task_list` is shown below.

```cpp
#include <array>

typedef
std::array<task_control_block, 3U> task_list_type;

void task_a() { /* ... */ }
void task_b() { /* ... */ }
void task_c() { /* ... */ }

task_list_type task_list
{{
  task_control_block
  {
    task_a,
    task_control_block::timer_type::milliseconds(2),
    task_control_block::timer_type::milliseconds(0)
  },
  task_control_block
  {
    task_b,
    task_control_block::timer_type::milliseconds(8),
    task_control_block::timer_type::milliseconds(7)
  },
  task_control_block
  {
    task_c,
    task_control_block::timer_type::milliseconds(16),
    task_control_block::timer_type::milliseconds(13)
  }
}};
```

The task_list is stored in an std::array containing three objects of type task_control_block. These represent the task control blocks of task_a(), task_b() and task_c(), and they are to be scheduled with cycles of 2, 8, and 16 ms and offsets of 0, 7, and 13 ms, respectively.

11.5   The Scheduler

Armed with our task_control_block and the task_list, we will now write a multitasking scheduler(). In particular,

```
#include <algorithm>

void scheduler()
{
  for(;;)
  {
    // Find the next ready task using std::find_if.
    std::find_if(task_list.begin(),
                 task_list.end(),
                 [](task_control_block& tcb) -> bool
                 {
                   // Call the ready task.
                   return tcb.execute();
                 });
  }
}
```

In this multitasking scheduler(), the outer for(;;)-loop continuously polls the task_list and never pauses, breaks or returns. The std::find_if() algorithm sequentially loops through the task_list. If a ready task is found, it is called via lambda function in combination with the execute() method of the task_control_block.

A ready task that is called thereby breaks the loop in std::find_if(). If no ready task is found, the outer for(;;)-loop continues polling the task_list waiting for the next ready task.

The STL's std::find_if() algorithm implements a simple task priority mechanism. Recall that std::find_if() locates the iterator of the first occurrence of an element in a range that satisfies the given find condition. In other words, it finds the iterator to the reference of a task_control_block in the task_list whose execute() function returns **true**. If, however, no task is ready, the iterator at the end of the task_list is found. All of this means that `std::find_if()` performs a priority-based search. The order of the tasks in the `task_list` defines the priority of the tasks.

The multitasking scheduler implemented with the `scheduler()` function is designed to be called one time only, for example, in `main()`. For instance, the multitasking scheduler might be called after initializing the MCAL. This has been discussed previously in Sect. 8.8. In particular,

```cpp
namespace mcal
{
  void init();
}

void scheduler();

int main()
{
  // Initialize the microcontroller layer.
  mcal::init();

  // Call the multitasking scheduler
  // and never return.
  scheduler();
}
```

Our multitasking scheduler can be used with a wide variety of projects ranging from small to large. It is efficient. In fact, the entire size of the multitasking scheduler including the implementation of the `task_control_block` and the `task_list` including three tasks only requires a few hundred bytes of code.

Our multitasking scheduler also has a high degree of portability. The only things needed to port to another microcontroller are the system-tick and the `timer`'s conversion to milliseconds.

11.6 Extended Multitasking

The example of the multitasking scheduler shown in the previous sections has called its tasks in a *top-down* fashion. This means that tasks have been implemented as run-capable entities that are called by the scheduler via top-down subroutine call. Each task always runs to completion before returning control to the scheduler.

At times, such basic tasks are insufficient for certain multitasking design needs. For example, it is often desired to wait in a task for an indefinite time within a deeply nested, polling loop. Perhaps the task needs to wait for a critical communication response or a reaction from a hardware device. This is shown in the code sample below.

```cpp
// External functions in the application.
bool initialize_state();
bool response_ready();
void handle_response();

// An example of an extended task.
void extended_task()
{
  // The task initialization.
  const bool state_is_valid = initialize_state();

  // The task worker loop.
  for(;;)
  {
    if(state_is_valid)
    {
      // Wait indefinitely for a response.
      while(!response_ready())
      {
        // Yield control to the scheduler.
        os::yield();
      }

      // Handle the communication response.
      handle_response();
    }
  }
}
```

In this sample, the extended task initializes its state and then enters a loop that waits indefinitely for a communication response. When waiting for the response, `extended_task()` calls `os::yield()` in order to yield control to the scheduler.

The extended task's yield gives the scheduler the opportunity to check if any other tasks with higher priority are pending and execute them if so. In this way, a running task can hand over control to the scheduler, allowing other potentially ready tasks to run. The scheduler returns control to the task at the same place at which control was yielded and also ensures that the task has the same state as before. This form of multitasking is known as cooperative multitasking with extended tasks.

When switching from one task to another, the scheduler is responsible for saving and restoring the task's *context*, in other words its state. This is called context switching. Context switching can be understood in very simple terms. The scheduler

needs to remember *where the task was* and also *what the task was doing* at the time
of the yield in order to properly save and restore a context. In the listing above, *where
the task was* is in the **while**()-loop that calls response_ready(). *What the
task was doing* is waiting for a communication response. From the perspective of
the CPU, however, the *where* is represented by the value of instruction pointer (or an
equivalent CPU register). The *what* is described in terms of the values of the CPU
registers and, possibly, a task stack.

Be aware that context switching is written in target-specific assembly language.
Context switching also requires additional resources. This includes runtime for the
context save and restore, and, in particular, RAM for context storage and individual
task stacks. These efficiency factors should be taken into account when considering
the use of an extended multitasking scheduler.

11.7   Preemptive Multitasking

Certain applications may need preemptive multitasking and synchronization objects
such as mutexes. When deciding whether or not to employ preemptive multitasking,
however, it is essential to carefully consider the expected benefits compared with
the costs. This is because preemptive scheduling and the use of synchronization
mechanisms may lead to significantly increased resource consumption and design
complexity.

In particular, preemptive multitasking might result in a more obscure relation
between the written code and its runtime characteristics. Preemptive multitasking
requires added resources because each preemptive task requires its own individual stack and context storage. Furthermore, widespread use of synchronization
mechanisms introduces numerous potential sources of error related to re-entrance
and concurrency. Many experienced embedded systems programmers rarely use
preemptive multitasking. It is often possible to eliminate a perceived necessity for
preemptive multitasking. Keep a watchful eye on runtime characteristics and ensure
that object encapsulations and interrelations are clear and efficient. If the project,
nonetheless, really needs preemptive multitasking, then by all means use it.

For preemptive multitasking, one may consider using a third-party operating
system. In particular, LaBrosse's book [4] describes a popular and robust real-time
kernel that can optionally be used with preemptive scheduling and synchronization
objects. LaBrosse's kernel is written in C and assembly. It is stable, well-tested and
has been ported to a variety of architectures.

Another widely used free operating system of high-quality is FreeRTOS [1].
The FreeRTOS system has been ported to many CPU architectures and features
a clearly defined, simple interface to the underlying hardware timer and memory
resources. The FreeRTOS licensing also allows the use of FreeRTOS in proprietary
commercial products.

11.8   The C++ Thread Support Library

C++ offers support for multi-threading in its thread support library. Although implementation of the C++ thread support library can be difficult to find among microcontroller compilers.

Thread support is predominantly implemented in the <thread> library, which makes secondary use of the headers <condition_variable>, <chrono> and <ratio>. The specification of the <thread> library can be found in Chap. 30 of [3]. The <atomic> and <mutex> libraries can be used for synchronizing access to shared data if a preemptive threading environment is used.

The code sample below uses C++ threads.

```cpp
#include <chrono>
#include <thread>

void thread_1()
{
  for(;;)
  {
    // Do something in thread_1.
    // ...

    // Yield control to the scheduler for 2ms.
    constexpr auto two_ms
      = std::chrono::milliseconds(2);

    std::this_thread::sleep_for(two_ms);
  }
}

void thread_2()
{
  for(;;)
  {
    // Do something in thread_2.
    // ...

    // Yield control to the scheduler for 7ms.
    constexpr auto seven_ms
      = std::chrono::milliseconds(7);

    std::this_thread::sleep_for(seven_ms);
  }
}
```

```cpp
void do_something()
{
  // Create two threads, thread_1 and thread_2.
  std::thread t1(thread_1);
  std::thread t2(thread_2);

  // Wait for thread_1 and thread_2 to finish.

  // In this example, the join() functions will wait
  // indefinitely because neither thread returns.

  t1.join();
  t2.join();
}
```

This example creates two threads, t1 and t2. The threads are objects of type std::thread. The first thread carries out its internal work and subsequently yields control to the scheduler for 2 ms, whereas the second thread has a cycle time of 7 ms. The cooperative multitasking yield is accomplished with the standard library's sleep_for() subroutine. Notice how the convenient timing mechanisms from the <chrono> library can be used compatibly with the thread support library.

After creating the two threads, the do_something() subroutine waits for both threads to complete before returning. This is accomplished with the join() method. In this example, however, the program will wait indefinitely because both threads are programmed to run without return.

The syntax and design of the C++ thread support library were strongly influenced by the POSIX standard [2]. In addition, C++ threads were implemented in Boost's Boost.Thread library prior to becoming part of the C++ language in C++11. So anyone familiar with POSIX *pthreads* from <pthread.h> or who has worked with Boost.Thread, should be able to understand and use C++ threads with no trouble at all.

References

1. R. Barry, *FreeRTOS Home* (2012), http://www.FreeRTOS.org
2. ISO, *ISO/IEC 9945:2003: Information Technology—Portable Operating System Interface (POSIX)* (International Organization for Standardization, Geneva, 2003)
3. ISO/IEC, *ISO/IEC 14882:2011: Information Technology—Programming Languages—C++* (International Organization for Standardization, Geneva, 2011)
4. J. LaBrosse, *μC/OS-III, The Real-Time Kernel* (Micrium Press, Magalia, 2009)

Part III
Mathematics and Utilities
for Real-Time C++

Chapter 12
Floating-Point Mathematics

This chapter describes floating-point mathematics for real-time C++ using the built-in floating-point types such as **float** and **double**. The first sections of this chapter introduce floating-point arithmetic, mathematical constants, elementary transcendental functions and higher transcendental functions. The last sections of this chapter cover more advanced topics including complex-numbered mathematics, compile-time evaluation of floating-point functions and generic numeric programming.

12.1 Floating-Point Arithmetic

Floating-point arithmetic can be used effectively in real-time C++. For example, the simple function below computes the floating-point area of a circle of radius r, where the area a is given by $a = \pi r^2$.

```
float area_of_a_circle(float r)
{
  constexpr float pi = 3.14159265358979323846F;

  return (pi * r) * r;
}
```

The C++ standard specifies three built-in floating-point types, **float**, **double** and **long double**.[1] The standard, however, does not specify any details about the internal representation of these types. Basically, the standard merely states that **double** needs to provide at least as much precision as **float**, and that

---

[1] We primarily use **float** and **double** in this book.

C.M. Kormanyos, *Real-Time C++*, DOI 10.1007/978-3-642-34688-0__12,
© Springer-Verlag Berlin Heidelberg 2013

long double must provide at least as much precision as **double**. The way the compiler internally stores and treats floating-point types remains implementation-defined. See Sect. 3.9.1, Paragraph 8 in [9] for additional details.

Most suppliers of good compilers, however, strive to provide conformance with the floating-point standard, IEEE 754–2008 [6]. In this standard, single-precision, usually implemented as **float**, is required to be 4 bytes in width and provide 24 binary digits of precision ($\sim$7 decimal digits). Double-precision, usually implemented as **double**, must be 8 bytes wide and provide 53 binary digits of precision ($\sim$15 decimal digits).

The IEEE 754 floating-point standard specifies an enormous amount of information on single-precision, double-precision and quadruple-precision floating-point numbers including rounding characteristics, subnormal numbers such as infinity (∞) and *not-a-number* (NaN), conversion to and from integer, etc. We will not discuss all of these details here due to space considerations. A comprehensive treatment of floating-point arithmetic can be found in the definitive reference work on the topic by Muller et al. [12].

Some microcontrollers have hardware support for floating-point arithmetic using a *floating-point unit* (FPU). An FPU can make floating-point arithmetic as efficient as integer calculations—or even more so. Many small-to-medium microcontrollers, however, do not have an FPU, and floating-point calculations are performed with a software floating-point emulation library. Floating-point emulation can be slow and may introduce large amounts of library code in the executable program. The real-time C++ programmer should strive to be aware of the potentially high performance costs of floating-point arithmetic.

C++ supports many floating-point functions including transcendental functions, floating-point classification functions, rounding functions, absolute value functions, etc. These functions are predominantly included in the <cmath> and <cstdlib> libraries (Sect. 12.3). In addition, care was taken during the specifications of C++11 and C99 to improve consistency in floating-point functions in C and C++ [7, 9].

As mentioned above, floating-point arithmetic in C++ supports the concept of infinity and other non-representable subnormal floating-point values. Consider finite, positive x with $x \in \mathbb{R}$ and x representable in the compiler's floating-point implementation of IEEE 754-2008. In this floating-point system, for example, the result of $x/0$ is ∞ and $\sqrt{-x}$ is NaN. Subnormals and floating-point limits are supported in the C++ language with the std::numeric_limits template, as described in Sect. A.5.

Some developers use the symbol $\mathbb{F}$ to denote the set of numbers representable in a floating-point system. In this book, however, we simply use $\mathbb{R}$ for the sake of convenience.

We will now perform some more floating-point math using the built-in **float** type. Consider the sinc function that often arises in fields such as optics, scattering and radiation theory,

$$\text{sinc}\, x = \frac{\sin x}{x}. \tag{12.1}$$

We will use the following scheme to calculate the sinc function.

$$\text{sinc } x = \begin{cases} 1, & \text{for } -\epsilon < x < \epsilon \\ 1 - \dfrac{x^2}{6} + \dfrac{x^4}{120} - \dfrac{x^6}{540}, & \text{for } |x| < 0.03, \\ \dfrac{\sin x}{x}, & \text{otherwise}, \end{cases} \qquad (12.2)$$

where $x \in \mathbb{R}$ and x is of type **float**. Here, ϵ represents the smallest number distinguishable from 1 that can be represented by **float**, Sect. A.5.

The corresponding code for the sinc function is shown below.

```cpp
#include <limits>
#include <cmath>

float sinc(const float& x)
{
  if(    (x > -std::numeric_limits<float>::epsilon())
      && (x <  std::numeric_limits<float>::epsilon()))
  {
    return 1.0F;
  }
  else if(std::abs(x) < 0.03F)
  {
    const float x2 = x * x;

    const float sum = ((     - 1.984126984E-04F
                       * x2 + 8.333333333E-03F)
                       * x2 - 1.666666667E-01F)
                       * x2;

    return 1 + sum;
  }
  else
  {
    return sin(x) / x;
  }
}
```

As shown in Eq. 12.2, very small arguments with $|x| < \epsilon$ return 1. Small arguments with $|x| < 0.03$ use a truncated Taylor series. Larger arguments with $|x| \geq 0.03$ use the library function sin() combined with division (in other words, $\sin(x)/x$). The polynomial expansion in the Taylor series uses the

method of Horner, as described in [10], Vol. 2, Sect. 4.6.4 in the paragraph named
"Horner's Rule".

12.2 Mathematical Constants

Some numbers such as $\sqrt{2}$, π, $\log 2$, e, γ and others appear time and time again
in mathematical formulas. It makes sense, then, to implement these numbers in
a dedicated fashion. In C++, it is straightforward to implement mathematical
constants as scalable template functions returning compile-time constant values.

Here, we use approximately 40 decimal digits, which slightly exceeds the
precision of quadruple-precision floating-point with 113 binary digits, or $\sim$34
decimal digits. Even if the application does not need this many digits, the precision
is available for any extended-use situation that may arise. Since the values are
compile-time constant, the extra digits do not add any overhead.

The template `const_pi()` subroutine below, for example, returns a scalable
compile-time constant floating-point approximation of π.

```
template<typename T>
constexpr T const_pi()
{
    return T(3.1415926535897932384626433832795028841972);
}
```

Using templated constants in code is simple. For example, this new version of
`area_of_a_circle()` uses the `const_pi()` template to compute the **float**
area of a circle of radius r.

```
float area_of_a_circle(const float& r)
{
    return (const_pi<float>() * r) * r;
}
```

Additional useful mathematical constants are implemented in the templates
below. The template names used below are prefixed with `const_` to clearly indicate
to the user that they are compile-time constants.

```
template<typename T>
constexpr T const_sqrt2()
{
    return T(1.4142135623730950488016887242096980785697);
}
```

```
template<typename T>
constexpr T const_pi()
{
  return T(3.1415926535897932384626433832795028841972);
}

template<typename T>
constexpr T const_ln2()
{
  return T(0.6931471805599453094172321214581765680755);
}

template<typename T>
constexpr T const_e()
{
  return T(2.7182818284590452353602874713526624977572);
}

template<typename T>
constexpr T const_euler_gamma()
{
  return T(0.5772156649015328606065120900824024310422);
}
```

12.3 Elementary Functions

As mentioned previously, C++ supports many floating-point mathematical functions and elementary transcendental functions in its C-compatibility headers <cmath> and <cstdlib>. Basically, <cmath> and <cstdlib> include everything in the C99 library headers <math.h> <stdlib.h> and add overloaded versions of the functions for **float** and **long double**.

The <cmath> and <cstdlib> libraries have a host of functions related to the floating-point number system including, among others, trigonometric, exponential, logarithmic, power, hyperbolic, rounding, absolute value functions, etc. Again, see Sect. 26.8 in [9] for details on the specifications of <cmath> and <cstdlib>.

The code below, for example, computes sin(1.23) for **float**.

```
#include <cmath>

const float s = sin(1.23F);
```

Table 12.1 Resource consumptions for single-precision floating-point functions on our target with the 8–bit microcontroller are shown

Function	Result (`float`)	Result (known)	Runtime (μs)	Code size (byte)
1.23×3.45	4.2435	Exact	9	420
$1.23/3.45$	0.35652 17	0.35652 17391 $\cdots$	30	430
$\sqrt{1.23}$	1.10905 4	1.10905 36506 $\cdots$	32	290
$\sqrt{1.23^2 + 3.45^2}$	3.66270 4	3.66270 39192 $\cdots$	55	1,084
$\sin(1.23)$	0.94248 88	0.94248 88019 $\cdots$	107	886
$\log(3.45)$	1.23837 4	1.23837 42310 $\cdots$	141	1,052
$\exp(1.23)$	3.42123 0	3.42122 95363 $\cdots$	171	1,272
$\mathrm{acosh}(3.45)$	1.90982 3	1.90982 29687 $\cdots$	238	1,672
$\Gamma(3.45)$	3.14631 2	3.14631 20534 $\cdots$	279	2,550

Floating-point functions can require significant resources. The results of floating-point benchmarks on our target with the 8–bit microcontroller are shown in Table 12.1. Multiplication, division and square root are the fastest functions. More complicated functions such as hyperbolic arc-cosine and Gamma (Sect. 12.4) require significantly more resources.

An interesting perspective on the runtime characteristics of floating-point functions can be obtained by comparing the floating-point benchmark results in Table 12.1 with those of the MD5 calculation in Sects. 6.1 and 6.2. For our target with the 8–bit microcontroller, the MD5 is an exceptionally computationally intensive task that needs about 10 kB of code and more than 1,400 μs (1.4 ms). The floating-point hyperbolic arc-cosine computation needs about 1/6 of the resources required by the MD5 calculation on this target system.

The performance of floating-point elementary functions may vary considerably from one microcontroller to another. There can even be strong variations from one compiler to another or among different implementations of the underlying C-library. In order to understanding floating-point efficiency in the project, some simple benchmarking in hard real-time such as the kind summarized in Table 12.1 above can be performed.

12.4 Special Functions

Some special functions of pure and applied mathematics such as Bessel functions, orthogonal polynomials, elliptic integrals, the Riemann Zeta function, etc. are specified in the *optional* special functions part of the C++ library [8]. Here, the

Fig. 12.1 The Gamma
function $\Gamma(x)$ for $x \in \mathbb{R}$
with $0 \lesssim x \leq 4$ is shown.
The Gamma function $\Gamma(x)$
has a singularity at the origin
and grows rapidly for large x

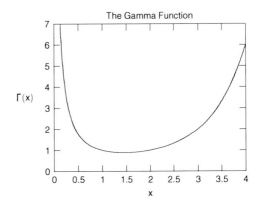

general term *special functions* means higher transcendental functions as described
in Erdélyi's three-volume treatise on the subject [3].

Since implementations of special functions are, in fact, optional in the C++
standard and because they can be quite difficult to calculate accurately and
efficiently, compiler support for them may be very limited among embedded targets.
So it may be necessary, at some point in time, to either write certain special functions
by oneself or arrange for dedicated compiler support for them in cooperation with
the compiler supplier.

In general, the complexity of computing special functions increases the *higher*
a function gets. In particular, the Gamma function $\Gamma(x)$ is often considered the
simplest special function of all to compute. Even though some compilers do not
include Gamma functions, both $\Gamma(x)$ as well as $\log \Gamma(x)$ are mandatory in C++11
for $x \in \mathbb{R}$ for **float**, **double** and **long double**. Orthogonal polynomials are
considered more difficult than the Gamma function. The Bessel functions $J_\nu(x)$,
which require the Gamma function, are often considered more difficult to compute
still, etc.

Writing a library of special functions that is accurate, efficient and supports
correct range checking and handling of subnormals is a task beyond the scope of
this book. To get better acquainted with the ways of programming special functions
in real-time C++, though, we will write an implementation of the Gamma function
$\Gamma(x)$ for $x \in \mathbb{R}$ for **float**.

The Gamma function $\Gamma(x)$ is the extension of the integer factorial function to
both real as well as complex numbers x with $x \in \mathbb{C}$. The relation between the
Gamma function and the factorial is $\Gamma(n + 1) = n!$, where $n \in \mathbb{Z}^+$ is a positive
integer or zero. The behavior of the Gamma function is shown in Fig. 12.1 for $x \in \mathbb{R}$
with $0 \lesssim x \leq 4$. The Gamma function has a complex-valued singularity at the
origin and grows rapidly for increasing argument (i.e., like the factorial). Notice at
the right-hand side of the graph the expected value of $\Gamma(4) = 3! = 6$.

Our computational scheme for computing $\Gamma(x)$ is primarily based on polynomial
expansion. In particular, we use

$$\Gamma(x) = \begin{cases} \text{Reflection of } \Gamma(x) \text{ for } x < 0 \\ \text{NaN for } x = 0 \\ \text{Taylor series of } 1/\Gamma(x) \text{ for } 0 < x < 0.1 \\ \text{Polynomial expansion of } \Gamma(x+1) \text{ for } 0.1 \le x < 1 \\ 1 \text{ for } x = 1, 2 \\ \text{Recursion of } \Gamma(x) \text{ for } x > 1 \\ +\infty \text{ for overflow when } x \text{ is large or near } 0 \end{cases} \qquad (12.3)$$

We have chosen to use polynomial expansion and recursion in this book because the resulting code is compact and easy-to-understand. Many numerical specialists prefer to use a Lanczos-type approximation for small-to-medium values combined with an asymptotic Stirling-type expansion for large arguments to compute $\log \Gamma(x)$ and subsequently take the exponent of it for $\Gamma(x)$. This is, for example, done in GCC for targets that support the Gamma function.

The small-argument Taylor series for $\dfrac{1}{\Gamma(x)}$ is given by

$$\frac{1}{\Gamma(x)} = x + \gamma\, x^2 - 0.65587\,80715\,x^3 - 0.04200\,26350\,x^4$$

$$+ 0.16653\,86114\,x^5 - 0.04219\,77346\,x^6 + \dots, \qquad (12.4)$$

where $\gamma = 0.57721\,56649\dots$ is the Euler-Mascheroni constant.

The polynomial expansion for $\Gamma(x+1)$ is given by[2]

$$\Gamma(x+1) = \left(\sum_{n=0}^{9} a_n x^n \right) + \epsilon(x), \qquad (12.5)$$

where the relative error $|\epsilon(x)| \lesssim 3 \times 10^{-8}$ and the coefficients a_n are given by

$$\begin{aligned} a_0 &= 0.99999\,99703 & a_5 &= -0.86491\,08124 \\ a_1 &= -0.57720\,69549 & a_6 &= 0.67213\,15341 \\ a_2 &= 0.98875\,89417 & a_7 &= -0.38608\,71683 \\ a_3 &= -0.90350\,83713 & a_8 &= 0.14050\,04023 \\ a_4 &= 0.95390\,74630 & a_9 &= -0.02358\,50272\,. \end{aligned} \qquad (12.6)$$

---

[2] A similar polynomial expansion for $\Gamma(x+1)$ is given in Sect. 6.1.36 of [1]. This polynomial approximation originates from the work of C. Hastings [5]. In my book, I have increased the number of coefficients from Hastings' original 8 up to 10 in order to reach precision better than the approximate 7 decimal digits of single-precision `float`.

These coefficients have been computed with a computer algebra system. A least-squares curve-fit of a table of $\Gamma(x + 1)$ with 81 equidistant points in the range $0 \leq x \leq 1$ has been used. The polynomial fit has been performed with 50 decimal digits of precision.

For our calculation, we also need both reflection of the Gamma function

$$\Gamma(-x) = -\frac{\pi}{x\,\Gamma(x)\,\sin \pi x}, \tag{12.7}$$

as well as upward recursion of the Gamma function

$$\Gamma(x + 1) = x\,\Gamma(x). \tag{12.8}$$

Armed with all these mathematical equations, we are finally ready to implement the core-part of our Gamma function, gamma1(), which computes the **float** value of $\Gamma(x)$ for $0 < x < 1$. In particular,

```
float gamma1(const float& x)
{
   // Compute Gamma(x) for 0 < x < 1 (float).

   if(x < 0.1F)
   {
      // Small-argument Taylor series for 1/gamma.
      const float sum = (((((((    + 0.0072189432F
                          * x -   0.0096219715F)
                          * x -   0.0421977346F)
                          * x +   0.1665386114F)
                          * x -   0.0420026350F)
                          * x -   0.6558780715F)
                          * x +   0.5772156649F)
                          * x +   1)
                          * x;

      return 1 / sum;
   }
   else
   {
      // Do the order-9 polynomial fit.
      const float g = (((((((((    - 0.0235850272F
                          * x +   0.1405004023F)
                          * x -   0.3860871683F)
                          * x +   0.6721315341F)
                          * x -   0.8649108124F)
                          * x +   0.9539074630F)
```

```
                                    * x -  0.9035083713F)
                                    * x +  0.9887589417F)
                                    * x -  0.5772069549F)
                                    * x +  0.9999999703F;

  // Note: We use one downward recursion here.
  return g / x;
  }
}
```

To make the complete implementation of tgamma(), we need to include
range checks, handling of subnormals, possible upward recursion of the result and
reflection for negative arguments. For example,

```
float tgamma(float x)
{
  // Is the argument a subnormal?
  if(!isfinite(x))
  {
    return x;
  }

  // Check for pure zero argument.
  if(0 == x)
  {
    return std::numeric_limits<float>::quiet_NaN();
  }

  // Check for overflow and underflow.
  if(    (x > 35)
      || ((x > -1.0E-4F) && (x < 1.0E-4F))
     )
  {
    return std::numeric_limits<float>::infinity();
  }

  // Is the argument 1 or 2?
  if((1 == x) || (2 == x))
  {
    return 1.0F;
  }

  // Use a positive argument for the Gamma calculation.
  const bool b_neg = (x < 0);
```

```
x = (b_neg ? -x : x);

// Get any integer recursion and scale the argument.
const std::uint16_t nx = std::uint16_t(::floor(x));
x -= float(nx);

float g = gamma1(x);

// Do the recursion if necessary.
for(std::uint16_t recur = 0U; recur < nx; ++recur)
{
  g *= x;
  ++x;
}

// Return (and possibly reflect) the result.
if(false == b_neg)
{
  return g;
}
else
{
  const float sin_pi_x = sin(const_pi<float>() * x);

  return -const_pi<float>() / ((x * g) * sin_pi_x);
}
}
```

This implementation of the tgamma() function is relatively complete. In practice, though, it should throw an std::out_of_range exception for arguments that are too large or so close to zero or negative integers that the results will be subnormal. In addition, it may be preferable to switch from recursion to Stirling's approximation for arguments above, say, $x \geq 10$ since many upward recursions can be costly. Even with its limitations, though, this version of tgamma() is a compact efficient Gamma function for **float** that may be adequate if the compiler does not include one. This version of tgamma() is included in the reference project of the companion code.

The numerical results of our tgamma() function are compared with known control values in Table 12.2. The relative deviations of the calculated values are $|\epsilon(x)| \lesssim 10^{-7}$, which is accurate to within the approximate 7 decimal digits of precision of **float**.

Another example of a special function often needed in real-time C++ is the Bessel function $J_v(x)$.

Table 12.2 Calculations of `tgamma(x)` are compared with known values of $\Gamma(x)$

x	`tgamma(x)`	$\Gamma(x)$
0.5	1.77245 38	1.77245 38509 ...
8.76	24203.830	24203.81462 ...
0.02	49.44221 1	49.44221 01631 ...
−0.345	0.29302 791	0.29302 79565 ...

The Taylor series for $J_\nu(z)$ is

$$J_\nu(z) = \left(\frac{1}{2}z\right)^\nu \sum_{k=0}^{\infty} \frac{\left(-\frac{1}{4}z^2\right)^k}{k!\,\Gamma(\nu + k + 1)}, \tag{12.9}$$

where $z, \nu \in \mathbb{C}$.

Equation 12.9 is a simple enough series. Accurately calculating Bessel functions over a wide range of arguments and orders is, however, relatively complicated. Numerical methods for computing the Bessel function $J_\nu(x)$ and other special functions are described in detail in [4] (language-neutral) and [13] (in Fortran 77). In addition, Boost [2] includes portable and well-tested C++ implementations of numerous higher transcendental functions for built-in floating-point types in its `Boost.Math` library.

12.5 Complex-Valued Mathematics

The C++ standard library supports complex-valued mathematics with its templated data type `std::complex`. The `std::complex` data type is defined in `<complex>` and specified for (and *only* for) the built-in types **float, double** and **long double**.

The public interface of the `std::complex` class supports basic arithmetic operators, elementary transcendental functions, the norm, polar coordinates, etc. See Sects. 26.4.1–26.4.9 in [9] for a complete synopsis of the `<complex>` library.

Consider x and y of type `std::complex<`**float**`>` given by

$$x = 1.23 + 3.45i$$

$$y = 0.77 + 0.22i. \tag{12.10}$$

The following code computes the complex values

$$z_1 = x/y$$

$$z_2 = \sin(x),\qquad\qquad (12.11)$$

where z_1 and z_2 are of type `std::complex<float>`.

```
std::complex<float> x(1.23F, 3.45F); // (1.23 + 3.45 I)
std::complex<float> y(0.77F, 0.22F); // (0.77 + 0.22 I)

std::complex<float> z1;
std::complex<float> z2;

z1 = x / y;       // (2.6603774 + 3.7204117 I)
z2 = std::sin(x); // (14.859343 + 5.2590045 I)
```

The `<complex>` library also supports, among others, common complex operations such as norm and absolute value. For the same complex values x and y, consider the norm and absolute value given by

$$n_x = \|x\| = (\Re x)^2 + (\Im x)^2$$

$$a_y = |y| = \sqrt{(\Re y)^2 + (\Im y)^2}.\qquad\qquad (12.12)$$

The following code computes the **float** values of n_x and a_y.

```
std::complex<float> x(1.23F, 3.45F); // (1.23 + 3.45 I)
std::complex<float> y(0.77F, 0.22F); // (0.77 + 0.22 I)

float nx = std::norm(x); // 13.415400
float ay = std::abs(y);  // 0.80081209
```

Setting and retrieving the real and imaginary parts of a complex number is done with the member functions `real()` and `imag()`. For instance,

```
std::complex<float> z(0); // (0 + 0 I)

z.real(1.23F); // Set the real part.
z.imag(3.45F); // Set the imag part.

float zr = z.real(); // Get the real part, 1.23.
float zi = z.imag(); // Get the imag part, 3.45.
```

In general, complex-valued floating-point calculations are at least four times slower than corresponding real-valued computations. The rule of thumb here is that mathematical software does the majority of its work with multiplication— an $O(N^2)$ operation. Since complex numbers have two components, real and imaginary, the computational effort of complex-valued math can be expected to be at least four times that of real-valued math because $2^2 = 4$.

For two cases in point, consider the work of multiplying two complex numbers

$$(a + ib) \times (c + id) = (ac - bd) + i(ad + bc), \qquad (12.13)$$

and that of evaluating the sine of a complex number

$$\sin(x + iy) = \sin x \cosh y + i \cos x \sinh y. \qquad (12.14)$$

The multiplication algorithm in Eq. 12.13 requires four real-valued multiplications and two additions.[3] The computation of the trigonometric sine function in Eq. 12.14 requires the evaluation of four real-valued elementary transcendental functions.[4]

Table 12.3 shows the runtime and code size for various complex-valued functions performed with `std::complex<float>` on our target with the 8–bit microcontroller. Comparison of the runtimes and code sizes with those of the corresponding real-valued floating-point calculations shown in Table 12.3 confirm that complex-valued math is 4–20 times bulkier than real-valued math.

Aside from potential resource consumption issues that need to be kept in mind, however, there are no other significant technical reasons to avoid using complex-valued floating-point math in real-time C++. So if a project can benefit from complex-valued math and the performance constraints can be satisfied, then the `<complex>` library can safely be used.

---

[3]There is also a well-known alternate scheme for multiplication of complex numbers that requires only *three* real-valued multiplications, but five additions. In particular,

$$(a + ib) \times (c + id) = (\alpha - \beta) + i(\alpha + \gamma),$$

where

$$\alpha = a(c + d)$$

$$\beta = d(a + b)$$

$$\gamma = c(b - a).$$

This scheme for multiplication of complex numbers may or may not be faster than the original $O(N^2)$ scheme on a given CPU architecture.

[4]Note here, however, that the sometimes supported function `sincos()` may boost efficiency because both $\sin x$ as well as $\cos x$ are required. In addition, only one calculation of e^y is needed because $\cosh y = (e^y + e^{-y})/2$ and $\sinh y = (e^y - e^{-y})/2$.

Table 12.3 Timing of complex-valued floating-point calculations

Function	Runtime (μs)	Code Size (byte)
$(1.23 + 3.45i) \times (0.77 + 0.22i)$	210	940
$\sqrt{1.23 + 3.45i}$	740	3,280
$\sin(1.23 + 3.45i)$	1,320	3,000
$\log(1.23 + 3.45i)$	940	3,760
$\exp(1.23 + 3.45i)$	1,110	2,840
$\mathrm{acosh}(1.23 + 3.45i)$	3,630	5,470

12.6 Compile-Time Evaluation of Functions with `constexpr`

Compile-time evaluation of floating-point functions uses the **`constexpr`** keyword. For example, we can re-factor the `area_of_a_circle()` function from Sects. 12.1 and 12.2.

```
template<typename T>
constexpr T const_area_of_a_circle(T r)
{
   return (const_pi<T>() * r) * r;
}
```

This function returns the floating-point value representing the approximate area of a circle with radius r as a compile-time constant. For example, to compute the area of a circle with approximate **float** radius 1.23 ($a \sim 4.752916$), we simply use

```
constexpr float a = const_area_of_a_circle(1.23F);
```

Using **`constexpr`** floating-point values in this way allows for portable and legible compile-time evaluation of even non-trivial floating-point functions such as trigonometric functions.

Consider, for instance, an order–19 polynomial approximation of the sine function,

$$\sin x = \sin\left(\frac{\pi}{2}\chi\right) = \left(\sum_{n=1,\, n\ \mathrm{odd}}^{n=19} a_n \chi^n\right) + O\left(10^{-20}\right), \qquad (12.15)$$

using the scaled argument

$$\chi = x \left(\frac{2}{\pi} \right) \tag{12.16}$$

in the range $-1 \leq \chi \leq 1$, where the coefficients a_n are given by

$$
\begin{aligned}
a_1 &= 1.57079\ 63267\ 94896\ 61922\ 76341 \\
a_3 &= -6.45964\ 09750\ 62462\ 53373\ 25359\ 10^{-1} \\
a_5 &= 7.96926\ 26246\ 16703\ 87700\ 53004\ 10^{-2} \\
a_7 &= -4.68175\ 41353\ 18622\ 85169\ 58362\ 10^{-3} \\
a_9 &= 1.60441\ 18478\ 69923\ 28124\ 60184\ 10^{-4} \\
a_{11} &= -3.59884\ 32339\ 70852\ 51537\ 71884\ 10^{-6} \\
a_{13} &= 5.69217\ 26597\ 22165\ 75609\ 94942\ 10^{-8} \\
a_{15} &= -6.68800\ 01786\ 32981\ 94595\ 55395\ 10^{-10} \\
a_{17} &= 6.06408\ 55645\ 94093\ 05881\ 23490\ 10^{-12} \\
a_{19} &= -4.24681\ 71354\ 84152\ 33794\ 93663\ 10^{-14} .
\end{aligned}
\tag{12.17}
$$

These coefficients have also been computed with a computer algebra system using a least-squares fitting technique.

It takes a bit of typing and some careful considerations about argument reduction, reflection and the like. It is, however, relatively straightforward to write a compile-time sine function for floating-point arguments based on Eqs. 12.15–12.17.

In particular, the subroutine below performs a compile-time computation of sin x for floating-point argument x with better than 20 decimal digits of precision.[5]

```
template<typename T>
constexpr T const_sin(T x)
{
  // Scale x to CHI (+-pi/2 to +-1).
  #define CHI_S T(x / const_pi_half<T>())

  // Take the absolute value of CHI.
  #define IS_NEG bool(CHI_S < T(0))
  #define CHI_A  T(IS_NEG ? -CHI_S : CHI_S)

  // Do the argument reduction.
  #define NPI2 std::uint32_t(CHI_A / 2)
```

[5]This implementation uses solely range reduction, reflection and the polynomial approximation. To obtain the highest possible precision conserving characteristics, it may be better to use Taylor series approximations near the turning points at $x = 0$ and $x = \pi/2$ after the range reduction. See [11] for further details on techniques for range reduction.

```
#define NPI   std::uint32_t(                        \
                (CHI_A - (NPI2 * 2) > T(1)) \
                ? NPI2 + 1                          \
                : NPI2)

#define CHI   T(CHI_A - T(NPI * 2))
#define CHI2 T(CHI * CHI)

// Do the order-19 polynomial expansion.
#define SUM                                                  \
  ((((((((( - T(4.246817135484152337949366 3E-14)  \
      * CHI2 + T(6.0640855645940930588123490E-12)) \
      * CHI2 - T(6.6880001786329819459555395E-10)) \
      * CHI2 + T(5.6921726597221657560994942E-08)) \
      * CHI2 - T(3.5988432339708525153771884E-06)) \
      * CHI2 + T(1.6044118478699232812460184E-04)) \
      * CHI2 - T(4.6817541353186228516958362E-03)) \
      * CHI2 + T(7.9692626246167038770053004E-02)) \
      * CHI2 - T(6.4596409750624625337325359E-01)) \
      * CHI2 + T(1.5707963267948966192276341E+00)) \
      * CHI

// Reflect the result if necessary.
#define NEEDS_REFLECT bool((NPI % 2)  != 0)

  return ((NEEDS_REFLECT == IS_NEG) ? SUM : -SUM);
}
```

Using `const_sin()` for compile-time calculations of the sine function in code is simple. In the example below, for instance, the compiler computes the approximate double-precision representation of sin (0.5).

```
constexpr double y = const_sin(0.5);
```

If y is subsequently used in a subroutine, the compiler should be able to compute the value of the sine function at compile time. In my benchmark, investigations of the compiler-generated assembly code revealed that the compiler directly replaced the variable y with the 8–byte hexadecimal representation of

$$\sin (0.5) \approx 0.47942\,55386\,04203\,01 = 0x3FDEAEE8744B05F0. \quad (12.18)$$

In this example, the floating-point representation of **double** is 8 bytes wide and conforms with IEEE-754. This is an extremely efficient form of constant folding. In fact, the `const_sin()` subroutine reduces the runtime effort for computing sin x

for constant x to that of merely loading a constant value computed by the compiler into CPU registers.

With a bit of additional effort, compile-time constant versions of cosine and tangent can also be written. In particular,

```
template<typename T>
constexpr T const_cos(T x)
{
    return -const_sin<T>(x - const_pi_half<T>());
}

template<typename T>
constexpr T const_tan(T x)
{
    return const_sin<T>(x) / const_cos<T>(x);
}
```

It is possible to use compile-time evaluation of functions to compute essentially any function, bounded only by the compiler's internal limits. It is possible to extend the number of coefficients in polynomial expansions and the like to obtain even higher precision. In addition, template metaprogramming can be employed for more complicated range reduction if needed. Compile-time evaluation of floating-point functions may potentially be a new research topic in the area of high-performance numerical computing made possible by the abilities of **constexpr** in C++11.

12.7 Generic Numeric Programming

Generic numeric programming employs templates to use the same code for different floating-point types and functions. We have already encountered generic numeric programming previously in this chapter. In particular, recall the templated function const_area_of_a_circle() from Sect. 12.6.

```
template<typename T>
constexpr T const_area_of_a_circle(T r)
{
    return (const_pi<T>() * r) * r;
}
```

This subroutine has strong generic character because it can be used with different floating-point types to provide results with differing precision. For example, if

float, **double** and **long double** are 4, 8 and 16 bytes wide, respectively, on a given system, then the following results are obtained for the area of a circle with radius 1.23.

```
// 4.7529155
float area_f = const_area_of_a_circle(1.23F);

// 4.752915525615998
double area_d = const_area_of_a_circle(1.23);

// 4.752915525615998190470133174563599
long double area_ld = const_area_of_a_circle(1.23L);
```

We will now add even more power to generic numeric programming using not only different floating-point types but also function objects as template parameters. Consider some well-known central difference rules for numerically computing the first derivative of a function $f'(x)$ with $x \in \mathbb{R}$.

$$f'(x) \approx m_1 + O(dx^2)$$

$$f'(x) \approx \frac{4}{3}m_1 - \frac{1}{3}m_2 + O(dx^4)$$

$$f'(x) \approx \frac{3}{2}m_1 - \frac{3}{5}m_2 + \frac{1}{10}m_3 + O(dx^6), \qquad (12.19)$$

where the difference terms m_n are given by

$$m_1 = \frac{f(x + dx) - f(x - dx)}{2\,dx}$$

$$m_2 = \frac{f(x + 2dx) - f(x - 2dx)}{4\,dx}$$

$$m_3 = \frac{f(x + 3dx) - f(x - 3dx)}{6\,dx}, \qquad (12.20)$$

and dx is the step-size of the derivative.

The third formula in Eq. 12.19 is a three-point central difference rule. It calculates the first derivative of $f(x)$ to $O(dx^6)$, where dx is the given step-size. For example, if the step-size is 0.01 this derivative calculation has at least 6 decimal digits of precision—just about right for the 7 decimal digits of **float**.

We will now make a generic template subroutine using this three-point central difference rule. In particular,

```
template<typename value_type,
         typename function_type>
value_type derivative(const value_type x,
                       const value_type dx,
                       function_type function)
{
  // Compute the derivative using a three point
  // central difference rule of O(dx^6).

  const value_type dx1 = dx;
  const value_type dx2 = dx1 * 2;
  const value_type dx3 = dx1 * 3;

  const value_type m1
    = (  function(x + dx1)
       - function(x - dx1)) / 2;

  const value_type m2
    = (  function(x + dx2)
       - function(x - dx2)) / 4;

  const value_type m3
    = (  function(x + dx3)
       - function(x - dx3)) / 6;

  const value_type fifteen_m1 = 15 * m1;
  const value_type six_m2     =  6 * m2;
  const value_type ten_dx1    = 10 * dx1;

  return ((fifteen_m1 - six_m2) + m3) / ten_dx1;
}
```

The `derivative()` template function can be used to compute the first derivative of any continuous function to $O(dx^6)$. For example, consider the first derivative of $\sin x$ evaluated at $x = \pi/3$. In other words,

$$\frac{d}{dx} \sin x \bigg|_{x=\frac{\pi}{3}} = \cos\left(\frac{\pi}{3}\right) = \frac{1}{2}. \tag{12.21}$$

The code below computes this derivative with about 6 decimal digits of precision using the `derivative()` function.

```
float x = const_pi<float>() / 3.0F;

// Should be very near 0.5.
float y = derivative(x,
                     0.01F,
                     [](const float& x) -> float
                     {
                         return sin(x);
                     });
```

The expected value is 0.5. The compiler that was used to test this code sequence obtained 0.50000286. This result is within the expected tolerance of $O\left(dx^6\right)$ with $dx = 0.01$. This code also makes use of the const_pi() function from Sect. 12.2 and a lambda expression, both C++ language elements with strong generic character as well.

The derivative() function can also be used with function objects. Consider the quadratic equation,

$$ax^2 + bx + c = 0. \tag{12.22}$$

The code below implements a templated function object that encapsulates the left-hand side of the quadratic equation.

```
template<typename T>
class quadratic
{
public:
  const T a;
  const T b;
  const T c;

  quadratic(T A, T B, T C) : a(A), b(B), c(C) { }

  T operator()(const T& x) const
  {
    return ((a * x + b) * x) + c;
  }
};
```

The first derivative of the quadratic equation can be computed in closed form. In other words,

$$\frac{d}{dx}\left(ax^2 + bx + c\right) = 2ax + b. \tag{12.23}$$

The `derivative()` function can handily compute the first derivative of the `quadratic` function object. In particular, the code below computes

$$\frac{d}{dx}\left(1.2x^2 + 3.4x + 5.6\right)\Bigg|_{x=\frac{1}{2}} = 1.2 + 3.4 = 4.6. \qquad (12.24)$$

```
float x = 0.5F;

// Should be very near 4.6.
float y
  = derivative(x,
               0.01F,
               quadratic<float>(1.2F, 3.4F, 5.6F));
```

The versatile `derivative()` template function exemplifies generic numeric programming because both the floating-point type (`value_type`) as well as the function-type (`function_type`) are template parameters. This means that `derivative()` can be used with **float**, **double**, **long double**, an extended precision type, a fixed-point type (Chap. 13), etc. Furthermore, `derivative()` can be used with functions having static linkage, lambda expressions and function objects alike.

A similar generic template method for computing the numerical integral of a function

$$\int_a^b f(x)\,dx \qquad (12.25)$$

is shown below.

```
template<typename value_type,
         typename function_type>
value_type integral(const value_type a,
                    const value_type b,
                    const value_type tol,
                    function_type function)
{
  std::uint_fast8_t n = 1U;

  value_type h = (b - a);
  value_type I = (function(a) + function(b)) * (h / 2);

  for(std::uint_fast8_t k = 0U; k < 8U; k++)
  {
```

```cpp
    h /= 2;

    value_type sum(0);
    for(std::uint_fast8_t j = 1U; j <= n; j++)
    {
      sum +=
        function(a + (value_type((j * 2) - 1) * h));
    }

    const value_type I0 = I;
    I = (I / 2) + (h * sum);

    const value_type ratio = I0 / I;
    const value_type delta = std::abs(ratio - 1);

    if((k > 1U) && (delta < tol))
    {
      break;
    }

    n *= 2;
  }

  return I;
}
```

This function uses a recursive trapezoid rule to perform numerical integration. See Sect. 5.2.2 in [4] for additional information on this recursive trapezoid rule.

Generic numeric programming can be quite useful in real-time C++ because it is flexible and scalable. Since generic numeric programming utilizes template methods, the results can be highly optimized by the compiler resulting in exceptionally efficient algorithms.

References

1. M. Abramowitz, I.A. Stegun, *Handbook of Mathematical Functions, 9th Printing* (Dover, New York, 1972)
2. B. Dawes, D. Abrahams, *Boost C++ Libraries* (2012), http://www.boost.org
3. A. Erdélyi, W. Magnus, F. Oberhettinger, F.G. Tricomi, *Higher Transcendental Functions*, vol. 1–3 (Krieger, New York, 1981)
4. A. Gil, J. Segura, N.M. Temme, *Numerical Methods for Special Functions* (Society for Industrial and Applied Mathematics, Philadelphia, 2007)
5. C. Hastings, *Approximations for Digital Computers* (Princeton University Press, Princeton, 1955)

6. IEEE Computer Society, *IEEE Std 1003.1 – 2008*, IEEE Standard 754-2008 (2008). Available at http://ieeexplore.ieee.org/servlet/opac?punumber=4610933
7. ISO/IEC, *ISO/IEC 9899:1999: Programming Languages—C* (International Organization for Standardization, Geneva, 1999)
8. ISO/IEC, *ISO/IEC 29124:2010: Information Technology—Programming Languages, Their Environments and System Software Interfaces—Extensions to the C++ Library to Support Mathematical Special Functions* (International Organization for Standardization, Geneva, 2010)
9. ISO/IEC, *ISO/IEC 14882:2011: Information Technology—Programming Languages—C++* (International Organization for Standardization, Geneva, 2011)
10. D.E. Knuth, *The Art of Computer Programming Volumes 1–3*, 3rd edn. (Addison Wesley, Reading, 1998)
11. J.M. Muller, *Elementary Functions: Algorithms and Implementation* (Birkhäuser, Boston, 2006)
12. J.M. Muller, N. Brisebarre, F. de Dinechin, C.M. Jeannerod, V. Lefèvre, G. Melquiond, N. Revol, D. Stehlé, T. Torres, *Handbook of Floating-Point Arithmetic* (Birkhäuser, Boston, 2010)
13. S. Zhang, J. Jin, *Computation of Special Functions* (Wiley, New York, 1996)

Chapter 13
Fixed-Point Mathematics

Many embedded systems applications need to perform floating-point calculations. As mentioned in the previous chapter, however, small-scale microcontrollers may not have hardware support for floating-point calculations with a floating-point unit (FPU). To avoid potentially slow floating-point emulation libraries manipulating 32–bit single-precision **float** or even 64–bit double-precision **double**, many developers elect to use integer-based fixed-point arithmetic. The first part of this chapter describes fixed-point data types and presents a scalable template class representation for fixed-point. In the second part of this chapter, we will use our fixed-point class to compute some elementary transcendental functions, discuss fixed-point efficiency and develop a specialization of std::numeric_limits.

13.1 Fixed-Point Data Types

A fixed-point number is a specialized real data type, optionally signed, that has a fixed number of digits before the decimal point and another fixed number of digits after the decimal point. Fixed-point numbers are often implemented in base–2 or base–10. For example, a base–10 fixed-point system could represent 3.456 as an integer with value 3,456, where the scaling factor is 1/1,000 (see [6]).

Fixed-point representations in base–2 are also common. For example, a base–2, signed, 16–bit fixed-point representation is shown in Fig. 13.1. It has one sign bit, seven binary integer digits to the left of the decimal point and eight binary fraction digits to the right of the decimal point.

This is known as a Q7.8 fixed-point type using the *Q-notation*. In the unambiguous Q-notation, the entire word is a two's complement integer with an implicit sign bit. For example, Q15.16 describes a fixed-point type with one sign bit, 15 integer bits and 16 fractional bits. The Q15.16 representation is stored in a 32–bit two's complement signed integer.

Fixed-point numbers generally do not have an exponent field, lending them a near-integer representation. Therefore, manipulations of fixed-point numbers

C.M. Kormanyos, *Real-Time C++*, DOI 10.1007/978-3-642-34688-0_13,
© Springer-Verlag Berlin Heidelberg 2013

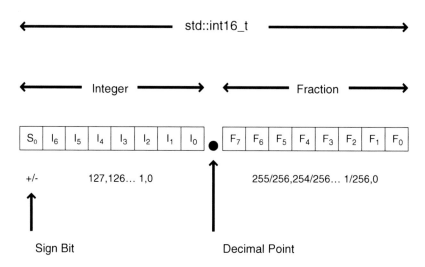

Fig. 13.1 A representation of the Q7.8 fixed-point type is shown

such as addition, multiplication and division use integer algorithms which can be simpler and potentially more efficient than those of conventional floating-point representations.

The Q7.8 representation can hold real numbers ranging from

$$\pm \left\{ \texttt{0x00.01} \ldots \texttt{0x7F.FF} \right\}, \tag{13.1}$$

in other words from

$$\pm \left\{ \frac{1}{2^8} \ldots \left(2^7 - \frac{1}{2^8} \right) \right\}, \tag{13.2}$$

which is approximately equal to

$$\pm \left\{ 0.004 \ldots 127.996 \right\}. \tag{13.3}$$

The decimal point has been symbolically included in the hexadecimal representation of Eq. 13.1 in an intuitive fashion. The Q7.8 fixed-point representation has slightly more than two decimal digits of precision both to the left of the decimal point as well as to the right of the decimal point. Note that the fractional part of the Q7.8 representation has one binary digit more of precision than the integer part due to the sign bit in the integer part.

Since the decimal point has a fixed position in the underlying integer data type, smaller numbers have decreased precision. In fact, the minimum value of the Q7.8 representation is $\left(1/2^8\right) \approx 0.004$, with merely *one* binary digit of precision. In addition, fixed-point representations lacking an exponent usually have smaller range than floating-point types. In particular, the maximum value of the Q7.8 representation is approximately $+127.996$.

Fixed-point types generally have less range and reduced precision compared with floating-point representations. The underlying reason for this is the near-integer representation of fixed-point types. This is, however, exactly what lends them their improved performance. Fixed-point trades reduced range and decreased precision in favor of potentially improved efficiency using simpler integer algorithms.

It is possible to vary the fundamental integer size and/or the decimal-split characteristics when defining fixed-point types. This can be done in order to obtain different performances or other numerical ranges. For example, a signed, 32–bit Q15.16 representation could be used for a fixed-point type with optimized performance on a 32–bit architecture. If storage size or performance on an 8–bit platform are considerations, then an unsigned, 8–bit Q0.8 representation could be used. The Q0.8 representation is able to store fixed-point numbers with positive values less than one with about two decimal digits of precision. The Q0.8 representation could be useful, for example, if the application only needs to implement a couple of trigonometric calculations, such as sine and cosine functions with just a few digits of precision. Whatever the fixed-point representation, one must be aware of its range. In addition, utmost care must be taken to remain within the numerical limitations at all times when performing fixed-point calculations.

It is also possible to dynamically vary the characteristics of a fixed-point type's decimal-split during runtime. This may be desired for optimizing the results of numerical calculations within specific ranges. For example, calculations of the exponential function of, say, $e^2 \ldots e^3$ have results that range from about $7 \ldots 20$. Comparing these values with the results of calculations of the sine or cosine functions, for instance, shows that the exponential function benefits from more digits to the left of the decimal point and fewer to the right. So preferentially shifting the decimal point of the fixed-point type a few places to the right in order to make room for more digits in the integer part will generally improve fixed-point calculations of the exponential function.

In this book, however, dynamic modification of the decimal-split is not done because it can lead to additional sources of error and a more complicated implementation. In my opinion, it may be best to consider the kinds of calculations planned for a particular application up front and, based on the analysis, limit the required range to some reasonable values, such as $0.001 \ldots 1,000$. Once the fixed-point range has been defined, a dedicated fixed-point type adequate for the given range can be selected up front.

13.2 A Scalable Fixed-Point Template Class

A class representation of a specialized numeric type in C++ should behave like a built-in type as closely as possible. In other words, it should be possible to perform operations on the specialized type such as assignment, binary arithmetic, comparison, etc. In order to accomplish this, the author of a specialized numeric class usually needs to implement some or all of the following features.

- Make a copy constructor from the self-type and additional constructors from other built-in types.
- Implement assignment operators from the self-type and other built-in types.
- Write overloads for the assignment operator and arithmetic compound assignment operators such as **operator**+=(), **operator**-=(), **operator**∗=(), **operator**/=().
- Make the global unary operators **operator**+() and **operator**-() as well as the operators for the pre-forms and post-forms of increment and decrement **operator**++() and **operator**--().
- Implement standard global operators for binary arithmetic operations including **operator**+(), **operator**-(), **operator**∗(), **operator**/(), etc.
- Make the global comparison operators for the specialized type as well as other built-in types such as **operator**<(), **operator**<=(), **operator**==(), **operator**!=(), **operator**>=(), **operator**>().
- Optionally implement a template specialization of std::numeric_limits for the numeric type.

These steps have been carried out in the reference project of the companion code to make a specialized fixed_point class. The fixed_point class implements a relatively complete representation of fixed-point arithmetic in C++. This class is based on a scalable template that supports varying decimal digits of precision depending on the width of the underlying template parameter.

A partial synopsis of the fixed_point template class is shown in the listing below. Complete implementation details can be found in the source code of the reference project.

```
// The scalable fixed_point template class.
template<typename integer_type>
class fixed_point
{
public:
  // Signed representation of the fixed_point type.
  typedef integer_type signed_value_type;

  // Default constructor.
  fixed_point();

  // Constructors from POD.
  fixed_point(const char);
  fixed_point(const signed char);
  fixed_point(const unsigned char);
  fixed_point(const signed short);
```

```
fixed_point(const unsigned short);
fixed_point(const signed int);
fixed_point(const unsigned int);
fixed_point(const signed long);
fixed_point(const unsigned long);
fixed_point(const float&);
fixed_point(const double&);

// Copy constructor.
fixed_point(const fixed_point&);

// Copy construction from another fixed-point type.
template<typename other_type>
fixed_point(const fixed_point<other>&);

// Copy assignment operators from POD.
fixed_point& operator=(const char);
fixed_point& operator=(const signed char);
fixed_point& operator=(const unsigned char);
fixed_point& operator=(const signed short);
fixed_point& operator=(const unsigned short);
fixed_point& operator=(const signed int);
fixed_point& operator=(const unsigned int);
fixed_point& operator=(const signed long);
fixed_point& operator=(const unsigned long);
fixed_point& operator=(const float&);
fixed_point& operator=(const double&);

// Copy assignment operator.
fixed_point& operator=(const fixed_point&);

// Copy assignment from another fixed-point type.
template<typename other>
fixed_point& operator=(const fixed_point<other>&);

// Negation.
void negate();

// Pre-increment and pre-decrement.
fixed_point& operator++();
fixed_point& operator--();

// Compound assignment operations.
fixed_point& operator+=(const fixed_point&);
```

```
  fixed_point& operator-=(const fixed_point&);
  fixed_point& operator*=(const fixed_point&);
  fixed_point& operator/=(const fixed_point&);

  // Conversion operations.
  float              to_float() const;
  double             to_double() const;
  signed_value_type to_int() const;
  std::int8_t        to_int8() const;
  std::int16_t       to_int16() const;
  std::int32_t       to_int32() const;

private:
  // Internal data representation.
  signed_value_type data;

  // Internal structure for special constructor.
  typedef nothing internal;

  // Special constructor from data representation.
  fixed_point(const internal&,
              const signed_value_type&);

  // Comparison functions.
  // ...

  // Other private implementation details.
  // ...
};

// Global post-increment and post-decrement.
// Global binary mathematical operations.
// Global binary comparison operations.
// Global math functions and transcendental functions.

// ...
```

In the fixed_point class, the decimal-split is always in the middle of the underlying integer representation of the type. The size of the template parameter integer_type sets the scale of the fixed_point class. Here, the integer_type parameter is assumed to be one of the signed fixed-size integer types such as std::int16_t, std::int32_t, etc. If integer_type is std::int16_t, for example, then the fixed_point class represents Q7.8

fixed-point numbers. With a larger `integer_type` such as `std::int32_t`, the `fixed_point` class represents Q15.16 fixed-point numbers.

Dedicated types have been defined for the fixed-point representations that can be made from the `fixed_point` class. In particular,

```
// Define four scalable fixed_point types.
typedef fixed_point<std::int8_t>  fixed_point_3pt4;
typedef fixed_point<std::int16_t> fixed_point_7pt8;
typedef fixed_point<std::int32_t> fixed_point_15pt16;
typedef fixed_point<std::int64_t> fixed_point_31pt32;
```

For our target with the 8–bit microcontroller, the first three can be used effectively. On this 8–bit platform, though, the manipulation of signed 64–bit integers required for the Q31.32 representation is excessively costly and this fixed-point type should be avoided. On our target with the 32–bit microcontroller, however, the Q31.32 representation can be quite efficient. When selecting the right fixed-point types for a system, it may be beneficial to analyze runtimes and assembly listings in order to find the right trade-off between performance, range and precision.

13.3 Using the `fixed_point` Class

Using the `fixed_point` class is straightforward. For example, we will set the value of a Q7.8 fixed-point variable `r` to approximately 1.23.

```
// r is approximately 1.23.
const fixed_point_7pt8 r(1.23F);
```

Here, the fixed-point variable `r` is constructed from the **float** representation of 1.23. It can, however, be more efficient to construct fixed-point values using pure integers instead of, say, **float** or **double**. In particular, we will create the variable `r` again—this time using an integer constructor.

```
// r is approximately 1.23.
const fixed_point_7pt8 r(fixed_point_7pt8(123) / 100);
```

In this case, `r` uses an intermediate fixed-point object created from the integer 123 which is subsequently divided by the integer 100. In general, this kind of fixed-point construction should offer the best performance, even with subsequent integer division. In fact, depending on the compiler's capabilities and the characteristics of the underlying fixed-point type, the compiler may be able to directly initialize this kind of expression using constant-folding. One does need to carefully benchmark the results in order to verify that this is, in fact, the case for a particular fixed-point type on a given architecture.

It is also essential to be aware of the range limitations of fixed-point types. For example, when setting the intermediate value in the constructor shown above to 123, we are not far away from the maximum value of 127 that can fit in the integer part of the Q7.8 representation. An initial value of, say, 234 would overflow the integer part of the Q7.8 representation.

It is easy to write functions using the `fixed_point` class. Consider the template function below that computes the fixed-point area of a circle.

```
template<typename fixed_point_type>
fixed_point_type
  area_of_a_circle(const fixed_point_type& r)
{
  return (fixed_point_type::value_pi() * r) * r;
}
```

In particular, we will use this template with the Q7.8 fixed-point type to compute the approximate area of a circle with radius 1.23.

```
// r is approximately 1.23.
const fixed_point_7pt8 r(fixed_point_7pt8(123) / 100);

// a is approximately 4.723.
const fixed_point_7pt8 a = area_of_a_circle(r);
```

The result for the area a is ~4.723, which differs from the actual value of $4.752915526\ldots$ by merely $0.6\,\%$.

The `fixed_point` class can be seamlessly mixed with other built-in integral and floating-point types in mathematical expressions. For example, a simple template subroutine that implements the left-hand side of a cubic equation with signed integer polynomial coefficients could be implemented like this.

```
template<typename fixed_point_type,
         const int_fast8_t c0,
         const int_fast8_t c1,
         const int_fast8_t c2,
         const int_fast8_t c3>
fixed_point_type cubic(const fixed_point_type& x)
{
  return (((c3 * x + c2) * x + c1) * x) + c0;
}
```

As mentioned above, the `fixed_point` class can also be used with built-in **float**. In particular, consider an order–5 polynomial approximation of the trigonometric sine function

$$\sin x = 1.57041\ 28\ \chi - 0.64256\ 39\ \chi^3 + 0.07227\ 39\ \chi^5 + \epsilon(x) , \quad (13.4)$$

where

$$\chi = x \left(\frac{2}{\pi} \right) . \qquad (13.5)$$

This polynomial approximates $\sin x$ in the range $-\pi/2 \le x \le \pi/2$ (in other words $-1 \le \chi \le 1$) with relative error $|\epsilon(x)| \lesssim 0.0002$.

The polynomial approximation in Eq. 13.4 can be implemented with a template subroutine using the `fixed_point` class as follows.[1]

```
template<typename fixed_point_type>
fixed_point_type sin(const fixed_point_type& x)
{
    // Scale x to chi (+-pi/2 to +-1).
    fixed_point_type chi(x * 0.6366198F);

    // Calculate chi^2 for the polynomial expansion.
    fixed_point_type chi2 = chi * chi;

    // Do the order-5 polynomial expansion.
    return ((          0.0722739F
            * chi2 -   0.6425639F)
            * chi2 +   1.5704128F)
            * chi;
}
```

We will now use the Q15.16 fixed-point representation to compute the approximate value of $\sin(1/2)$.

```
// 0.47937
fixed_point_15pt16 y = sin(fixed_point_15pt16(1) / 2);
```

The result for y is 0.47937, which differs from the actual value of approximately 0.4794255386 ... by less than 1 part in 10,000.

---

[1] This is, though, a somewhat naive and incomplete fixed-point implementation of the sine function. It loses performance via use of **float** and is missing range reduction and reflection. A more efficient and complete fixed-point implementation of the sine function will be shown in the following section.

13.4   Fixed-Point Elementary Transcendental Functions

Fixed-point math can be used to create elementary transcendental functions such
as trigonometric functions, exponential functions or logarithmic functions. Such
functions can be quite efficient and might significantly outperform corresponding
functions using built-in floating-point types such as **float** or **double**.

For example, we will now re-design the naive fixed-point implementation of the
trigonometric sine function from the previous section to use more efficient *integer*
construction of the polynomial coefficients (instead of construction from **float**)
and also to include range reduction and reflection.

The algorithm for computing the fixed-point sine function uses the following
scheme.

- Argument transformation from x to χ according to Eq. 13.5.
- Argument reduction via removing multiples of π.
- Reflection for negative arguments and odd integral multiples of π.
- Polynomial expansion according to Eq. 13.4.

A possible implementation of the fixed-point sine function according to this
scheme is shown below.

```cpp
friend inline fixed_point sin(const fixed_point& x)
{
  // This function makes uses fixed_point's internals
  // and is, therefore, a friend of fixed_point.

  // Transform x to chi (+-pi/2 to +-1).
  fixed_point
    chi(x * fixed_point::value_two_over_pi());

  // Take the absolute value for argument reduction.
  const bool is_neg = (chi < 0);

  if(is_neg)
  {
    chi.negate();
  }

  // Do the argument reduction.
  std::uint_fast8_t npi = 0U;

  // Remove multiples of pi (1 in the units of chi).
  if(chi.data > fixed_point::decimal_split_value)
  {
    const std::uint_fast8_t npi1 =
      (chi.data >> 1) >> fixed_point::decimal_split;
```

```
    npi = ((chi - (npi1 * 2U) > 1) ? npi1 + 1
                                   : npi1);

    chi -= fixed_point(npi * 2);
  }

  const fixed_point chi2 = chi * chi;

  // Do the polynomial expansion in terms of chi.
  const fixed_point sum =
    ((
       fixed_point(internal(), // near 0.072273923
           0x012808B37ULL >> (32U - decimal_split))
       * chi2 -
       fixed_point(internal(), // near 0.642563935
           0x0A47F11EEULL >> (32U - decimal_split)))
       * chi2 +
       fixed_point(internal(), // near 1.570412766
           0x19206922FULL >> (32U - decimal_split)))
       * chi;

  // Reflect the result if necessary.
  const bool needs_reflect = ((npi % 2) != 0);

  return ((is_neg == needs_reflect) ? sum : -sum);
}
```

The sin() function has been implemented as a **friend** of the fixed_point class because it makes use of the private decimal-split value and a private constructor from fixed_point. These are optimizations specifically intended to improve the performance of this implementation of the sine function. In general, one should try to find and incorporate these and similar kinds of optimizations when devising fixed-point functions because they can drastically improve the efficiency of fixed-point functions.

Using the fixed-point sine function in code is straightforward. For example, the code sequence below computes the approximate fixed-point values of sin (1/2) for several different fixed-point representations.

```
// 0.438: relative error 960/10,000
fixed_point_3pt4 y0 = sin(fixed_point_3pt4(1) / 2);

// 0.4766: relative error 60/10,000
fixed_point_7pt8 y1 = sin(fixed_point_7pt8(1) / 2);
```

```
// 0.47937: relative error 1/10,000
fixed_point_15pt16 y2 = sin(fixed_point_15pt16(1) / 2);

// actual value:
// 0.4794255386...
```

This implementation of the fixed-point sine function includes range reduction and reflection and can, therefore, be used in a robust computational environment. There are, however, potential improvements including proper handling of excessively large arguments and subnormal numbers such as infinity and NaN. These features can be optionally included in the sine function if the underlying fixed-point class supports subnormals.

The computational complexity of fixed-point transcendental functions increases with increasing precision and width of the underlying fixed-point type used in the computations. Table 13.1 compares the performance and efficiency characteristics of the computation of $\sin(1.23)$ for various fixed-point types and **float** on our target with the 8–bit microcontroller. On this architecture, the fixed-point calculations are significantly faster and generally smaller than the corresponding **float** implementation in the C++ standard library.[2]

Another common elementary transcendental function that can be readily implemented in fixed-point is the exponential function e^x for $x \in \mathbb{R}$. The exponential function has a very wide range of results that are of interest to the user. One of the most effective methods for reaching a large part of the range of e^x is based on argument scaling via removing integral multiples of $\log 2$ from x.

In particular, we start with

$$e^x = e^{\alpha - n \log 2}, \tag{13.6}$$

where we select

$$n = \frac{x}{\log 2}, \tag{13.7}$$

such that $-\log 2 \leq \alpha \leq \log 2$. The final result of the exponential function is obtained from

$$e^x = e^\alpha 2^n. \tag{13.8}$$

After approximating e^α, the final multiplication by 2^n requires only a shift operation. This is very efficient in binary fixed-point arithmetic.

For our calculation, we will approximate e^α for $-\log 2 \leq \alpha \leq \log 2$ using the polynomial

$$e^\alpha = 1 + c_1 \alpha + c_2 \alpha^2 + c_3 \alpha^3 + c_4 \alpha^4 + \epsilon(\alpha), \tag{13.9}$$

where the relative error $|\epsilon(\alpha)| \lesssim 2 \times 10^{-4}$.

---

[2]As mentioned previously, though, our fixed-point sine function does not properly treat subnormals. Whereas the **float** version in the C++ standard library does include this formal correctness.

Table 13.1 The performance and efficiency of the computation of $\sin(1.23)$ for various fixed-point types and **float** on our target with the 8–bit microcontroller are shown. The runtime values exclude the time needed for **float** construction from 1.23

fp Type	$\sin(1.23)$	Error	Runtime (μs)	Relative time $\left(\dfrac{\text{fixed\_point}}{\text{float}}\right)$	Code size (byte)
Q3.4	0.438	10^{-1}	8	0.08	300
Q7.8	0.4766	10^{-3}	17	0.16	520
Q15.16	0.47937	10^{-4}	50	0.48	1,170
float	0.47942 55	10^{-8}	105	–	890
Known value	0.47942 55386 ...	–			

The coefficients c_n are given by

$$c_1 = 0.99785\ 46$$
$$c_2 = 0.49947\ 21$$
$$c_3 = 0.17637\ 23 \qquad\qquad (13.10)$$
$$c_4 = 0.04351\ 08\,.$$

The code corresponding to Eqs. 13.6 through 13.10 for the fixed-point exponential function can be implemented as shown below.

```
friend fixed_point exp(const fixed_point& x)
{
  // Scale the argument by removing multiples of ln2.
  fixed_point x_over_ln2(x);
  x_over_ln2 *= fixed_point::value_one_over_ln2();

  const std::int_fast8_t n = x_over_ln2.to_int8();

  fixed_point alpha(x);
  alpha -= (fixed_point::value_ln2() * n);

  // Do the polynomial expansion in terms of alpha.
  fixed_point sum =
    (((
        fixed_point(internal(), // near 4.3510841353E-2
            0x0B238740ULL >> (32U - decimal_split))
```

```
      * alpha +
      fixed_point(internal(),  // near 1.7637226246E-1
          0x2D26bC00ULL >> (32U - decimal_split)))
      * alpha +
      fixed_point(internal(),  // near 4.9947209750E-1
          0x7FDD6C80ULL >> (32U - decimal_split)))
      * alpha +
      fixed_point(internal(),  // near 9.9785463267E-1
          0xFF735F00ULL >> (32U - decimal_split)))
      * alpha;

  sum.data += decimal_split_value;

  // Scale the result by 2^n if necessary.
  if(n > 0)
  {
    sum.data <<= n;
  }
  else if(n < 0)
  {
    sum.data >>= (-n);
  }

  return sum;
}
```

Using the fixed-point exponential function is easy. The code sample below, for instance, computes the approximate fixed-point values of exp (3.7) for both the Q7.8 as well as the Q15.16 fixed-point representations. The result of exp (3.7), however, overflows the Q3.4 representation so Q3.4 can not be used for this calculation.

```
fixed_point_7pt8 y1
  = exp(fixed_point_7pt8(37) / 10);
// 40.625: relative error 44/10,000

fixed_point_15pt16 y2
  = exp(fixed_point_15pt16(37) / 10);
// 40.4341: relative error 3/10,000

// Actual value:
// 40.4473043601...
```

To complement the exponential function, we will compute the logarithm function $\log x$ for $x \in \mathbb{R}$ and $x > 0$. In our approximation, we will first compute the base-2 logarithm $\log_2 (x + 1)$ in the range $0 \leq x \leq 1$. Argument scaling is done by removing integer powers of 2 from x. After scaling, the result of the natural logarithm is obtained from the well-known relation

$$\log x = \log 2 \times \log_2 x . \tag{13.11}$$

The logarithm function calculates $\log_2 (x + 1)$ using the polynomial approximation

$$\log_2 (x + 1) = d_1 x + d_2 x^2 + d_3 x^3 + d_4 x^4 + \epsilon (x) , \tag{13.12}$$

where the coefficients d_n are given by

$$
\begin{aligned}
d_1 &= 1.43841\ 89 \\
d_2 &= -0.67719\ 00 \\
d_3 &= 0.32185\ 38 \\
d_4 &= -0.08322\ 29 ,
\end{aligned}
\tag{13.13}
$$

and the relative error $|\epsilon(x)| \lesssim 1 \times 10^{-4}$.

Arguments ranging from $0 < x < 1$ use the negated result from one recursive call of the logarithm function with the argument inverted. In other words,

$$\log (x) = -\log \left(\frac{1}{x} \right) . \tag{13.14}$$

A `fixed_point` implementation of the logarithm function based on Eqs. 13.12–13.14 is shown below.

```
friend inline fixed_point log(const fixed_point& x)
{
  // Check for negative arguments.
  if(x.data < 0)
  {
    return fixed_point(0);
  }

  unsigned_value_type x2_data(x.data);

  if(x2_data == decimal_split_value)
  {
    // The argument is identically equal to one.
```

```cpp
    return fixed_point(0);
  }
  else if(x2_data < decimal_split_value)
  {
    // Invert and negate for 0 < x < 1.
    return -log(1 / x);
  }

  std::uint_fast8_t n2 = 0U;

  // Remove even powers of two from the argument.
  while(x2_data > (decimal_split_value * 2))
  {
    ++n2;
    x2_data >>= 1;
  }

  const fixed_point my_x2 =
    fixed_point(internal(),
                x2_data - decimal_split_value);

  // Do the order-4 polynomial expansion.
  const fixed_point sum =
    (((
      - fixed_point(internal(), // near 8.3222941295E-2
             0x0154E1943ULL >> (32U - decimal_split))
      * my_x2 +
      fixed_point(internal(), // near 3.2185380545E-1
             0x0526502D0ULL >> (32U - decimal_split)))
      * my_x2 -
      fixed_point(internal(), // near 6.7718997268E-1
             0x0AD5C5271ULL >> (32U - decimal_split)))
      * my_x2 +
      fixed_point(internal(), // near 1.4384189488
             0x1703C3967ULL >> (32U - decimal_split)))
      * my_x2;

  // Account for 2^n, scale the result and return.
  return (sum + n2) * value_ln2();
}
```

We now have fixed-point implementations for the sine, exponential and logarithm functions. We can use these basic functions to compute other associated functions such as the remaining trigonometric functions and the hyperbolic trigonometric functions.

For example, it is straightforward to derive the fixed-point cosine and tangent functions from the sine function. In particular,

```cpp
friend inline fixed_point cos(const fixed_point& x)
{
  return -sin(x - value_pi_half());
}

friend inline fixed_point tan(const fixed_point& x)
{
  const fixed_point s(sin(x));
  const fixed_point c(cos(x));

  if(s.data >= decimal_split_value || c.data == 0)
  {
    return fixed_point(0);
  }
  else
  {
    return
      fixed_point( internal(),
                   (s.data << decimal_split) / c.data);
  }
}
```

The hyperbolic trigonometric functions can be derived from the exponential function using the well-known algebraic relations

$$\sinh x = \frac{e^x - e^{-x}}{2} \tag{13.15}$$

$$\cosh x = \frac{e^x + e^{-x}}{2} \tag{13.16}$$

$$\tanh x = \frac{\sinh x}{\cosh x} = \frac{e^x - e^{-x}}{e^x + e^{-x}}. \tag{13.17}$$

When computing hyperbolic trigonometric functions, the computation of e^{-x} can be replaced with more efficient division using the reflection relation

$$e^{-x} = \frac{1}{e^x}.$$ (13.18)

The corresponding code for the fixed-point hyperbolic trigonometric functions is shown below.

```
friend inline fixed_point sinh(const fixed_point& x)
{
  // Compute exp(x) and exp(-x)
  const fixed_point ep = exp(x);
  const fixed_point em = 1 / ep;

  // Subtract exp(-x) from exp(x) and divide by two.
  fixed_point result(ep - em);
  result.data >>= 1;

  return result;
}

friend inline fixed_point cosh(const fixed_point& x)
{
  // Compute exp(x) and exp(-x)
  const fixed_point ep = exp(x);
  const fixed_point em = 1 / ep;

  // Add exp(x) and exp(-x) and divide by two.
  fixed_point result(ep + em);
  result.data >>= 1;

  return result;
}

friend inline fixed_point tanh(const fixed_point& x)
{
  // Compute exp(x) and exp(-x)
  const fixed_point ep = exp(x);
  const fixed_point em = 1 / ep;

  // Do the division and return the result.
  return (ep - em) / (ep + em);
}
```

Inverse trigonometric functions can be computed from polynomial approximations as well. For instance, the reference project in the companion code uses[3]

$$\sin^{-1} x = \frac{\pi}{2} - (1 - x)^{\frac{1}{2}} \left(a_0 + a_1 x + a_2 x^2 + a_3 x^3 \right) + \epsilon(x), \quad (13.19)$$

for $0 \le x \le 1$. The coefficients a_n are given by

$$
\begin{aligned}
a_0 &= \quad 1.57072\ 88 \\
a_1 &= -0.21211\ 44 \\
a_2 &= \quad 0.07426\ 10 \\
a_3 &= -0.01872\ 93,
\end{aligned}
\qquad (13.20)
$$

and the relative error $|\epsilon(x)| \lesssim 5 \times 10^{-5}$.
   The inverse cosine function is derived from the inverse sine function using

$$\cos^{-1} x = \frac{\pi}{2} - \sin^{-1} x. \qquad (13.21)$$

The inverse tangent function uses

$$\frac{\tan^{-1} x}{x} = 1 - 0.32825\ 30\, x^2 + 0.16175\ 71\, x^4 - 0.04849\ 48\, x^6 + \epsilon(x), \quad (13.22)$$

for $0 \le x \le 1$. The coefficients have been derived with computer algebra and the
relative error is $|\epsilon(x)| \lesssim 1 \times 10^{-4}$. Arguments greater than 1 use

$$\tan^{-1} x = \frac{\pi}{2} - \tan^{-1}\left(\frac{1}{x}\right). \qquad (13.23)$$

The inverse hyperbolic trigonometric functions can be computed with relations
involving logarithmic functions. In particular,

$$\sinh^{-1} x = \log\left(x + \sqrt{x^2 + 1}\right) \qquad (13.24)$$

$$\cosh^{-1} x = \log\left(x + \sqrt{x - 1}\sqrt{x + 1}\right) \qquad (13.25)$$

$$\tanh^{-1} x = \frac{1}{2}\left[\log(1 + x) - \log(1 - x)\right]. \qquad (13.26)$$

---

[3]This polynomial has been taken from Abramowitz and Stegun [1], paragraph 4.4.45. It originally
comes from from C. Hastings [4].

In this section, we have used polynomial approximations combined with argument reduction and reflection to compute real-valued fixed-point elementary transcendental functions. Excellent results for calculating transcendental function in fixed-point can be obtained from numerous other techniques including table-lookup methods, Taylor series, Newton iteration, Padé approximations, Chebyshev polynomial expansions, CORDIC (COordinate Rotation DIgital Computer), algorithms etc.

CORDIC algorithms provide efficient shift-and-add methods for computing hyperbolic and trigonometric functions. CORDIC methods are commonly used when the cost of multiplication is significantly higher than addition, subtraction, shift and table lookup. Fast CORDIC algorithms have the potential disadvantage of requiring large tables, making scalability difficult and resulting in potentially large code size.

For further information on efficient algorithms for elementary transcendental functions, the interested reader can consult [2, 3, 5].

13.5 A Specialization of `std::numeric_Limits`

Numeric limits are only provided for built-in types including floating-point types, integer types and **bool**. The author of a specialized numeric type such as the `fixed_point` class is, therefore, responsible for providing a template specialization of `std::numeric_limits`.

Consider, for example, the Q15.16 fixed-point representation. It has 15 binary digits to the left of the decimal point and 16 binary digits to the right of the decimal point. A possible implementation of the `std::numeric_limits` template class the Q15.16 fixed-point representation is listed below.

```
namespace std
{
  template<>
  class numeric_limits<fixed_point_15pt16>
  {
  public:
    static constexpr bool is_specialized = true;
    static constexpr fixed_point_15pt16 min()
    { return fixed_point_15pt16(nothing(), 1); }
    static constexpr fixed_point_15pt16 max()
    { return fixed_point_15pt16(nothing(),
                                0x7FFFFFFFL); }
    static constexpr fixed_point_15pt16 lowest()
    { return min(); }
```

```
static constexpr int digits = 16;
static constexpr int digits10 = 4;
static constexpr int max_digits10 = 5;
static constexpr bool is_signed = true;
static constexpr bool is_integer = false;
static constexpr bool is_exact = false;
static constexpr int radix = 2;
static constexpr T epsilon()
{ return fixed_point_15pt16(nothing(), 7); }
static constexpr T round_error()
{ return fixed_point_15pt16(nothing(), 0x8000); }

static constexpr int min_exponent = -15;
static constexpr int min_exponent10 = -4;
static constexpr int max_exponent = 14;
static constexpr int max_exponent10 = 4;

static constexpr bool has_infinity = false;
static constexpr bool has_quiet_NaN = false;
static constexpr bool has_signaling_NaN = false;
static constexpr float_denorm_style has_denorm
    = denorm_absent;
static constexpr bool has_denorm_loss = false;
static constexpr T infinity()
{ return fixed_point_15pt16(); }
static constexpr T quiet_NaN()
{ return fixed_point_15pt16(); }
static constexpr T signaling_NaN()
{ return fixed_point_15pt16(); }
static constexpr T denorm_min()
{ return fixed_point_15pt16(); }

static constexpr bool is_iec559 = false;
static constexpr bool is_bounded = false;
static constexpr bool is_modulo = false;
static constexpr bool traps = false;
static constexpr bool tinyness_before = false;
static constexpr float_round_style round_style
    = round_toward_zero;
};
}
```

Certain members of `numeric_limits<fixed_point_15pt16>`, such as the value of **true** for `is_specialized`, are self-explanatory. Understanding the values of other class members can be more subtle. The `digits` member, for example, contains only the binary digits to the right of the decimal point. This is fair because any non-trivial fixed-point calculations will lose about half their digits due to truncation or argument reduction.

The `digits10` member is derived from `digits`. The maximum and minimum values are given by the internal representations of `0x7FFFFFFF` and 1, respectively. The `nothing` structure, as described in Sect. 15.1, is used in the fixed-point constructor to set these values without left-shifting them.

The `epsilon()` member is the smallest number that, when subtracted from one, results in a value different from one. Since this fixed-point type has four decimal digits of precision to the right of the decimal point, `epsilon()` for this type is equal to 0.0001. In other words, `epsilon()` should return

$$\frac{\text{0xFFFF}}{10,000} \approx 7.$$

(13.27)

Specializations of `std::numeric_limits` for the `fixed_point` types in the reference project of the companion code are implemented as a generic template. Details can be found in the source code.

References

1. M. Abramowitz, I.A. Stegun, *Handbook of Mathematical Functions, 9th Printing* (Dover, New York, 1972)
2. W.J. Cody, W. Waite, *Software Manual for the Elementary Functions* (Prentice Hall, Upper Saddle River, 1980)
3. J.W. Crenshaw, *Math Toolkit for Real-Time Programming* (CMP Books, Kansas, 2000)
4. C. Hastings, *Approximations for Digital Computers* (Princeton University Press, Princeton, 1955)
5. J.M. Muller, *Elementary Functions: Algorithms and Implementation* (Birkhäuser, Boston, 2006)
6. Wikipedia, *Fixed-point arithmetic* (2012), http://en.wikipedia.org/wiki/Fixed-point_arithmetic

Chapter 14
High-Performance Digital Filters

There may be no other signal-processing tool more widely used in embedded software than the digital filter because even the simplest applications usually read some kinds of input signals that need filtering. In this chapter, we will implement several types of finite impulse response (FIR) filters. The first section of this chapter presents a simple order–1 floating-point FIR filter. In order to obtain high performance for filters on microcontrollers without a floating-point unit or digital signal processor (DSP), however, the filters in the rest of this chapter use pure-integer mathematics combined with template design.

14.1 A Floating-Point Order–1 Filter

Consider the floating-point filter

$$y_1 = (1 - \beta)\, x_0 + \beta x_1 , \qquad (14.1)$$

where the weight β ranges from $0 \dots 1$. The index convention here uses the highest index for the newest sample in the delay line. Successively lower indexes are used for older samples, reaching index 0 for the oldest sample.

Equation 14.1 is a floating-point order–1 low-pass FIR filter. The frequency response of this filter is given by

$$H\left(e^{i\omega}\right) = \frac{1}{\beta} + \frac{e^{-i\omega}}{1 - \beta} , \qquad (14.2)$$

where ω is the frequency in radians per sample.

At this point, we could investigate a host of theoretical characteristics of this filter, such as the Z–transform of the impulse response, the absolute value of the frequency response or the phase response. The rich theory of digital filters and digital signal processing are, however, beyond the scope of this book. So we will

C.M. Kormanyos, *Real-Time C++*, DOI 10.1007/978-3-642-34688-0_14,
© Springer-Verlag Berlin Heidelberg 2013

just concentrate on how to program digital filters. Readers can find additional information on digital filters in references [1–3].

The order–1 FIR low-pass filter from Eq. 14.1 can be implemented with a template class. For example,

```cpp
template<typename T>
class fir_01_fp
{
public:
  typedef T result_type;
  typedef T value_type;

  fir_01_fp(const value_type val = 0)  : result(val)
  {
    std::fill(values.begin(), values.end(), val);
  }

  void new_sample(const std::array<value_type, 2U>& b,
                  const value_type& val)
  {
    // Shift the delay line.
    values[0U] = values[1U];

    // Put the new sample in the delay line.
    values[1U] = val;

    // Calculate the FIR algorithm.
    result =   (b[0U] * values[0U])
             + (b[1U] * values[1U]);
  }

  const result_type& get_result() const
  {
    return result;
  }

private:
  result_type result;
  std::array<value_type, 2U> values;
};
```

The class fir_01_fp is a template filter class. As indicated by the trailing "fp" in its name, fir_01_fp is designed for floating-point types. For instance, fir_01_fp can be effectively used with floating-point types such as **float**, **double**, **long double**, the fixed_point class from the previous chapter, etc.

The fir_01_fp class has member variables for both the delay line (values) as well as the filter result (result). Notice how the delay line in values is stored as an array. The public interface of fir_01_fp has two functions, one called new_sample() and another called get_result().

Using fir_01_fp in code is straightforward. For example,

```
fir_01_fp<float> f(4.0f);

constexpr std::array<float, 2U> b
{
  { 0.875F, 0.125F }
};

void do_something()
{
  // The result of the first call is 16.0.
  f.new_sample(b, 100.0F);
}
```

The filter coefficients β and $(1 - \beta)$ from Eq. 14.1 are $\frac{1}{8}$ and $\frac{7}{8}$, respectively. They are stored in the array as the floating-point values 0.125 and 0.875. The filter f is initialized with 4.0. Thereby, both values of the delay line are initialized to 4.0.

In the first call to the new_sample() function, f's member variable result is set to

$$\text{result} = (0.875 \times 4.0) + (0.125 \times 100.0) = 16.0. \qquad (14.3)$$

The new_sample() function executes the filter algorithm and sets the new value of the filter result each time it is called. Users of fir_01_fp are expected to call the new_sample() method in a periodic cycle, thereby providing the value of the new sample and the desired filter coefficients as input parameters. The sum of the filter coefficients should always be equal to 1.0.

The template coefficients stored in b are passed to the new_sample() function as a constant reference to std::array. In this case, using a pass-by-reference (instead of pass-by-value) is essential for maintaining the performance of the filter function.

The filter's get_result() member function can be used for accessing the filtered result at any time. For example,

```
const float my_filter_result = f.get_result();
```

The fir_01_fp template filter class could potentially be used on micro-controller platforms that support fast floating-point math. However, many small microcontrollers lack a hardware floating-point unit (FPU) and floating-point math is emulated with software. This can be very inefficient. Double-precision math is excruciatingly slow on embedded microcontrollers without a hardware FPU. Even single-precision and fixed-point math are often unduly inefficient for many practical microcontroller applications.

For this reason, a floating-point filter such as `fir_01_fp` may be too slow for microcontrollers. In order to reach the desired high performance for embedded systems, we need to design filters that use integer math.

14.2   An Order–1 Integer Filter

When implementing integer filters instead of floating-point filters, one of the first design steps encountered is to express the floating-point sample values and coefficients in terms of normalized integer values. This can be accomplished by rewriting the order–1 FIR filter expression from Eq. 14.1 in integer form,

$$y_1 = \frac{\beta_0 x_0 + \beta_1 x_1 + \frac{1}{2}(\beta_0 + \beta_1)}{\beta_0 + \beta_1}, \qquad (14.4)$$

where y_1, x_0, x_1, β_0 and β_1 are unsigned integer values and the extra term in the numerator, $\frac{1}{2}(\beta_0 + \beta_1)$, handles unsigned integer rounding.

Equation 14.4 can be implemented in a scalable, optimized fashion using the template class shown below.

```
template<const std::size_t resol = 4U,
         typename sample_t       = std::uint16_t,
         typename value_t        = sample_t,
         typename result_t       = sample_t>
class fir_01
{
public:
  typedef sample_t            sample_type;
  typedef value_t             value_type;
  typedef result_t            result_type;
  typedef std::int_fast16_t   weight_type;

  fir_01(const sample_type& val = 0U)
    : result(val * resol)
  {
    std::fill(values.begin(),
              values.end(),
              result);
  }
```

```
template<const weight_type B0,
         const weight_type B1>
void new_sample(const sample_type& val)
{
  values[0U] = values[1U];

  values[1U]
    = val * static_cast<value_type>(resol);

  value_type new_val =   (B0 * values[0U])
                       + (B1 * values[1U]);

  result = (new_val + ((B0 + B1) / 2)) / (B0 + B1);
}

result_type get_result() const
{
  return (result + (resol / 2U)) / resol;
}

private:
  result_type result;
  std::array<value_type, 2U> values;
};
```

The class `fir_01` is a scalable template filter class. The last three template parameters, `sample_t`, `value_t` and `result_t`, are scaling parameters that can be used to define the dimension of the filter. They can be set to 8–bit, 16–bit, 32–bit or even 64–bit. These three template parameters provide for scalability with several degrees of freedom because the sizes of the variables representing the filter sample, the delay line and the filter result can be set independently.

The first template parameter, `resol`, provides a resolution scale by multiplying each new sample with a constant integer. Closer approximation to the analog filter regime is obtained for higher values of the `resol` parameter. The resolution scale is removed from the filter result in the `get_result()` function.

Care should be taken to ensure that `resol` is a multiple of two. Only then will the rounding correction (given by `resol/2`) be exact. Furthermore, the best performance can be achieved if `resol` is a power of 2^n, where n is a small positive integer value. This is because the compiler can replace the division with a fast, efficient shift operation. See Sect. 6.11.

The class `fir_01` is a template, and its `new_sample()` function is a template function within a template class. The template parameters of `new_sample()` are the filter coefficients, `B0` and `B1`. These are constant signed integers of type `std::int_fast16_t`. Since the filter coefficients are compile-time constants, the filter algorithm can be optimized to a high degree, see Sect. 6.12. Just as described above for the `resol` parameter, the sum of ($|B0| + |B1|$) should also be a small integer power of two such that the rounding correction is exact and such that the compiler can replace division by ($|B0| + |B1|$) with an efficient shift operation.

Care must be taken to select the proper dimension of a filter such that the entire range of sample values can be filtered without numerical overflow. At the same time, the filter operations need to be matched to the CPU architecture.

For example, we will dimension a filter running on a 16–bit machine. Imagine a filter that should be designed to sample 10–bit ADC values ranging from $0 \ldots 1{,}023$. Furthermore, say that this filter will be sampled with a high frequency, such as in an interrupt service routine. For this 16–bit microcontroller, the high performance of 16–bit math is mandatory, as opposed to costly 32–bit operations. In this case, all three template parameters (`sample_t`, `value_t` and `result_t`) should be set to `std::uint16_t`. The samples need 10 bits. Therefore, there are 6 bits remaining to be split among the coefficients and the resolution. The resolution could be set to 4, requiring 2 bits. This leaves 4 bits for the filter coefficients. Thus, the filter coefficients, `B0` and `B1` can range from $1 \ldots 15$, whereby the sum of ($|B0| + |B1|$) should always be equal to 16.

A filter with larger sample values or higher valued coefficients may need to be dimensioned with wider data types for one or more of the template parameters. For example, the following template parameters could be selected for a high-frequency filter running, for example, on a 32–bit machine.

$$sample\_t = std::uint16\_t$$

$$value\_t = std::uint32\_t$$

$$result\_t = std::uint16\_t. \qquad (14.5)$$

A filter with these dimensions can be used to filter samples within the entire range of `std::uint16_t` ($0 \ldots 65{,}535$) because the type of `value_t` is `std::uint32_t`. This is large enough to hold the internal values of the filter algorithm without overflow. Examples showing how significantly a filter's dimension impacts its runtime performance will be shown in Sect. 14.4.

Using an `fir_01` object in code is straightforward. For example,

```
typedef fir_01<> filter_type;
filter_type f(4U);

void do_something()
{
  // The result of the first call is 16.
  f.new_sample<7, 1>(100U);
}
```

This sample code creates an `fir_01` object called `f`. The type of its first template parameter, `sample_t`, is `std::uint16_t`, which is the default template parameter. By way of default, the other two template parameters, `value_t` and `result_t` are also set to the type of `sample_t` (i.e., `std::uint16_t`).

This example has numerical values similar to the example of the floating-point filter in the previous section. The filter is initialized with an initial value of 4. The sample function of the filter is called in `do_something()` with a sample value of 100. The filter coefficients (`B0` and `B1`) are 7 and 1, respectively. The `new_sample()` function places the new sample value of 100 at the top of the delay line. It is weighted with the coefficient 1. The old value in the delay line is the initialization value of 4. It is weighted with the coefficient 7. The result of calling the filter's template subroutine `new_sample<7, 1>(100)` is

$$\frac{(7 \times 4) + (1 \times 100) + (8/2)}{8} = 16, \tag{14.6}$$

where 16 is a rounded pure integer result.

It is interesting to study the disassembled source code listing which the compiler produces when compiling the code of this example. The constructor code is efficient because the compiler can unroll the loop in `std::fill()`. Thereby, the values of `result` and those in the delay line can be directly initialized with 16, evaluated via constant folding from $|resol| \times 4 = 16$.

Similarly, the filter algorithm of the `new_sample()` subroutine can be highly optimized. The compiler can replace all of the multiplication operations in the inner product of the filter algorithm with fast shift-and-add operations. This, combined with constant folding, makes the filter code extremely efficient. This is a very significant result which is essential for obtaining high performance with integer template filters. A further optimization is the normalization with the coefficient sum. The division by $(|B0| + |B1|) = 8$ can be replaced with a right shift of 3.

In this example, every part of the filter sampling function can been inlined and optimized by the compiler. There is no function call to `new_sample()` and there are no parameters passed to the subroutine. The disassembled source of `new_sample()` is near to, or possibly even is, as optimally efficient as compiled code can be—approaching the efficiency of assembly programming itself.

The sampling subroutine can be used with equal efficiently in both interrupt service routines as well as normal task levels. This is a very satisfying result which exemplifies how the power of C++ templates can be utilized to obtain the highest possible filter performance.

14.3   Order–N Integer FIR Filters

We will now extend the techniques used for the order–1 FIR filter in the previous section to order–N FIR filters. The order–N FIR filter is defined by the difference equation

$$y_n = b_0\, x[n] + b_1\, x[n-1] + \ldots + b_N\, x[n-N], \qquad (14.7)$$

where $x[n]$ are the delay line values, y_n is the filter result, b_i are the coefficients and N is the filter order. An order–N FIR filter has $N + 1$ terms on the right hand side. These are the filter samples weighted with their coefficients. They are commonly referred to as *taps*. Equation 14.7 can also be expressed as

$$y_n = \sum_{i=0}^{N} b_i\, x[n-i]. \qquad (14.8)$$

The order–1 filter template class from the previous section can be extended to order–N using Eqs. 14.7 and 14.8. A synopsis of a template class that can be used to implement these filter algorithms is shown below.

```
template<const std::size_t order,
         const std::size_t resol = 4U,
         typename sample_t = std::uint16_t,
         typename value_t  = sample_t,
         typename result_t = sample_t>
class fir_order_n
{
public:
  static_assert((order > 0U) && (order < 48U),
         "error: filter order must be from 1 to 48");

  fir_order_n() { }

  explicit fir_order_n(const sample_t&) { }

  template<typename... dummy_parameters>
  void new_sample(const sample_t&) { }

  result_t get_result() const { return result_t(0); }
};
```

The template class `fir_order_n` has the same template parameters as the template class `fir_01`, plus one additional template parameter `order` that represents the order of the filter. As can be deduced from the class synopsis, this class is meant to serve only as a template for further specializations of the `order`.

Each individual class implementation of the *N*th filter `order` must be explicitly programmed as separate template specialization.

An example of the template class specialization of `fir_order_n` for order–5 is shown below.

```
template<const std::size_t resol,
         typename sample_t,
         typename value_t,
         typename result_t>
class fir_order_n<5U,
                  resol,
                  sample_t,
                  value_t,
                  result_t>
{
public:
  typedef sample_t sample_type;
  typedef value_t  value_type;
  typedef result_t result_type;

  fir_order_n() : result(0)
  {
    std::fill(data.begin(), data.end(), result);
  }

  explicit fir_order_n(const sample_type& x)
    : result(value_type(x) * resol)
  {
    std::fill(data.begin(), data.end(), result);
  }

  template<const std::int_fast16_t B0,
           const std::int_fast16_t B1,
           const std::int_fast16_t B2,
           const std::int_fast16_t B3,
           const std::int_fast16_t B4,
           const std::int_fast16_t B5>
  void new_sample(const sample_type& x)
  {
    // Shift the delay line.
    std::copy(data.begin() + 1U,
              data.end(),
              data.begin());
    // Store the new sample at top of delay line.
```

```
      *(data.end() - 1U) = value_type(x) * resol;

      // Calculate the FIR algorithm.
      const value_type new_val
        =   value_type(data[0U] * B0)
          + value_type(data[1U] * B1)
          + value_type(data[2U] * B2)
          + value_type(data[3U] * B3)
          + value_type(data[4U] * B4)
          + value_type(data[5U] * B5);

      constexpr std::int_fast16_t weight
        = B0 + B1 + B2 + B3 + B4 + B5;

      result = (new_val + (weight / 2)) / weight;
    }

    result_type get_result() const
    {
      return (result + (resol / 2U)) / resol;
    }

private:
    result_type result;
    std::array<value_type, 6U> data;
};
```

Aside from the constructor and some convenient type definitions, the template class specialization of fir_order_n<5, /*...*/> has only one function with significant algorithmic complexity, new_sample(). It is in the new_sample() method that the FIR algorithm in Eq. 14.7 is implemented. Notice how the delay line is shifted and the new sample, weighted with the resolution, is put at the top of the delay line.

The new_sample() function in fir_order_n<5, /*...*/> is a template function with six integral template parameters. This explains why each individual order–N filter needs to be implemented as a template class specialization. It is because every different value of the template parameter N needs to have its own specific template variation of the new_sample() subroutine with N+1 template parameters for the filter coefficients.

This design choice could be considered somewhat inconvenient. There are not very many ways to accomplish this without making template specializations defining the individual template implementations of new_sample(). A variadic template could be considered. This would, however, allow the template user to supply non-integer template parameter types for the filter coefficients, potentially resulting in undefined behavior. In light of these conditions, each individual order–*N* fir_order_n class has been explicitly specialized in order to provide a place in code at which the individual template variations of new_sample() can be defined.

A collection of fir_order_n filters including filter order ranging from 1 ... 48 is available in the reference project of the companion code. In order to avoid tedious typing work and to ensure that the implementations are error free, these template specializations have been created with a simple, automatic code generator which has been specifically written for this purpose.

Using fir_order_n objects in code is simple and intuitive. The following sample code, uses an order–5 low-pass filter that is dimensioned for 16–bit unsigned math with a coefficient sum of 32 and a resolution scale of 4. The coefficient sum uses 5 bits and the resolution scale uses 2 bits. Together, they use a total of 7 bits from the 16 bits available, leaving 9 bits remaining for the range of the sample values. This filter can filter 9–bit unsigned integer values ranging from 0 ... 511.

```
typedef fir_order_n<5U> filter_type;

filter_type f(4U);

void do_something()
{
   f.new_sample<5, 5, 6, 6, 5, 5>(100U);
}
```

The result of the filter operation is

$$\frac{(5 \times 4) + (5 \times 4) + (6 \times 4) + (6 \times 4) + (5 \times 4) + (5 \times 100) + 16}{32} = 19,$$

(14.9)

where 19 is the rounded pure integer result.

As is the case for the order–1 filter in the previous section, the examination of the disassembled source code listing for this filter operation reveals highly optimized code. The generation and investigation of this listing are left as exercises for the reader. In the benchmark carried out, all parts of the new_sample() function were sucessfully inlined by the compiler. Furthermore, because the filter coefficients are available at compile time and since the coefficient sum is a power of 2, the compiler replaced slow multiply and divide operations with fast shift-and-add operations in the FIR algorithm.

A filter with larger dimensions and a greater number of filter parameters is shown in the code sample below.

```
typedef fir_order_n<17U,
                    64U,
                    std::uint16_t,
                    std::uint32_t> filter_type;

filter_type f(4U);

void do_something()
{
  f.new_sample<-2, -2, -2, -1, 3, 9, 15, 20, 24,
               24, 20, 15, 9, 3, -1, -2, -2, -2>(100U);
}
```

This is an order–17 low-pass FIR filter. It is also known as an 18–tap filter because it has 18 filter coefficients. The sum of the filter coefficients is 128 and the resolution scale is 64. The symmetry of the coefficients has been exploited to write all 18 template parameters of the `new_sample()` function in a legible fashion. This filter uses `std::uint32_t` to represent the internal algorithm values because they do not always fit within `std::uint16_t`. This filter can filter input values within the entire range of `std::uint16_t`.

The order–17 filter in this example requires significantly more code and runtime than the order–5 filter from the previous example. This is not only because the filter has more coefficients, but also because the delay line values are 32 bits wide instead of 16. With the numerous 32–bit operations of its `new_sample()` function, this order–17 filter is *definitely* over-dimensioned for 8–bit or 16–bit targets. It would be more appropriate for 32–bit targets. However, it is possible to get the same filter quality with much less code and runtime expense using two or more cascaded filters of lower order. This technique will be discussed in Sect. 14.4. This order–17 filter can be comfortably used with 32–bit targets and examination of its disassembled source code listing shows the same kind of high-performance optimizations that were observed for the order–5 filter above—inlining, unrolling, shift-and-add, etc.

The filter coefficients for the order–17 filter operation have been obtained with a *filter design tool*. Scaling and rationalization of the coefficients has done with the filter design tool to obtain pure integer coefficients. Thereby care has been taken to ensure that the coefficient sum of 128 is an unsigned integer power of two.

14.4   Some Worked-Out Filter Examples

This section presents some worked out filter examples. The results have been prepared for visualization within a PC environment and also tested in real-time on two different microcontrollers.

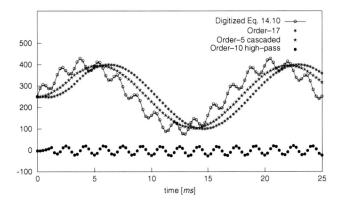

Fig. 14.1 Test results for various filters are shown. The connected *open circles* (○) show the digitized test data. The *asterisks* (∗) show the results of an order–17 low-pass filter. The *stars* (⋆) show the results of two cascaded order–5 low-pass filters. The *solid circles* (●) show the results of an order–11 high-pass filter

Consider the unfiltered raw signal shown with connected open circles (○) in Fig. 14.1. This signal could, for example, result from a voltage measurement fed to a 10–bit ADC input. The main component of the signal is a sine wave with a frequency of 60 Hz, an amplitude of 150 and an offset of 250. Added to this underlying sine wave is a strong, asynchronous noise component. The noise has 10 times the signal's frequency ($10 \times 60 = 600\,\mathrm{Hz}$), $\frac{1}{5}$ of its amplitude ($150/5 = 30$) and an offset of 0.317 ms.

The mathematical representation of this signal S is given by

$$S = 250 + 150 \times \left[\sin(0.12\pi t) + \frac{1}{5}\sin(0.317 + 1.2\pi t) \right], \qquad (14.10)$$

where t is the time in ms.

We will now filter this signal with an order–N, low-pass FIR filter such that the noise component with a frequency of 600 Hz is strongly suppressed and the main component at 60 Hz passes through the filter with as little attenuation as possible. This is a typical filter design problem. The first step in designing the filter is to consider the sampling frequency. Imagine that about 3–4 samples should be taken per half-wave of noise. As mentioned above, the noise has a frequency of 600 Hz. So, if there should be, say, $3\frac{1}{2}$ samples per half-wave of noise, then the resulting sampling frequency T_s is given by

$$T_s = 3\frac{1}{2}\,(2 \times 600\,\mathrm{Hz}) = 4,200\,\mathrm{Hz} \approx 4,000\,\mathrm{Hz}, \qquad (14.11)$$

where T_s has been rounded down to 4 kHz. The corresponding sampling period is 250 μs.

To design this filter, we will select a pass-band upper frequency of 200 Hz and a stop-band lower frequency of 600 Hz, with a stop-band attenuation of 40 dB. A ripple of 1 dB is allowed within the pass-band. The pass-band upper frequency of 200 Hz is high enough to expect good signal passing at 60 Hz, and the stop-band lower frequency of 600 Hz with 40 dB attenuation should effectively suppress the noise.

Supplying these filter parameters to the filter design tool and instructing the tool to compute the unbound optimum number of taps produces 18 double-precision coefficients for an 18–tap, order–17 filter. These double-precision coefficients correspond to the scaled integer coefficients in the order–17 filter of Sect. 14.3. In fact, these filter parameters have been used to generate them.

For the purpose of testing this order–17 filter, a PC-based simulation has been written. A separate program has been used to generate 101 digitized points from Eq. 14.10 using the desired sampling frequency of 4 kHz. These are the test data. They are shown in Fig. 14.1. The test data span $1\frac{1}{2}$ full periods of the 60 Hz signal and about 15 full periods of the signal's noise. The code below shows the test data, stored in a static constant STL array with 101 elements.

```cpp
#include <cstdint>
#include <array>

const std::array<std::uint16_t, 101U> data =
{
  {
    250U, 288U, 306U, 301U, 287U, 288U, 312U, 351U,
    381U, 386U, 371U, 354U, 357U, 381U, 412U, 428U,
    417U, 390U, 370U, 372U, 392U, 411U, 409U, 383U,
    347U, 326U, 328U, 343U, 350U, 333U, 296U, 258U,
    241U, 246U, 258U, 256U, 231U, 190U, 158U, 150U,
    162U, 176U, 170U, 141U, 106U,  87U,  93U, 116U,
    132U, 125U, 100U,  77U,  75U,  97U, 129U, 147U,
    141U, 123U, 113U, 127U, 162U, 198U, 215U, 209U,
    195U, 197U, 224U, 264U, 297U, 306U, 296U, 285U,
    293U, 325U, 363U, 386U, 383U, 364U, 352U, 363U,
    392U, 420U, 427U, 409U, 381U, 368U, 377U, 400U,
    414U, 403U, 371U, 338U, 324U, 332U, 348U, 348U,
    322U, 282U, 250U, 240U, 250U
  }
};
```

The code below uses the order–17 filter that we have just designed to filter these test data.

```
#include <iostream>
#include <math/filters/fir_order_n.h>

typedef fir_order_n<17U,
                    64U,
                    std::uint16_t,
                    std::uint32_t> filter_type;

void do_something()
{
  filter_type f(data[0U]);

  std::cout << f.get_result() << "\n";

  std::for_each(
    data.begin() + 1U,
    data.end(),
    [&f](const std::uint16_t& s)
    {
      f.new_sample
      <-2, -2, -2, -1, 3, 9, 15, 20, 24,
       24, 20, 15, 9, 3, -1, -2, -2, -2>(s);

      std::cout << f.get_result() << "\n";
    });
}
```

The order–17 filter, f, sequentially filters the test data in do_something() using STL's for_each() algorithm in combination with a lambda expression. The filter results are printed to the standard output.

The results of this filter simulation are shown in Fig. 14.1. As can be seen in the figure, the filter quality is excellent. The main component of the signal at 60 Hz passes through the filter essentially unattenuated. The noise at 600 Hz has, for all practical purposes, been eliminated. The filtered signal has a phase shift corresponding to the delay line of the 18–tap filter.

The new_sample() function of the order–17 filter runs quickly on 32–bit targets, requiring just a few microseconds. For example, it requires approximately 9.6 μs on our target with the 32–bit microcontroller. Since the sample rate is 4 kHz and the corresponding sample period is 250 μs, the filter operation requires approximately $9.6 / 250 \approx 3.8\%$ of the total CPU power. This filter can, therefore, be comfortably used with this target. The sample rate could even be doubled or four-folded if higher frequencies need to be filtered.

However, this order–17 filter has many 32–bit operations. In fact, it needs at least nineteen 32–bit move operations alone for shifting the delay line. In addition, roughly twice again as many operations are required for the filter algorithm itself, and most of these are also 32–bit operations. So this filter is actually over dimensioned for most applications using 16–bit or 8–bit architectures. In comparison with the runtime of 9.6 μs on the 32–bit target, the new_sample() function requires approximately 56 μs on our 8–bit target, and this corresponds to $56/250 \approx 22\%$ of the total CPU power with a 4 kHz sampling rate. This is too much CPU load for the filter function on this target.

Similar filter quality can be obtained using 16–bit operations that are more appropriate for smaller architectures such as our target with the 8–bit microcontroller. One way to accomplish this is by using two or more cascaded filters with much lower order. For example, we will use two cascaded, 16–bit order–5 filters instead of the order–17 filter. When using these, it should be possible to significantly reduce the CPU load on the 8–bit target.

To design an order–5 filter for this purpose, the filter parameters previously used to design the order–17 filter can be used. This time, however, the number of taps is limited to 6. The resulting integer coefficients are (5, 5, 6, 6, 5, 5). The code sample below shows how to use two cascaded 16–bit, order–5 filters with these coefficients.

```cpp
#include <iostream>

typedef fir_order_n<5U> filter_type;

void do_something()
{
  filter_type f1(data[0U]);
  filter_type f2(f1.get_result());

  std::cout << f2.get_result() << std::endl;

  std::for_each(
    data.begin() + 1U,
    data.end(),
    [&f1, &f2](const std::uint16_t& s)
    {
      f1.new_sample<5, 5, 6, 6, 5, 5>(s);

      filter_type::result_type r = f1.get_result();

      f2.new_sample<5, 5, 6, 6, 5, 5>(r);

      std::cout << f2.get_result() << std::endl;
    });
}
```

This code uses two filters, f1 and f2. The filter result of f1 is supplied to the new_sample() function of f2. In this way, the filters are cascaded.

The results of this filter operation on the test data are also shown in Fig. 14.1. The filter quality is just as good as that of the order–17 filter. However, the required CPU power has been significantly reduced. This cascaded filter operation is acceptable for 16–bit architectures with a sampling frequency of 4 kHz. The runtime of the new_sample() function on the 8–bit target has been reduced from 56 μs for the order–17 filter to 22 μs for two cascaded order–5 filters. In other words, with a sampling period of 250 μs, the fraction of the total CPU power invested in filter sampling has been reduced from the unacceptably high level of approximately 22 % to the tolerable amount of $22/250 \approx 9\%$.

As a final example, we will filter the test data with a high-pass filter. This time, the filter design tool needs parameters for a high-pass filter. We use a stop-band upper frequency of 80 Hz with an attenuation of 40 dB and a pass-band lower frequency of 600 Hz with a pass-band ripple of 1 dB. The result is an order–10, eleven tap high-pass filter with the integer coefficients $(1, 2, 4, 6, 8, -40, 8, 6, 4, 2, 1)$.

The results of this filter are signed. Therefore, precautions for signed arithmetic and rounding need to be included in the filter algorithms. This has been done in the companion code, but not explicitly listed here.

Programming the PC simulation with the signed high-pass filter is left as an exercise for the reader. The results that have been obtained when researching for this book are shown in Fig. 14.1. A few samples are needed before the high-pass filter attenuates the 60 Hz part of the signal, leaving only the ripple at 600 Hz part— as per design goal for this high-pass filter.

References

1. R.G. Lyons, *Understanding Digital Signal Processing* (Prentice Hall, Upper Saddle River, 2004)
2. A.V. Oppenheim, R.W. Schafer, *Digital Signal Processing* (Prentice Hall, Upper Saddle River, 1975)
3. L. Thede, *Analog and Digital Filter Design Using C* (Prentice Hall, Upper Saddle River, 1996)

Chapter 15
C++ Utilities

This chapter presents a selection of C++ utilities that are useful for solving recurring problems in microcontroller programming.

15.1 The `nothing` Structure

Consider the implementation of the `nothing` structure below.

```
struct nothing { };
```

The `nothing` structure contains no members and encapsulates no functionality whatsoever. Although the `nothing` structure does not actually do anything itself, it can be quite useful as a place holder for other function and template parameters.

Recall the `fixed_point` class from Sect. 13.2. The constructors of the `fixed_point` class from integral types perform a left-shift of their input parameter before using it to initialize the internal representation of the fixed-point number. This accounts for the fixed position of the decimal point. For a simplified version of the Q7.8 fixed-point representation, for example, we have something like the following.

```
// A simplified Q7.8 fixed-point representation.
class fixed_point
{
public:
  fixed_point(std::uint16_t u) : value(u << 8) { }

private:
  std::uint16_t value;
};
```

C.M. Kormanyos, *Real-Time C++*, DOI 10.1007/978-3-642-34688-0__15,
© Springer-Verlag Berlin Heidelberg 2013

266 15 C++ Utilities

At the same time, the values of special fixed-point numbers such as mathematical constants have a known integral representation in this fixed-point system. The integral representation of the numerical constant π in this fixed-point system, for example, is 0x0324. To accommodate construction from a known integral value that is not supposed to be left-shifted, the fixed_point class has an additional private constructor that takes an integral type parameter and a nothing-type structure. In other words,

```cpp
// A simplified Q7.8 fixed-point representation.
class fixed_point
{
public:
  // Construct from integer with left-shift.
  fixed_point(std::uint16_t u) : value(u << 8) { }

  // Create pi with the special constructor.
  static fixed_point value_pi()
  {
    return fixed_point(nothing(), 0x0324U);
  }

private:
  std::uint16_t value;

  // Constructor from integer without left-shift.
  fixed_point(const nothing&,
              std::uint16_t u) : value(u) { }
};
```

Here, the nothing structure provides for unambiguous differentiation between the normal constructor from std::uint16_t having left-shift and the private constructor from std::uint16_t without left-shift. If the nothing structure were not used, the two constructors would be ambiguous. The special private constructor from an integer without left-shift is used to efficiently return the value of π in the value_pi() method.

We will now use the nothing structure to create a template class that represents a collection of three things. We will call this class a triple. The triple class can be made by using three template parameters, and supplying defaults for them. For instance,

```cpp
struct nothing {};

template <typename first_type  = nothing,
          typename second_type = nothing,
          typename third_type  = nothing>
```

```
class triple
{
public:
  // Constructor with default values.
  triple(const first_type&  t1_ = first_type(),
         const second_type& t2_ = second_type(),
         const third_type&  t3_ = third_type())
    : t1(t1_),
      t2(t2_),
      t3(t3_)
  {
  }

  // Element access.
  first_type&  first()  { return t1; }
  second_type& second() { return t2; }
  third_type&  third()  { return t3; }

private:
  first_type  t1;
  second_type t2;
  third_type  t3;
};
```

The triple class is similar to the standard std::pair class in the standard library's <utility> header. The triple class, however, has three elements, whereas std::pair has two.

Using the triple class is straightforward. The code below, for example, uses a triple containing a **char**, an **int** and an instance of a structure.

```
struct something
{
  something() { }
};

triple<char, int, something>
  things('a', 123, something());

void do_something()
{
  if(things.first() == 'a')
  {
  }
}
```

Techniques using a nothing-like class type are often employed to implement std::tuple for compilers that lack C++11 support for variadic templates.

15.2   The noncopyable Class

In Sect. 4.8, we first discussed non-copyable classes. Often times, we would like to prohibit intentional and unintentional copying of a class object. A potential implementation of a non-copyable mechanism for classes is shown in below. This implementation is based on the noncopyable class in Boost.

```
class noncopyable
{
protected:
  noncopyable()  {}
  ~noncopyable()  {}

// Emphasize: The following members are private.
private:
  noncopyable(const noncopyable&) = delete;

  const noncopyable& operator=(const noncopyable&)
    = delete;
};
```

Here, the copy constructor and copy assignment operator have been declared private and explicitly qualified with **delete**. This renders both the noncopyable class as well as any class that is privately derived from it non-copyable because derived classes inherit the private non-copyable members.

It is common in microcontroller programming to purposely prohibit class copying. Consider, once again, an LED mapped to a port pin. We will use an led class similar to the one in Sect. 1.1.

```
class led
{
public:
  // The led class constructor.
  led(const port_type p,
      const bval_type b)  : port(p),
                            bval(b)
  {
    // ...
  }
```

```
  void toggle() const
  {
    // ...
  }

private:
  // Private member variables of the class.
  port_type port;
  bval_type bval;
};
```

As in Sect. 1.1, we can create an instance of the led class on microcontroller port bin portb.5. In particular,

```
// Create led_b5 on portb.5.
led led_b5
{
  mcal::reg::portb,
  mcal::reg::bval5
};
```

Here, led_b5 is directly associated with portb.5 and with no other pin. In the present form, however, it is possible to copy led_b5. The copy operation below, for instance, can successfully be compiled.

```
// Create led_b5 on portb.5.
led led_b5
{
  mcal::reg::portb,
  mcal::reg::bval5
};

// Copy led_b5 to another led instance.
led led_other = led_b5;
```

Probably, though, we would prefer to prohibit copying the led class in this fashion. This policy will help ensure that only one class instance uses the hardware pin at one time. The modified version of the led class shown below inherits privately from the noncopyable class.

```
class noncopyable { /* ... */ };

// Make the led class noncopyable.
```

```
class led : private noncopyable
{
  // ...
};
```

Here, the led class has been made non-copyable by simply inheriting privately from noncopyable.

The noncopyable utility simplifies typing and reduces the burden of code upkeep because the non-copyable attribute can simply be inherited via private derivation. This eliminates the need to manually implement a private copy constructor and copy assignment operator for each non-copyable class, as was shown in Sect. 4.8.

15.3 A Template timer Class

A timer class can be used for diverse timing applications in real-time C++. For example, the visible LED toggling in Sect. 2.3 has used a 1 s blocking delay to create a toggle frequency of 1/2 Hz. In addition, the multitasking scheduler in Sect. 11.2 has included interval timing for task scheduling.

We will now present a template timer class. The synopsis of the public interface of our timer class is shown below.

```
template<typename unsigned_tick>
class timer
{
public:
  // A class-specific tick type.
  typedef unsigned_tick tick_type;

  // Utility functions for creating timespans.
  template<typename other>
  static tick_type microseconds(const other&);

  template<typename other>
  static tick_type milliseconds(const other&);

  template<typename other>
  static tick_type seconds(const other&);

  template<typename other>
  static tick_type minutes(const other&);
```

```
template<typename other>
static tick_type hours(const other&);

// Constructors.
timer();
explicit timer(const tick_type&);
timer(const timer&);

// Copy assignment operator.
timer& operator=(const timer&);

// Interval and relative timeout functions.
void start_interval(const tick_type&);
void start_relative(const tick_type&);

// The timeout, now, and delay functions.
bool timeout() const;
static tick_type now();
static void blocking_delay(const tick_type&);
};
```

This timer class provides the following operations in its public interface.

- Query the current time point with now().
- Set relative timeouts with start_relative().
- Set interval timeouts with start_interval().
- Wait in a blocking delay with blocking_delay().

This implementation of the timer class requires a timebase in hard real-time. This may, for example, originate from an underlying microcontroller peripheral timer. Here, we use the procedural get_time_elapsed() function from the MCAL, as described in Sect. 9.3. In particular, the timer's now() function simply returns the elapsed time from get_time_elapsed(). In other words,

```
template<typename unsigned_tick>
class timer
{
public:
  typedef unsigned_tick tick_type;

  // ...

  static tick_type now()
  {
    // Return the elapsed time in microseconds.
```

```
   return mcal::gpt::get_time_elapsed();
  }
};
```

In our example, the resolution of the underlying timebase is microseconds. The overlying `timer` class obtains the same microsecond resolution.

Since the `timer` class is a template, it can be scaled to various widths such as 16–bit or 32–bit. For example, we can set a relative timeout for a time point that lies $250\,\mu s$ in the future using a 16–bit timer. In particular,

```
// Use a convenient type definition.
typedef timer<std::uint16_t> timer_type;

// Set a time point 250us in the future.
timer_type time(timer_type::microseconds(250U));
```

A polling task can query if the `timer` object has timed out by calling the `timeout()` member function. For instance,

```
void do_something()
{
  if(time.timeout())
  {
    // Do something at this time.
  }
}
```

The `timer` class, or a class similar to it, can also be used as a building block together with callbacks to encapsulate the functionality of event and alarm objects. To do this, a `timer` object might be included as a member of a larger alarm or event object. These composite objects may be stored in a container and manipulated with a scheduling mechanism to fully implement events and alarms.

15.4   Linear Interpolation

Linear interpolation is a method of curve fitting on data points using linear polynomials. The need to perform linear interpolation on an ordered set of data points arises frequently in real-time microcontroller programming. Operations like sensor calibration and analysis of position data can often be carried out quickly and with sufficient accuracy using linear interpolation. The data points shown in Fig. 15.1, for example, are suitable for linear interpolation.

Fig. 15.1 A set of data
points suitable for linear
interpolation is shown

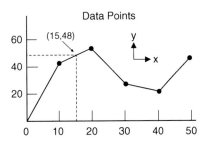

An example of linear interpolation using Eq. 15.2 is shown in Fig. 15.1. Linear interpolation with a straight line between the two (x, y) points $(10, 44)$ and $(20, 53)$ gives $y = 48$ at $x = 15$. Here, we are using integer calculations.

We will consider linear interpolation using a straight line between two points (x_0, y_0) and (x_1, y_1). The equation for the straight line between these two points is

$$\frac{y - y_0}{x - x_0} = \frac{y_1 - y_0}{x_1 - x_0} . \tag{15.1}$$

Solving Eq. 15.1 for an unknown value y at a known value x results in

$$y = y_0 + (x - x_0) \frac{y_1 - y_0}{x_1 - x_0} . \tag{15.2}$$

A template subroutine for straight line linear interpolation based on Eq. 15.2 is shown in the code below.

```
template<typename point_iterator,
         typename x_type,
         typename y_type = x_type>
y_type linear_interpolate(point_iterator pts_begin,
                          point_iterator pts_end,
                          const x_type& x,
                          const y_type& offset)
{
  if(pts_begin == pts_end)
  {
    // There are no data points to interpolate.
    return y_type();
  }
  else if(   (x <= pts_begin->x)
          || (pts_begin + 1U == pts_end))
  {
    // We are beneath the lower x-range or there
```

```
    // is only one data point to interpolate.
    return pts_begin->y;
  }
  else if(x >= (pts_end - 1U)->x)
  {
    // We are above the upper x-range.
    return (pts_end - 1U)->y;
  }
  else
  {
    // Find interpolation pair with binary search.
    point_iterator it
      = std::lower_bound(pts_begin,
                         pts_end,
                         point<x_type>(x));

    // Do the linear interpolation.
    const x_type xn       = (it - 1U)->x;
    const x_type delta_xn = it->x - xn;
    const x_type delta_x  = x - xn;
    const y_type yn       = (it - 1U)->y;
    const y_type delta_yn = it->y - yn;

    const y_type delta_y
      = (delta_x * delta_yn) / delta_xn;

    return (yn + delta_y) + offset;
  }
}
```

Following some elementary bounds checking, the core of this linear interpolation function uses the `std::lower_bound()` algorithm to find the pair of interpolation points. The `linear_interpolate()` subroutine thereby profits from the high efficiency of `std::lower_bound()` which uses a binary search for sequences having random access iterators.

The fourth input parameter to `linear_interpolate()` called `offset` has a dual role. It allows an optional non-zero offset to be applied to the result of the linear interpolation. In addition, the `offset` parameter provides the compiler with enough information to automatically deduce all of the template parameters.

The `linear_interpolate()` subroutine is designed to work particularly well with a template point class type such as the one shown in Sect. 5.4. The lower-bound algorithm tests for inequality using **operator**<(). In order to be used with `linear_interpolate()`, then, the `point` class needs to have an implementation of **operator**<(). Here, the sense of *less-than* is based on the

x-value of a point. In other words, the point (x_i, y_i) is less than the point (x_j, y_j) if $x_i < x_j$.

A modified implementation of the `point` class that supports **operator<()** is shown below.

```
template<typename x_type,
         typename y_type = x_type>
class point
{
public:
  x_type x;
  y_type y;

  point(const x_type& x_ = x_type(),
        const y_type& y_ = y_type()) : x(x_),
                                       y(y_) { }

  bool operator<(const point& other) const
  {
    return (x < other.x);
  }
};
```

Using `linear_interpolate()` with a collection of points is straightforward. The sample below, for instance, performs the linear interpolation that is depicted in Fig. 15.1.

```
// The data points.
const std::array<point<std::uint16_t>, 6U> points
{
  {
    point<std::uint16_t> {  0U,  0U },
    point<std::uint16_t> { 10U, 44U },
    point<std::uint16_t> { 20U, 53U },
    point<std::uint16_t> { 30U, 28U },
    point<std::uint16_t> { 40U, 22U },
    point<std::uint16_t> { 50U, 47U }
  }
};

const std::uint16_t y
  = linear_interpolate(points.begin(),
                       points.end(),
                       std::uint16_t(15U),
```

std::uint16_t(0U));

// The value of y is 48.

The linear_interpolate() subroutine can be used with built-in integral and floating-point types. It can also be used with user-defined types such as the fixed_point class in Sect. 13.2. If used exclusively for integral types, it may be beneficial to include a simple rounding correction in the division of the linear interpolation equation.

15.5 A Circular Buffer Template Class

A circular buffer can be an efficient storage queue that is useful for communication interfaces and other input-output operations. The SPI™ driver class in Sect. 9.5, for example, uses circular buffers for its transmit and receive queues.

A possible implementation of a template circular buffer class is shown below.

```cpp
template<typename T,
         const std::size_t N>
class circular_buffer
{
public:
  typedef T value_type;
  typedef value_type* iterator;
  typedef std::size_t size_type;

  circular_buffer() : in_ptr(buffer),
                      out_ptr(buffer) { }

  constexpr size_type size() const { return N; }

  bool empty() const { return (in_ptr == out_ptr); }

  size_type inque() const
  {
    const bool is_wrap = (in_ptr >= out_ptr);

    return (is_wrap ? in_ptr - out_ptr
                    : size() - (out_ptr - in_ptr));
  }

  void flush()
```

```cpp
  {
    in_ptr = out_ptr = buffer;
  }

  void in(const value_type by)
  {
    *in_ptr = by;

    ++in_ptr;

    if(in_ptr >= (buffer + N))
    {
      in_ptr = buffer;
    }
  }

  value_type out()
  {
    if(empty())
    {
      return static_cast<value_type>(0);
    }
    else
    {
      const value_type by = *out_ptr;

      ++out_ptr;

      if(out_ptr >= (buffer + N))
      {
        out_ptr = buffer;
      }

      return by;
    }
  }

private:
  value_type buffer[N];
  iterator in_ptr;
  iterator out_ptr;
};
```

The `circular_buffer` class supports input and output queuing of elements. There are some STL-like members such as `size()` and `empty()`. Full support for STL iterators, however, has not been included in this implementation. A more refined circular buffer class with iterator support and STL compliance is included in Boost [1].

Using the `circular_buffer` class is simple. For instance,

```cpp
typedef
circular_buffer<std::uint8_t, 4U> buffer_type;

void do_something()
{
  buffer_type buffer;

  // Put three bytes into the buffer.
  buffer.in(1U);
  buffer.in(2U);
  buffer.in(3U);

  // The size of the buffer is 3.
  auto count = buffer.size();

  // The buffer is not empty.
  const bool is_empty = buffer.empty();

  // Extract the first element.
  const buffer_type::value_type value = buffer.out();

  // The size of the buffer is now 2.
  count = buffer.size();
}
```

15.6   The Boost Library

The Boost library is a large collection of generic utilities aimed at a wide range of C++ users and application domains. The Boost libraries extend the functionality of C++ beyond the language specification. Boost contains many individual libraries, including libraries for generic utilities, numeric and lexical operations, mathematics, random numbers, threading, image processing, regular expressions, etc. The Boost libraries are known for their high quality, partly because a candidate library is subjected to peer reviews before being accepted to Boost.

Some of the concepts in this chapter originate from Boost. For example, the concept of the `noncopyable` class in Sect. 15.2 has been taken from the utilities part of Boost. The `circular_buffer` class in Sect. 15.5 is similar to Boost's `circular_buffer`.

The Boost website indicates that Boost aims to provide reference implementations potentially suitable for standardization [1]. This makes Boost a great place to follow the development of the C++ language. In fact, some of Boost's active members are on the C++ standards committee, and ten Boost libraries have been included in the C++11 standard [2], see [3].

References

1. B. Dawes, D. Abrahams, *Boost C++ Libraries* (2012), http://www.boost.org
2. ISO/IEC, *ISO/IEC 14882:2011: Information Technology—Programming Languages—C++* (International Organization for Standardization, Geneva, 2011)
3. B. Karlsson, *Beyond the C++ Standard Library: An Introduction to Boost* (Addison Wesley, Reading, 2005)

Chapter 16
Extending the C++ Standard Library and the STL

The C++ standard library and the STL provide a wide selection of functions, classes and generic containers that can be used in common programming situations. There are, however, times when just the right container or function for a particular programming task is missing from the standard library and the STL. In the first part of this chapter, we will extend the C++ standard library and the STL by developing a custom `dynamic_array` container that has a functionality that lies between those of `std::array` and `std::vector`. Furthermore, one often encounters a good C++ compiler that lacks large parts of the C++ standard library such as the STL, C99 compatibility, the time utilities in `<chrono>` or the thread support library. The second half of this chapter shows how to emulate partial standard library support with certain self-written parts of the C++ standard library and the STL.

16.1 Defining the Custom `dynamic_array` Container

The `std::array` container can be used when the number of elements is known at compile time. For instance,

```
// Fixed-size array of four counters init. to 1.
std::array<unsigned, 4U> counters
{
  { 1U, 1U, 1U, 1U }
};

void do_something()
{
  // Increment the counters.
  std::for_each(std::begin(counters),
                std::end(counters),
```

C.M. Kormanyos, *Real-Time C++*, DOI 10.1007/978-3-642-34688-0_16,
© Springer-Verlag Berlin Heidelberg 2013

```
            [] (unsigned& u)
            {
              ++u;
            });

    // It is not possible to resize the array.
}
```

On the other hand, the `std::vector` container is designed for dynamic allocation. Using vector's constructors or member functions such as `push_back()`, `resize()`, `insert()`, `erase()`, etc., the number of elements in a vector can be changed from zero to the maximum capacity during the entire lifetime of the object. For example,

```
// Dynamic vector of four counters init. to 1.
std::vector<unsigned> counters(4U, 1U);

void do_something()
{
    // Increment the counters.
    std::for_each(std::begin(counters),
                  std::end(counters),
                  [] (unsigned& u)
                  {
                     ++u;
                  });

    // We can resize the vector.
    counters.push_back(counters.front());
}
```

Basically, `std::array` is efficient but has the limitation of constant compile-time size. While `std::vector` does offer flexible resizing during runtime, it also has slight performance and storage disadvantages caused by its dynamic allocation mechanisms.

At times it may be convenient to use a container with characteristics that lie *between* those of `std::array` and `std::vector`. For example, consider a container that can be dynamically allocated one time in the constructor and retains its size for the lifetime of the object. This container offers the flexibility of dynamic sizing at creation time without the added overhead needed for reallocation. We will call this container `dynamic_array`. For example,

```
// A dynamic array of four counters initialized with 1.
dynamic_array<unsigned> counters(4U, 1U);

void do_something()
{
  // Increment the counters.
  std::for_each(std::begin(counters),
                std::end(counters),
                [](unsigned& u)
                {
                  ++u;
                });

  // It is not possible to resize the dynamic_array.
}
```

Here, we have created a dynamic_array of counters and initialized them with one. Although it is possible to dynamically set the number of elements in this container during construction, the size can not be modified thereafter. In this way, dynamic_array is a kind of hybrid container that combines the efficiency of an array with the dynamic sizing (albeit via one-shot allocation) of std::vector.

As will be described below, the custom dynamic_array container will be designed to fulfill the general requirements for sequential STL containers.[1] In this way, the dynamic_array container is consistent with the STL and also fills a functional niche between the fixed-size std::array and that of the dynamic std::vector. This can be considered a kind of user-defined *extension* of the STL that, even though not formally standardized in ISO/IEC [1], can potentially be very useful in generic programming.

16.2 Implementing and Using dynamic_array

We will now present an implementation of dynamic_array. The class definition of dynamic_array is similar to that of std::array but also has features in its constructors closely resembling those of the constructors of std::vector.[2] The class synopsis of a possible implementation of dynamic_array is shown in the code sample below.

---

[1] The general requirements for STL containers are specified in Paragraph 23.2.1 of [1] and listed in Tables 96 and 97 therein.

[2] Consult Sect. 23.3.2 in [1] for an overview of std::array and Sect. 23.3.6 for a summary of std::vector.

```cpp
#include <algorithm>
#include <iterator>
#include <initializer_list>
#include <memory>

template<typename T,
         typename alloc = std::allocator<T>>
class dynamic_array
{
public:
  // Type definitions:
  typedef alloc          allocator_type;
  typedef T&             reference;
  typedef const T&       const_reference;
  typedef T*             iterator;
  typedef const T*       const_iterator;
  typedef std::size_t    size_type;
  typedef std::ptrdiff_t difference_type;
  typedef T              value_type;
  typedef T*             pointer;
  typedef const T*       const_pointer;
  typedef std::reverse_iterator<iterator>
    reverse_iterator;
  typedef std::reverse_iterator<const_iterator>
    const_reverse_iterator;

  // Constructors:
  explicit dynamic_array(size_type n)

  dynamic_array(size_type count, const T& val);

  dynamic_array(const dynamic_array& other);

  dynamic_array(std::initializer_list<T> lst);

  // Destructor:
  ~dynamic_array();

  // Iterator members:
  iterator              begin();
  iterator              end();
  const_iterator        begin() const;
  const_iterator        end() const;
  const_iterator        cbegin() const;
```

```
const_iterator          cend() const;
reverse_iterator        rbegin();
reverse_iterator        rend();
const_reverse_iterator rbegin() const;
const_reverse_iterator rend() const;
const_reverse_iterator crbegin() const;
const_reverse_iterator crend() const;

// Size and capacity:
size_type size() const;
size_type max_size() const;
constexpr bool empty();

// Element access members:
reference        operator[](const size_type i);
const_reference operator[](const size_type i) const;

reference        at(const size_type i);
const_reference at(const size_type i) const;

reference        front();
const_reference front() const;

reference        back();
const_reference back() const;

// Element manipulation members:
void fill(const T& u);
void swap(dynamic_array<T>& u);

private:
  // Data members:
  const size_type N;
  pointer elems;
};
```

The dynamic_array has the type definitions and iterator support required for a sequential STL container. In addition, dynamic_array has several constructors responsible for allocation and initialization of the elements. For example, the second of dynamic_array's constructors shown in the class synopsis above can be implemented as follows.

```
dynamic_array(size_type count, const T& val)
  : N(count),
    elems(allocator_type().allocate(N))
{
  std::fill_n(begin(), N, val);
}
```

Here, the elements of the dynamic array are allocated and initialized with the value stored in the second parameter of the constructor. None of the functions in dynamic_array other than the constructors modify the number of elements in the container, meaning that once a dynamic_array is created, it keeps its size for its entire lifetime. The remaining implementation details of the dynamic_array class can be found in the companion code.

The dynamic_array container fulfills most of the general requirements for sequential STL containers. It can, therefore, be used with the standard algorithms of the STL. The code sample below, for instance, initializes a dynamic_array with three data bytes from an std::initializer_list and calculates the byte checksum thereof.

```
util::dynamic_array<int> values ( { 1, 2, 3 } );

int sum = std::accumulate(values.begin(),
                          values.end(),
                          0);
```

The dynamic_array container can also be used with other functions and class types. Consider, for example, a potential interface to a communication class.

```
class communication
{
public:
  communication() { }
  ~communication() { }

  bool send(const dynamic_array<std::uint8_t>& cmd);
  bool recv(dynamic_array<std::uint8_t>& rsp);
};
```

Here, the communication class has member functions send() and recv() responsible for sending and receiving communication frames, respectively. Data transfer in transmission and reception is carried out using dynamic_array containers holding 8–bit data bytes.

16.3   Writing Parts of the C++ Library if None Is Available

Some C++ compilers, even very good ones, fail to provide implementations of the C++ library and the STL. At times, even if the C++ library and the STL are available, the implementations provided by the compiler may be incomplete and could lack some new and potentially useful C++ language features.

If certain components of the C++ library and the STL are missing, it may be possible to manually write them. This assumes, however, that the development and testing of these components can be carried out with the reliability mandated by real-time C++.

Throughout this book, for example, the code samples have used many parts of the C++ library and the STL. For the most part, these samples have been successfully tested and executed on several 8– and 32–bit microcontrollers. Some of the GCC ports used for these tests, however, include only an incomplete C++ standard library and lack the STL entirely. In order to resolve this problem, parts of the C++ library and STL components were explicitly written for this book. The implementations of these can be found in the reference project of the companion code.

Writing a complete implementation of the C++ library and the STL that closely adheres to the standard and provides optimal efficiency is a large-scale programming endeavor. In fact, this is generally considered to be a task for the most experienced C++ specialists because it requires the utmost in programming skill, deep understanding of compiler optimization techniques, meticulous attention to detail and an extensive testing effort.

Writing a complete standards-adherent C++ library might be a task that lies beyond the capabilities of most of us. It can, nonetheless, be feasible and practical to write a small subset of the C++ standard library and the STL. In the following section, we will consider a strategy for writing a subset of the C++ library.

16.4   Implementation Notes for Parts of the C++ Library and STL

It may make sense to select a single location for storage of library headers and any necessary source files when writing a subset of the C++ library and the STL. This can, for example, be a single root directory combined with additional subdirectories for the platform-specific library parts. For instance, the directory structure for the self-written subset of the C++ library for the GCC port for our target with the 8–bit microcontroller is shown in Fig. 16.1. Selecting a single location for self-written library headers simplifies the process of adding the path information to the compiler's default search paths, as described in Sect. 1.6.

The selection of which C++ library components to write may be primarily based on usefulness and ease of implementation. Consider the subset of the C++ library and the STL listed below.

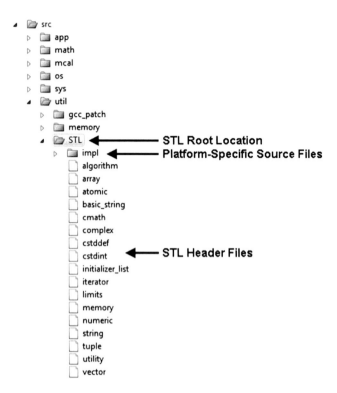

Fig. 16.1 The directory structure for the self-written subset of the C++ library and the STL written for this book is shown

- The fixed-size integer types including those with an exact number of bits, those with at least a specific number of bits and the fastest types with at least a certain number of bits.
- Partial support for `std::array`, optionally not including reverse iterators.
- Commonly used yet simple-to-write functions from the `<algorithm>` library such as the minimax functions, `std::min()` and `std::max()`, and others operating on sequential iterators such as `std::for_each()`, `std::fill()`, `std::copy()`, `std::find_if()` and others.

Fixed-size integer types are defined in `<cstdint>`. If the C++ compiler has C99 compatibility and supports the C99 fixed-size integer types, then it is a simple matter to inject these types into the namespace `std`. For example,

```
// A partial implementation of <cstdint>

// Include the C99 fixed-size integers.
#include <stdint.h>
```

```
namespace std
{
  // Types with an exact number of bits.
  typedef uint8_t   ::uint8_t;
  typedef uint16_t  ::uint16_t;
  typedef uint32_t  ::uint32_t;
  typedef uint64_t  ::uint64_t;

  // Types with at least a certain number of bits.
  typedef uint_least8_t   ::uint_least8_t;
  typedef uint_least16_t  ::uint_least16_t;
  typedef uint_least32_t  ::uint_least32_t;
  typedef uint_least64_t  ::uint_least64_t;

  // Fastest types with at least a certain
  // number of bits.
  typedef uint_fast8_t   ::uint_fast8_t;
  typedef uint_fast16_t  ::uint_fast16_t;
  typedef uint_fast32_t  ::uint_fast32_t;
  typedef uint_fast64_t  ::uint_fast64_t;
}
```

If the C++ compiler does not have C99 compatibility, then the fixed-size integer types must be defined. This can be readily accomplished using simple **typedef**s of platform-dependent built-in types such as **char**, **short**, **int**, **long** and possibly **long long**. This does, however, result in slight portability issues because the widths of the built-in types are compiler-dependent. These portability issues can, however, be managed because the fixed-size integer types need be set up only once for a given platform. Once this is done, it is relatively straightforward to separate processor-specific versions of header files such as <cstdint> in different directories or to use preprocessor definitions to achieve separation within larger header files.

A partial implementation of std::array is shown in the listing below. This implementation does not include support for reverse iterators.

```
// A partial implementation of <array>
#include <algorithm>
#include <cstddef>

namespace std
{
  template <typename T, size_t N>
  struct array
  {
    // Type definitions:
```

```cpp
typedef T&           reference;
typedef const T&     const_reference;
typedef T*           iterator;
typedef const T*     const_iterator;
typedef size_t       size_type;
typedef ptrdiff_t    difference_type;
typedef T            value_type;
typedef T*           pointer;
typedef const T*     const_pointer;

// Data elements:
T elems[N];

// iterators:
iterator begin() { return elems; }
iterator end()   { return elems + N; }
const_iterator begin() const
{ return elems; }
const_iterator end() const
{ return elems + N; }
const_iterator cbegin() const
{ return elems; }
const_iterator cend() const
{ return elems + N; }

// Size-related members:
constexpr size_type size() { return N; }
constexpr size_type max_size() { return N; }
constexpr bool empty() { return false; }

// Element access members:
reference operator[](size_type n)
{ return elems[n]; }
const_reference operator[](size_type n) const
{ return elems[n]; }
const_reference at(size_type n) const
{ return elems[n]; }
reference        at(size_type n)
{ return elems[n]; }
reference front()
{ return elems[0U]; }
const_reference front() const
{ return elems[0U]; }
reference back()
```

```
    { return elems[N - 1U]; }
    const_reference back() const
    { return elems[N - 1U]; }

    T* data() { return elems; }
    const T* data() const { return elems; }

    // Element manipulation members:
    void fill(const T& u) { fill_n(begin(), N, u); }
    void swap(const array<T, N>& other)
    { swap_ranges(begin(), end(), other.begin()); }
  };
}
```

This implementation of std::array makes use of other parts of the C++ standard library including the types std::size_t and std::ptrdiff_t as well as the algorithms std::fill_n() and std::swap_ranges(). So these parts of the library must also be available for this implementation of std::array.

The minimax algorithms std::min() and std::max() can be implemented as shown below.

```
namespace std
{
  template<typename T>
  const T& min(const T& a, const T& b)
  {
    return (a < b ? a : b);
  }

  template<typename T>
  const T& max(const T& a, const T& b)
  {
    return (a > b ? a : b);
  }
}
```

Some examples of sequential STL algorithms that navigate through iterators include std::fill(), std::for_each() and std::find_if(). These algorithms have linear complexity and are relatively easy to implement. The following code samples show possible implementations of these algorithms.

One potential implementation of std::fill() is shown below.

```
// Sample implementation of std::fill:
template<typename forward_iterator,
```

```
                    typename value_type>
void std::fill(forward_iterator first,
               forward_iterator last,
               const value_type& value)
{
  // Fill each element in [first, last) with value.
  while(first != last)
  {
    *first = value;
    ++first;
  }
}
```

A sample implementation of std::for_each() follows below. This version of std::for_each() was also shown previously in Sect. 5.8.

```
// Sample implementation of std::for_each:
template<typename iterator_type,
         typename function_type>
function_type std::for_each(iterator_type first,
                            iterator_type last,
                            function_type function)
{
  // Apply function to each element in [first, last).
  while(first != last)
  {
    function(*first);
    ++first;
  }

  return function;
}
```

A potential realization of std::find_if() is shown below.

```
// Sample implementation of std::find_if:
template<typename iterator_type,
         typename predicate_type>
iterator_type std::find_if(iterator_type first,
                           iterator_type last,
                           predicate_type predicate)
{
  // Find the first element satisfying predicate.
```

```
while(    (first != last)
      && (false == predicate(*first)))
{
  ++first;
}

return first;
}
```

16.5 Providing now() for <chrono>'s High-Resolution Clock

The C++ standard library supports chronological timing functions in its <chrono> library. Part of the <chrono> library includes support for various *clocks* such as a system clock and a high-resolution clock. See Sect. 20.11.7 in [1] for details on the specification of <chrono>. The standard library's high-resolution clock (called std::chrono::high_resolution_clock) may be well-suited for providing the timebase in a real-time C++ project.

A potential synopsis of std::chrono::high_resolution_clock in <chrono> is shown below.

```
namespace std { namespace chrono {

class high_resolution_clock
{
public:
  // The resolution of the clock is microseconds.
  typedef chrono::microseconds duration;

  // Types for representation, period and time point.
  typedef duration::rep rep;
  typedef duration::period period;
  typedef chrono::time_point<high_resolution_clock,
                             duration> time_point;

  // The counter is steady: A call to now() always
  // returns a later timer than a previous call.
  static const bool is_steady = true;

  // The platform-specific implementation of now().
```

```
// It is declared, but not implemented.
static time_point now();
};

} } // namespaces
```

Here, the timebase of the high-resolution clock is a static member function called now(). Any good microcontroller C++ compiler should have a definition of the high_resolution_clock class in <chrono>. The subroutine now(), however, could merely be declared, not implemented. In other words, the now() function of the high_resolution_clock might lack a function body. This makes perfect sense because it may be impossible for the C++ standard library authors to know which hardware timer or counter will be used for the timebase in now() or what its frequency is.

For this reason, it is often necessary to manually implement the now() subroutine of <chrono>'s std::chrono::high_resolution_clock class. This makes it possible to use the high-resolution chronological functions in the <chrono> library. One potential implementation of now() is shown below.

```
// Implement std::chrono::high_resolution_clock::now()
// for the standard library high-resolution clock.
std::chrono::high_resolution_clock::time_point
  high_resolution_clock::now()
{
  // The high-resolution clock source is microseconds.
  typedef
  std::chrono::time_point<high_resolution_clock,
                          microseconds> from_type;

  // Get the consistent tick in microseconds.
  // This function should be in the mcal.
  auto microsecond_tick
    = consistent_microsecond_tick();

  // Now obtain a time point in microseconds.
  auto from_micro
    = from_type(microseconds(microsecond_tick));

  // Return the duration in microseconds.
  return time_point_cast<duration>(from_micro);
}
```

The timebase in this implementation of now () has a resolution in microseconds. Here, the timebase of the high-resolution clock is microseconds. Based on the necessities of the project and the capabilities of the microcontroller, a different time-base can be selected. Other common choices include milliseconds and nanoseconds.

The consistent_microsecond_tick() subroutine is assumed to be a project-specific function that returns the underlying hardware system-tick in microseconds. This subroutine can, for example, be derived from a free-running timer or a timer interrupt service routine with a fixed period (Sect. 9.3).

Reference

1. ISO/IEC, *ISO/IEC 14882:2011: Information technology—Programming languages—C++* (International Organization for Standardization, Geneva, 2011)

Chapter 17
Additional Reading

This chapter provides additional references covering C++, the C++ standard library and STL, software design, C++ coding guidelines, the embedded systems toolchain and microcontroller hardware.

17.1 Literature List

Readers seeking additional information may find the following references helpful. Most of these references have also been mentioned in the previous chapters.

- The formal language specifications of C++98, C++03 and C++11 are available from ISO [11, 13, 16]. ISO-published norms may be prohibitively expensive for hobbyists and students. Cost-free draft versions are available on the Internet and final versions can be found in any good public library.
- The specification of the C language is in [12], and embedded extensions to C are specified in [15].
- A detailed description of the standard library extensions (TR1) can be found in [3]. The TR1 extensions were originally published in [14], and are now predominantly integrated in C++11.
- Comprehensive information on the C++ core language, object-oriented techniques and effective STL usage can be found in [5, 7, 8, 19, 23–25].
- See [17, 22] for in-depth coverage of the containers and algorithms of the STL.
- C++ templates and template metaprogramming are described in [1, 6, 30].
- See [21] for C++ I/O streams. Although not used extensively in this book, I/O streams are useful for PC-based applications, and a well-rounded understanding of C++ should include basic knowledge of I/O streams.
- The Boost libraries are intended to provide reference implementations potentially suitable for standardization [1]. This makes Boost a great place to track the future development of the C++ language. More information on the Boost libraries can be found in [18, 28].

C.M. Kormanyos, *Real-Time C++*, DOI 10.1007/978-3-642-34688-0_17,
© Springer-Verlag Berlin Heidelberg 2013

- A well-respected software design book is [10].
- C++ Coding guidelines can be found in [27].
- Information on microcontroller board design, tools, startup, processor architectures and memory topologies can be found in [4, 26].
- Information on microcontroller programming in C with GNU development tools can be found in [2, 20].
- Detailed coverage of GNU GCC is available in [29].
- The GCC sources are available at the GNU GCC website [9].

References

1. D. Abrahams, A. Gurtovoy, *C++ Template Metaprogramming: Concepts, Tools and Techniques from Boost and Beyond* (Addison Wesley, Reading, 2004)
2. M. Barr, *Programming Embedded Systems with C and GNU Development Tools*, 2nd edn. (O'Reilly, Sebastopol, 2006)
3. P. Becker, *The C++ Standard Library Extensions: A Tutorial and Reference* (Addison Wesley, Reading, 2006)
4. J. Catsoulis, *Designing Embedded Hardware* (O'Reilly, Sebastopol, 2005)
5. J.O. Coplien, *Advanced C++ Programming Styles and Idioms* (Addison Wesley, Reading, 1992)
6. D. Di Gennaro, *Advanced C++ Metaprogramming* (Addison Wesley, Reading, 2011)
7. B. Eckel, *Thinking in C++ Volume 1: Introduction to Standard C++*, 2nd edn. (Pearson Prentice Hall, Upper Saddle River, 2000)
8. B. Eckel, *Thinking in C++ Volume 2: Practical Programming* (Pearson Prentice Hall, Upper Saddle River, 2004)
9. Free Software Foundation, *The GNU Compiler Collection Version 4.6.2* (2012), http://gcc.gnu.org
10. E. Gamma, R. Helm, R. Johnson, J. Vlissides, *Design Patterns: Elements of Reusable Object-Oriented Software* (Addison Wesley, Reading, 1994)
11. ISO/IEC, *ISO/IEC 14882:1998: Programming languages—C++* (International Organization for Standardization, Geneva, 1998)
12. ISO/IEC, *ISO/IEC 9899:1999: Programming languages—C* (International Organization for Standardization, Geneva, 1999)
13. ISO/IEC, *ISO/IEC 14882:2003: Programming languages—C++* (International Organization for Standardization, Geneva, 2003)
14. ISO/IEC, *ISO/IEC TR 19768:2007: Information technology—Programming languages—Technical Report on C++ Library Extensions* (International Organization for Standardization, Geneva, 2007)
15. ISO/IEC, *ISO/IEC TR 18037:2008: Programming languages—C—Extensions to Support Embedded Processors* (International Organization for Standardization, Geneva, 2008)
16. ISO/IEC, *ISO/IEC 14882:2011: Information technology—Programming languages—C++* (International Organization for Standardization, Geneva, 2011)
17. N.M. Josuttis, *The C++ Standard Library: A Tutorial and Reference*, 2nd edn. (Addison Wesley, Reading, 2011)
18. B. Karlsson, *Beyond the C++ Standard Library: An Introduction to Boost* (Addison Wesley, Reading, 2005)
19. A. Koenig, B.E. Moo, *Accelerated C++: Practical Programming by Example* (Addison Wesley, Reading, 2000)

20. J. LaBrosse, *Embedded Systems Building Blocks: Complete and Ready-to-Use Modules in C* (CMP Books, Lawrence, 1999)
21. A. Langer, K. Kreft, *Standard C++ I/O Streams and Locales: Advanced Programmer's Guide and Reference* (Addison Wesley, Reading, 2008)
22. R. Lischner, *STL Pocket Reference* (O'Reilly, Sebastopol, 2004)
23. S. Meyers, *More Effective C++: 35 New Ways to Improve Your Programs and Designs* (Addison Wesley, Reading, 1996)
24. S. Meyers, *Effective STL: 50 Specific Ways to Improve Your Use of the Standard Template Library* (Addison Wesley, Reading, 2001)
25. S. Meyers, *Effective C++: 55 Specific Ways to Improve Your Programs and Designs*, 3rd edn. (Addison Wesley, Reading, 2005)
26. T. Noergaard, *Embedded Systems Architecture: A Comprehensive Guide for Engineers and Programmers* (Newnes Publishing, Burlington, 2005)
27. Programming Research Group, *High-Integrity C++ Coding Standard Manual* (2007), http://www.codingstandard.com/HICPPCM/index.html
28. B. Schäling, *The Boost C++ Libraries* (XML Press, Laguna Hills, 2011)
29. W. van Hagen, *The Definitive Guide to GCC* (Apress, Berkeley, 2006)
30. D. Vandevoorde, N.M. Josuttis, *C++ Templates: The Complete Guide* (Addison Wesley, Reading, 2003)

Appendices

Appendix A
A Tutorial for Real-Time C++

This appendix presents a short tutorial on C++. It is not a complete language tutorial, but rather a brief introduction to the most important parts of C++ for programming real-time embedded systems.

A.1 C++ Cast Operators

C++ has four template cast operators. The code below, for instance, uses the **static_cast** operator to cast from **float** to **int**.

```
float f = 3.14159265358979323846F;

int n = static_cast<int>(f);
```

The code sequence below uses the **reinterpret_cast** operator to set bit–5 in the microcontroller port register portb.

```
// The address of portb is 0x25.
constexpr std::uint8_t portb = 0x25U;

// Cast std::uint8_t to std::uint8_t*.
volatile std::uint8_t* pb
  = reinterpret_cast<volatile std::uint8_t*>(portb);

// Set portb.5.
*pb |= 0x20;
```

C.M. Kormanyos, *Real-Time C++*, DOI 10.1007/978-3-642-34688-0,
© Springer-Verlag Berlin Heidelberg 2013

The **reinterpret_cast**() operator is sometimes considered unsafe because it can convert unrelated types. For a detailed description of the potential dangers of **reinterpret_cast**(), see Eckel [1], Chap. 3, in the subsection on **reinterpret_cast**(). For direct memory access in microcontroller programming, however, **reinterpret_cast**() can be considered safe and appropriate.

This book only uses the **static_cast** and **reinterpret_cast** cast operators. C++ also has the **dynamic_cast** and **const_cast** operators. The **dynamic_cast** operator converts pointers and references. It also performs a costly but robust runtime check to ensure that the result of the cast is valid. The **const_cast** operator can change the *constness* of an object by either setting or removing its constant attribute.

A.2   Uniform Initialization Syntax

C++ has a syntax for fully uniform type initialization that works on any object. It was introduced with C++11. Uniform initialization syntax can be used alongside traditional constructor initialization with parentheses and initialization with **operator**=() alike.

Uniform initialization syntax uses curly braces to hold the initial values. The code below, for instance, initializes built-in types with uniform initialization syntax.

```
int n { 123 };

float f { 3.14159265358979323846F };
```

Aggregate types can also be initialized with uniform initialization syntax. The code below initializes a structure with two data members.

```
struct my_struct
{
  my_struct(const int n_ = 0,
            const float& f_ = 0.0F) : n(n_),
                                      f(f_) { }

  int n;
  float f;
}

my_struct instance_of_my_struct
```

```
{
  123,                          // Initial value for n.
  3.14159265358979323846F // Initial value for f.
};
```

In certain situations, the compiler can also deduce the type of an object based on uniform initialization syntax. For example,

```
struct my_struct
{
  // ...
}

my_struct my_function()
{
  // The compiler correctly deduces the return type.
  return
  {
    456,
    0.57721566490153286061F
  };
}
```

Uniform initialization syntax can be used in the constructor initialization list of a class type as well as to initialize an instance of a class type. For instance,

```
struct point
{
  point(const int x_ = 0,
        const int y_ = 0) : x{x_}, y{y_} { }

  int x;
  int y;
};

point pt { 123, 456 };
```

In addition, uniform initialization syntax can be used to conveniently initialize STL containers such as std::array and std::vector (Sect. A.6). Some examples are shown below.

```
std::array<int, 3U> a
{
  { 1, 2, 3 }
```

```
};

std::vector<char> v
{
  { 'a', 'b', 'c' }
};
```

A.3   Overloading

Function overloading in C++ allows creating several functions with the same name but different types of input and output parameters. For example,

```
// The area of a rectangle.
float area(const float& length,
           const float& width)
{
  return length * width;
}

// The area of a circle.
float area(const float& radius)
{
  constexpr float pi = 3.1415926535897932F;

  return (pi * radius) * radius;
}
```

Global functions and local functions as well as class member functions can be overloaded. It is essential, however, not to confuse class member overloading with dynamic polymorphism and the runtime virtual function mechanism, described in Sect. 4.4.

A.4   Compile-Time Assert

`static_assert()` performs a compile-time check of a constant expression. The syntax of `static_assert` is:

```
static_assert(expression, message);
```

where `expression` is a condition to be tested by the compiler and `message` is a character-based message text. If the result of the `expression` is non-zero, then `static_assert` has no effect and compilation continues unabatedly. If the result of `expression` is zero, then compilation fails and the `message` text is displayed like a regular compiler error.

`static_assert()` can be used to perform compile-time diagnostics. This can be convenient for checking platform-specific requirements. For example,

```
constexpr unsigned int version = 3U;

// Print error message if version is less than 2.
static_assert(version >= 2U, "Version is too low!");
```

In this example, `static_assert()` ensures that `version` is 2 or higher and issues a compiler error if not.

A.5 Numeric Limits

The C++ standard library supports numeric limits of built-in types in its `<limits>` header. The `<limits>` library provides the `std::numeric_limits` template, and specializations are provided for both built-in floating-point and integer types as well as **bool**. The member variable `is_specialized` is **true** for a specialization of `std::numeric_limits`.

The synopsis of the `std::numeric_limits` template class is shown below.

```
namespace std
{
  template<class T>
  class numeric_limits
  {
  public:
    static constexpr bool is_specialized = false;
    static constexpr T min() { return T(); }
    static constexpr T max() { return T(); }
    static constexpr T lowest() { return T(); }

    static constexpr int digits = 0;
    static constexpr int digits10 = 0;
    static constexpr int max_digits10 = 0;
    static constexpr bool is_signed = false;
    static constexpr bool is_integer = false;
    static constexpr bool is_exact = false;
```

```
        static constexpr int radix = 0;
        static constexpr T epsilon() { return T(); }
        static constexpr T round_error() { return T(); }

        static constexpr int min_exponent = 0;
        static constexpr int min_exponent10 = 0;
        static constexpr int max_exponent = 0;
        static constexpr int max_exponent10 = 0;

        static constexpr bool has_infinity = false;
        static constexpr bool has_quiet_NaN = false;
        static constexpr bool has_signaling_NaN = false;
        static constexpr float_denorm_style has_denorm
          = denorm_absent;
        static constexpr bool has_denorm_loss = false;
        static constexpr T infinity() { return T(); }
        static constexpr T quiet_NaN() { return T(); }
        static constexpr T signaling_NaN() { return T(); }
        static constexpr T denorm_min() { return T(); }

        static constexpr bool is_iec559 = false;
        static constexpr bool is_bounded = false;
        static constexpr bool is_modulo = false;
        static constexpr bool traps = false;
        static constexpr bool tinyness_before = false;
        static constexpr float_round_style round_style
          = round_toward_zero;
      };
    }
```

The specialization of `numeric_limits` for **int** on a 32–bit platform, for example, might be implemented as follows.

```
namespace std
{
  template<>
  class numeric_limits<unsigned int>
  {
  public:
    static constexpr bool is_specialized = true;

    static constexpr int min() { return -2147483648; }
    static constexpr int max() { return 2147483647; }
```

```
      static constexpr int lowest() { return 0; }

      static constexpr int digits = 31;
      static constexpr int digits10 = 9;
      static constexpr int max_digits10 = 9;
      static constexpr bool is_signed = true;
      static constexpr bool is_integer = true;
      static constexpr bool is_exact = true;
      static constexpr int radix = 2;
      static constexpr int epsilon() { return 0; }
      static constexpr int round_error() { return 0; }

      static constexpr int min_exponent = 0;
      static constexpr int min_exponent10 = 0;
      static constexpr int max_exponent = 0;
      static constexpr int max_exponent10 = 0;

      static constexpr bool has_infinity = false;
      static constexpr bool has_quiet_NaN = false;
      static constexpr bool has_signaling_NaN = false;
      static constexpr float_denorm_style has_denorm
        = denorm_absent;
      static constexpr bool has_denorm_loss = false;
      static constexpr int infinity() { return 0; }
      static constexpr int quiet_NaN() { return 0; }
      static constexpr int signaling_NaN() { return 0; }
      static constexpr int denorm_min() { return 0; }

      static constexpr bool is_iec559 = false;
      static constexpr bool is_bounded = false;
      static constexpr bool is_modulo = false;
      static constexpr bool traps = false;
      static constexpr bool tinyness_before = false;
      static constexpr float_round_style round_style
        = round_toward_zero;
  };
}
```

The std::numeric_limits templates allow the programmer to query information about the numeric limits of built-in types. For example,

```
constexpr int n_max = std::numeric_limits<int>::max();
```

Numeric limits can be conveniently used in other templates. For example,

```
template<typename unsigned_type>
struct hi_bit
{
  // The bit position of the high bit.
  static constexpr int bpos
    = std::numeric_limits<unsigned_type>::digits - 1;

  // The value of the type with the high-bit set.
  static constexpr unsigned_type value
    = static_cast<unsigned_type>(1) << bpos;
};
```

The scalable hi_bit template structure provides compile-time constant values.
For instance,

```
constexpr std::uint8_t hi08 =
  hi_bit<std::uint8_t>::value;   // (1 << 7)

constexpr std::uint16_t hi16 =
  hi_bit<std::uint16_t>::value; // (1 << 15)

constexpr std::uint32_t hi32 =
  hi_bit<std::uint32_t>::value; // (1 << 31)

constexpr std::uint64_t hi64 =
  hi_bit<std::uint64_t>::value; // (1 << 63)
```

Specializations of std::numeric_limits can also be written to provide
information about the numeric limits of user-defined types.

A.6   STL Containers

The C++ standard library has a collection of *container* types. Containers store
sequential elements in a single object. There are different kinds of containers. Some
are optimized for fast random access, others for fast insertion and deletion, etc. The
choice of which container to use depends on the programming situation.

The most important containers in this book are the standard sequential containers:

* std::array is a fixed-length sequential array aligned in memory.
* std::vector is like an std::array. However, a std::vector does
  not have fixed-length. It can grow or shrink dynamically. The std::vector
  container is designed for fast random access.

- `std::deque` is a double-ended queue. It is designed for fast insertion and deletion at the front and back ends.
- `std::list` is a sequence that can be traversed without random access.
- `std::basic_string, std::string` and `std::wstring` are character strings. Although strings do not formally fulfill all the requirements for sequential STL containers, they have many features in common with them.

STL containers are templated, meaning they have strong generic character. Containers have various constructors, a destructor and a selection of member functions. Using STL containers is straightforward. For example,

---

```
#include <vector>

void do_something()
{
  std::vector<int> v(3U, 0);

  v[0U] = 1;
  v[1U] = 2;
  v[2U] = 3;

  // Size is 3.
  std::vector<int>::size_type s = v.size();

  v.push_back(4);

  s = v.size(); // Size is 4.

  int v0 = v.at(0U); // Value is 1.
  int v3 = v.back(); // Value is 4.

  // copy ctor
  std::vector<int> v2(v);

  // iterator ctor
  std::vector<int> v3(v.begin(), v.end());

  // operator=
  std::vector<int> v4 = v;
}
```

This code creates a vector of integers, an `std::vector<int>` called v. The vector v is initially created with three elements set to zero. The three elements are subsequently set to (1,2,3) using the index operator (**operator**[] ()). A fourth element with a value of 4 is *pushed back* onto the back end of the vector using the member function push_back(). The code sample also illustrates some of std::vector's other methods such as size(), at() and back().

Containers can be copy constructed, created from another sequence of iterators and copy assigned. Additional member functions of containers include other access functions and sequence operations such as insertion, assignment, etc. See [4, 6] for complete documentation of containers and their member functions.

Templated containers use member type definitions to define common member types. An example is std::vector's size_type, shown above. Other common member types of containers include iterator types, pointer types, reference types and a value type. Again, consult [4, 6] for complete documentation of these.

STL containers are useful for embedded systems programming and are used extensively in this book and its companion code. Containers facilitate program organization and data localization. Containers of base class pointers or references allow for powerful sequential polymorphism. Containers are particularly useful in combination with STL algorithms (Sect. A.8).

A.7   STL Iterators

An *iterator* is the generalization of a pointer, used for pointing to the elements in sequential containers. Iterators can be used to manipulate the elements of standard STL containers. In particular, each standard STL container facilitates manipulation of its elements via iterators by providing dedicated iterator types and standardized iterator functions such as begin() and end(). For example,

```
#include <vector>

void do_something()
{
  std::vector<int> v(3U);

  // Set v to (1,2,3).
  v[0U] = 1;
  v[1U] = 2;
  v[2U] = 3;

  for(std::vector<int>::iterator it = v.begin();
      it != v.end();
      ++it)
  {
    *it += 5;
  }
```

```
    // Now v is (6,7,8).
}
```

This code uses `std::vector`'s `iterator` type to iterate through v in the range from `v.begin()` to the element just before `v.end()`. The loop statement adds 5 to each of v's elements.

An iterator pair that delimits a range in a sequence is denoted by

$$[\texttt{First, Last}), \qquad\qquad (A.1)$$

where established convention mandates that `First` points to the first element in the sequence and `Last` points to the element one increment past the final element. The STL's *standard algorithms* (Sect. A.8) use this convention. Using this convention consistently ensures compatibility with the STL and other code. The code sample below uses a range of input iterators with `std::copy()`.

```cpp
#include <algorithm>
#include <array>
#include <vector>

void do_something()
{
    // Initialized src with (101, 101, 101).
    const std::vector<int> src(3U, 101);

    // Uninitialized dst.
    std::array<int, 3U> dst;

    // Copy from vector src to array dst.
    // dst now also contains (101, 101, 101).
    std::copy(src.begin(), src.end(), dst.begin());
}
```

All iterators support incrementing (++) to advance the iterator to the next element in the sequence. Some STL iterators support decrementing (- -) to lower the iterator to the previous element. In general, the *pre*-increment and *pre*-decrement forms of (++) and (- -) are more efficient than the *post*-increment and *post*-decrement forms. Many programmers, therefore, preferentially use the *pre*-forms in situations for which *pre* and *post* are functionally identical. All STL iterators use the dereferencing operator (*) or the member selection operator (->) for element access.

C++ has several categories of iterators including (among others) forward iterators, bidirectional iterators and random access iterators.

There is a clear distinction between *constant* iterators and *non-constant* iterators. In particular, constant iterators are limited to read-only access. Non-constant iterators can read and write container elements.

```
container_type::iterator nonconst_iterator1
  = cnt.begin();

container_type::const_iterator const_iterator2
 = cnt.begin();

container_type::const_iterator const_iterator3
  = cnt.cbegin();

*nonconst_iterator1 = 1;  // OK
*const_iterator2    = 2;  // Error!
*const_iterator3    = 3;  // Error!
```

The "c" in cbegin() emphasizes that the iterator iterates over *constant* elements, as in const_iterator. Some special container member iterator functions such as begin() and end() are overridden, having both constant as well as non-constant versions. Others like cbegin() and cend() are solely constant. The STL has several iterator classes that can be used standalone or as base classes for custom iterators. The standard iterator classes are defined in <iterator>.

A.8   STL Algorithms

The STL has an extensive collection of templated algorithms specifically designed to operate on a range of iterators. Most of the standard algorithms are defined in <algorithm> and some others are defined in <numeric> and <memory>.

STL algorithms are highly versatile because they can be used generically with any kind of iterator—even with regular pointers. The standard algorithms can simplify many common coding situations by transferring program complexity from the user code to the STL. More information on STL algorithms can be found in [2, 4, 6].

There are several categories of algorithms.

- Non-modifying sequence operations like std::all_of(), std::count(), std::for_each(), std::search(), etc.
- Mutating sequence operations that modify the elements in the range including algorithms such as std::copy(), std::move(), std::fill() and the like.
- Sorting algorithms.

- Binary search algorithms operating on sorted ranges.
- Merge operations that act on sorted ranges.
- Heap operations.
- Comparison operations including algorithms such as the minimax functions std::min() and std::max() and the generalized alphabetical compare algorithm std::lexicographical_compare().

A typical function prototype of an STL algorithm is shown below.

```
template<typename iterator_type,
         typename function_type>
function_type std::for_each(iterator_type first,
                            iterator_type last,
                            function_type function);
```

This is the function prototype of std::for_each(), which was also shown in Sect. 5.8. The std::for_each() algorithm applies its function parameter (function) to each element in the range [first, last).

We will now present several examples showing how to use STL algorithms.

```
#include <algorithm>
#include <vector>

namespace
{
  void add_five(int& elem)
  {
    elem += 5;
  }
}

void do_something()
{
  std::vector<int> v(3U);

  // Set v to (1,2,3).
  v[0U] = 1;
  v[1U] = 2;
  v[2U] = 3;

  // Now v is (6,7,8).
  std::for_each(v.begin(), v.end(), add_five);
}
```

In this example, the add_five() subroutine is called for each element in
the range [v.begin(), v.end()). An algorithm's function parameter can be
a function with static linkage that has non-subroutine-local scope.

It is also possible to use a dedicated class type for an algorithm's function
parameter. This is called a *functor*, or a function object. In order to work properly,
the functor must support the function call operator, **operator**(). Dedicated
function objects incur overhead. It only makes sense to use one if its advantages
(i.e., encapsulation, data localization and reduction of complexity) justify its costs.

An example using a functor **struct** is shown below. Also in this code sample,
5 is added to each element in v using std::for_each().

```cpp
#include <algorithm>
#include <vector>

struct add_five
{
  add_five() { }

  void operator()(int& elem)
  {
    elem += 5;
  }
};

void do_something()
{
  std::vector<int> v(3U);

  // Set v to (1,2,3).
  v[0U] = 1;
  v[1U] = 2;
  v[2U] = 3;

  std::for_each(v.begin(), v.end(), add_five());

  // Now v is (6,7,8).
}
```

Algorithms can use a so-called *lambda expression* (Sect. A.9) for the function
object. For example,

```cpp
#include <algorithm>
#include <vector>
```

```cpp
void do_something()
{
  std::vector<int> v(3U);

  // Set v to (1,2,3).
  v[0U] = 1;
  v[1U] = 2;
  v[2U] = 3;

  std::for_each(v.begin(),
                v.end(),
                [](int& elem)
                {
                  elem += 5;
                });

  // Now v is (6,7,8).
}
```

Lambda expressions are efficient and elegant when used with algorithms because they integrate the entire functionality of the function object within the algorithm's call parameters. This also facilitates compiler optimization, see Sect. 6.18.

To complete the examples in this section, we will briefly look ahead to Sect. A.10 and initialize the vector with an std::initializer_list.

```cpp
#include <algorithm>
#include <vector>
#include <initializer_list>

void do_something()
{
  // Set v to (1,2,3).
  std::vector<int> v( { 1, 2, 3 } );

  std::for_each(v.begin(),
                v.end(),
                [](int& elem)
                {
                  elem += 5;
                });

  // Now v is (6,7,8).
}
```

In this coding example, the combined use of a standard algorithm, a lambda expression and an initializer list provides for a high degree of coding efficiency and performance in C++.

There are *many* algorithms in the STL and most developers do not rigorously maintain a complete mental list of all available algorithms and in which situations to use them. The most important things to remember about the standard algorithms is that there even *are* standard algorithms in the first place, and where to find help about them, for example, with help functions, additional literature, etc.

A.9   Lambda Expressions

A *lambda expression* is an anonymous function that has a body but does not have a name. Lambda expressions are stylistically eloquent and can be optimized particularly well when used with the standard algorithms of the STL.

A C++ lambda expression has the form shown below [7].

```
[capture](arguments) -> return-type { body }
```

We have already used lambda expressions with STL algorithms previously in this book. Lambda expressions can also be used as standalone function objects. The lambda expression shown below, for example, computes the **float** value of the hypotenuse,

$$h = \sqrt{x^2 + y^2}. \tag{A.2}$$

```
#include <cmath>

void do_something()
{
  const float x = 3.0F;
  const float y = 4.0F;

  // Capture x and y by reference.
  // The lambda expression has no input parameters.
  // The lambda expression returns float.

  const float h =
    [&x, &y]() -> float
    {
      return std::sqrt((x * x) + (y * y));
    }();

  // The value of h is 5.0F.
}
```

The local variables x and y are captured by reference. The body of the anonymous function is implemented within the scope of the curly braces. The trailing set of parentheses after the closing curly brace effects the function call.

A.10   Initializer Lists

C++11 added several useful templated container classes to the STL. One of these is std::initializer_list. An initializer list is a sequential list of constant objects or values. Elements in an initializer list must be type-identical or type-convertible. STL containers can be conveniently initialized with an initializer list. These convenient kinds of initializations were not possible prior to the inclusion of std::initializer_list in the STL.

For example,

```
// Initialization with operator=.
container c1 = { 1, 2, 3 };

// Initialization with the container's ctor.
container c2( { 1, 2, 3 } );

// Initialization with uniform initialization syntax.
container c3 {{ 1, 2, 3 }};
```

Functions can take initializer lists as parameters. In addition, initializer lists support iterators. For example,

```
#include <initializer_list>
#include <numeric>

constexpr std::initializer_list<int> lst {1, 2, 3};

const int sum = std::accumulate(std::begin(lst),
                                std::end(lst),
                                0);
```

Initializer lists are quite useful for embedded systems programming because, just like tuples, they provide a way to group objects while incurring low code overhead. Because their values are potentially compile-time constant, initializer lists lend themselves well to inlining and template metaprogramming.

A.11   Type Inference

What follows is a note for C and traditional C++ programmers. The meaning of
the **auto** keyword drastically changed as C++ evolved from C++03 to C++11. The
original legacy **auto** keyword was used, in both C as well as C++03 and C++98,
as a qualifier for local variables. It was a hint to the compiler to preferentially store
a local variable on the stack instead of in a CPU register.

C++11, however, uses the **auto** keyword for automatic compile-time *type
inference*. For example,

```
auto n = 3;                  // n is int.
auto u = std::uint8_t(3U);   // u is std::uint8_t.

// A bit more complicated... Here, the type
// of collection is std::initializer_list<int>.
auto collection { 1, 2, 3 };
```

Wikipedia astutely notes [8], **auto** *is also useful for reducing the verbosity of
the code*. In particular, instead of writing long iterator type names such as this:

```
for(std::vector<int>::iterator it = v.begin();
    it != v.end();
    ++it)
```

automatic type inference with **auto** can be used like this:

```
for(auto it = v.begin(); it != v.end(); ++it)
```

This can be made even more generic and simple with the STL's generic versions
of std::begin() and std::end(). See, for example, Sect. 23.4 in the C++
standard [3]. In particular,

```
for(auto it = std::begin(v); it != std::end(v); ++it)
```

This construction comes in handy for, among other things, generic template
programming.

A.12   Range-Based `for(:)`

C++11 added a simplified range-based `for(:)` short-hand notation for iterating over the elements of a list. This simplified range-based iteration statement allows for easy navigation through a list of elements. For example,

```
std::vector<char> v( {1, 2, 3} );

for(char& c : v)
{
   c += static_cast<char>(0x30);
}
```

This simplified loop basically means, iterate over every character in v, and add 0x30 to each one. The traditional `for(;;)`-loop and the `for_each()` algorithm still work and can be used for the same things. The new shorthand of the range-based `for(:)`-loop is, however, potentially more convenient and terse.

Range-based `for(:)`-loops work for C-style arrays, initializer lists, and any type that has the normal `begin()` and `end()` functions. This includes all of the standard library containers that have `begin()` and `end()`.

A.13   Tuple

A *tuple* is the generalization of an ordered group of objects, such as a pair or a triple, a quadruple, a quin-*tuple*, a sex-*tuple*, etc. While other programming languages such as Python and Perl have had tuples for quite a while, they are relatively new in C++, available with C++11. Tuples are implemented as template classes. The template parameters of a tuple define the number of tuple objects and their types.

For example, a tuple consisting of three objects, a **float**, a **char** and an **int**, can be created and used as shown below.

```
#include <tuple>

typedef std::tuple<float, char, int> tuple_type;

void do_something()
{
   // Make a tuple of a float, char and an int.
   tuple_type t(1.23F, 'a', 123);

   // Get element number 1 of the tuple ('a').
```

```
char c = std::get<1>(t);

// Get element number 2 of the tuple (123).
int n = std::get<2>(t);

// Use the type member of tuple_element to obtain
// the float value of the zero'th tuple element.
std::tuple_element<0, tuple_type>::type val
  = std::get<0>(t);

// Get the size of the tuple.
int size = std::tuple_size<tuple_type>::value;
}
```

Tuples can be created and initialized with their ctor using appropriate arguments. `tuple` also provides a default ctor which uses the default ctors of its respective elements. The Nth element of an ordered tuple or a reference thereto can be retrieved with the templated `std::get()` function. STL's `std::tuple_size` wraps the tuple element count by storing the number of elements in its member variable `value`. The `std::tuple_element` template wraps the type of a tuple element. Note in the listing that a convenient type definition has been used in order to avoid typing long and complicated tuple types.

Tuples can be copy assigned with **operator=()**. They can also be copy constructed. Copy and assign use member-wise assignment. Copy and assign also require that for each element pair the destination can be converted from the source.

Tuples can be assigned using STL's `std::make_tuple()` facility. For example, the tuple in the listing above could be created with `std::make_tuple()`. In particular,

```
#include <tuple>

typedef std::tuple<float, char, int> tuple_type;

tuple_type t = std::make_tuple(1.23F, 'a', 123);
```

Tuples can be compared. Comparison functions use relational operators and perform pair-wise comparison. Comparison stops when the first element pair comparison yields **true**.

The code sample below shows `tuple` copy and compare.

```
#include <string>
#include <tuple>
```

```
void do_something()
{
  std::tuple<int, std::string> t1(123, "identical");
  std::tuple<int, std::string> t2 = t1;
  std::tuple<int, std::string> t3(t1);

  bool result;
  result = (t1 == t2);   // true
  result = (t1 == t3);   // true

  std::get<0>(t2) += 1; // 123 -> 124
  result = (t2 > t1);    // true

  // Transform identical -> xdentical
  std::get<1>(t3).at(0U) = 'x';
  result = (t3 > t1);    // true
}
```

Tuples are immensely useful because they can group collections of objects together in a single representation. At the same time, tuples incur a minimum of code overhead because tuple elements are partly or completely available at compile-time. In particular, the template facilities `std::get()`, `std::tuple_size` and `std::tuple_element` can be optimized particularly well at compile time. Tuples lend themselves readily to template design and template metaprogramming, see Sect. 5.10.

A.14   Regular Expressions

Support for lexical parsing of regular expressions in C++ is implemented in the `<regex>` library. A complete implementation of `<regex>` involves extensive templates and a significant amount of object code. Therefore, `<regex>` is often too large-scale for most microcontroller projects.

Microcontroller programming, however, usually involves other associated PC-based programs and utilities used for a variety of purposes such as manipulating files, automatic code generation, designing specialized language parsers, etc. Lexical parsing with regular expressions can drastically simplify the implementations of these programs. Therefore, the microcontroller programmer should have basic competence with `<regex>`.

Consider a regular expression designed for parsing a composite string composed of three substrings. The first substring is an alphanumeric name including underscores. The second substring is a hexadecimal number. The third substring is a base–10 unsigned integer. For example,

`_My_Variable123    03FFB004    4`

A regular expression for parsing this composite string is shown below:

```
const std::regex
rx(  std::string("([_0-9a-zA-Z]+)")   // Alnum name.
   + std::string("[[:space:]]+")       // 1+ spaces.
   + std::string("([0-9a-fA-F]+)")     // Hex integer.
   + std::string("[[:space:]]+")       // 1+ spaces.
   + std::string("([0-9]+)"));         // Base-10 int.
```

This regular expression rx uses POSIX syntax. The <regex> library supports several syntaxes, POSIX being the default. The first, third and fifth strings in the definition of the regular expression are enclosed in parentheses. The parentheses indicate a *capture group* of the regular expression. A *capture group* contains an expression which should be *caught*, in other words stored, when checking for a regular expression match.

A program showing how to use this regular expression is shown in the sample code below.

```
#include <algorithm>
#include <iterator>
#include <iostream>
#include <string>
#include <regex>

int main()
{
  const std::regex rx(  std::string("([_0-9a-zA-Z]+)")
                      + std::string("[[:space:]]+")
                      + std::string("([0-9a-fA-F]+)")
                      + std::string("[[:space:]]+")
                      + std::string("([0-9]+)"));

  const std::string str("_My_Variable123 03FFB004 4");

  std::match_results<std::string::const_iterator> mr;

  if(std::regex_match(str, mr, rx))
  {
    std::copy(mr.begin(),
              mr.end(),
              std::ostream_iterator
                <std::string>(std::cout, "\n"));
  }
}
```

The `regex_match()` function is a Boolean subroutine with three input parameters. There are six different overwritten forms of `regex_match()`. The one in the listing checks if its input string, `str`, identically matches its input regular expression, `rx`. If the regular expression matches, then `regex_match()` returns **true**. The match results, `mr`, contain the results of the regular expression match.

The output of the program is:

```
_My_Variable123 03FFB004 4
_My_Variable123
03FFB004
4
```

A successful match has $N + 1$ elements in the match results, where N is the number of capture groups in the regular expression. The 0th match result always contains the entire string submitted to the match. In this example, there are four elements in the match results, one for the input string and three for the capture groups.

Regular expressions are templated. For example, `std::regex` is actually a type definition for `std::basic_regex<`**char**`>`. Therefore, regular expressions can be used with strings or sequences of other types. In addition, `match_results` are templated and support iterators allowing for convenient manipulation with STL standard algorithms.

Additional information on `std::regex` can be found in [5]. Even though this reference describes the `Boost.Regex` library, it is also applicable here because `std::regex` originates from Boost.

References

1. B. Eckel, *Thinking in C++ Volume 1: Introduction to Standard C++*, 2nd edn. (Pearson Prentice Hall, Upper Saddle River, 2000)
2. B. Eckel, *Thinking in C++ Volume 2: Practical Programming* (Pearson Prentice Hall, Upper Saddle River, 2004)
3. ISO/IEC, *ISO/IEC 14882:2011: Information Technology – Programming Languages – C++* (International Organization for Standardization, Geneva, 2011)
4. N.M. Josuttis, *The C++ Standard Library: A Tutorial and Reference*, 2nd edn. (Addison Wesley, Reading, 2011)
5. B. Karlsson, *Beyond the C++ Standard Library: An Introduction to Boost* (Addison Wesley, Reading, 2005)
6. R. Lischner, *STL Pocket Reference* (O'Reilly, Sebastopol, 2004)
7. Wikipedia, *Anonymous Function* (2012), http://en.wikipedia.org/wiki/Anonymous_function
8. Wikipedia, *C++11* (2012), http://en.wikipedia.org/wiki/C%2B%2B11

Appendix B
A Robust Real-Time C++ Environment

Real-time programming is characterized by demanding performance, size and safety constraints. This, combined with the large scope of the C++ language and a potentially complex set of development tools, can make the creation of high-quality real-time C++ software a truly challenging endeavor. In the harsh world of real-time C++, the stability of the development environment can contribute to the overall quality of the software as much or even more than the actual coding itself. This chapter discusses various aspects related to the robust real-time C++ environment.

B.1 Addressing the Challenges of Real-Time C++

Microcontroller software is usually cost-sensitive, safety-critical or both and demands the utmost in efficiency and robustness. The development environment and the executable program usually run on separate systems. In addition, flashing the microcontroller generally uses a connection with a hardware interface for in-system programming (ISP) with an on-chip debugger or an in-circuit emulator (ICE). This can make it particularly difficult to visualize, debug and test microcontroller software.

When addressing the challenges of real-time C++ programming, it may be best to start with a simple project and build up tools, coding competence and a collection of re-usable software components steadily and methodically. The brief checklist below describes some considerations that need to be made when doing real-time C++ programming.

✓ Select the right microcontroller for the application. Consider performance and cost aspects. Decide if the application needs a cost-sensitive 8–bit microcontroller or a more powerful, more expensive 32–bit or 64–bit microcontroller. Try to estimate how much program memory and RAM are needed and select the microcontroller accordingly. If future versions of the application are planned, it may be advisable to use a scalable microcontroller family that includes

C.M. Kormanyos, *Real-Time C++*, DOI 10.1007/978-3-642-34688-0,
© Springer-Verlag Berlin Heidelberg 2013

pin-compatible chip derivatives which can accommodate future extensions of
functionality.

✓ Get a microcontroller prototype up and running. Students and hobbyists may be
well served with a commercially available microcontroller starter kit including
a board, a debug interface and a demo compiler. Using a starter kit can ease the
learning curve by providing a functioning set of hardware, software and code
examples, all in one package. If working in a production environment, try to
ensure that a functioning prototype board is available early in the development
cycle.

✓ Obtain a high-quality C++ compiler. Compiler availability can be an issue
and successful development mandates that a good C++ compiler is available
for the microcontroller. GCC is cost free and known for having a high degree
of language standards conformance. Professionally supplied compilers might
beat the performance of GCC, particularly for low-level hardware programming
requiring intimate knowledge of the microcontroller architecture. At the same
time, professionally supplied compilers tend to be prohibitively expensive for
students and hobbyists. Those interested in assessing compiler price and performance may want to carry out market research in combination with compiler
benchmarks for the domain of the application.

✓ Depending on project necessities, make sure a microcontroller programmer, a
simulator, a debugger or an ICE, or several of these are available. If other test
and measurement devices such as an oscilloscope or logic analyzer are required,
verify that the equipment is available. One should verify that the equipment
works and that one has basic knowledge of how to use it, or knows where to
find help if not.

✓ Design and use a software architecture (Sect. B.2). The architecture significantly
influences the overall quality of the entire software. When doing any robust
microcontroller programming in C++, it is essential to use a layered software
architecture that shields the application layer from the low-level hardware-
specific, non-portable register manipulation code. In this way, application software can be used and re-used, thereby improving portability and localizing the
work of switching the microcontroller to the hardware layer.

✓ Establish coding competence. C++ is a rich, multifaceted language. If working
alone, try to learn the C++ language as best as possible through independent
study. Keep in touch with other programmers and best-practice in the community
e.g., via Internet forums, additional literature, etc.

✓ Software reliability can be improved by adhering to established coding guidelines, such as [1]. Conforming to guidelines can be mandatory when working in
a professional setting where proving reliability to customers may be required in
an assessment or audit situation. When working on projects that demand high
reliability, consider using a static syntax checker in addition to the compiler.

✓ Build up a library of re-usable code. Programming microcontrollers in C++
can be a long-term process based on years of effort. Over the course of time, a
body of re-usable, portable code can be built up for programming situations that

repeatedly arise. Some examples of components that I have collected in my own libraries, and partially in this book, include register manipulation mechanisms (Chap. 7), custom allocators (Chap. 10), timers (Sect. 15.3), multitasking schedulers (Chap. 11), filter functions (Chap. 14), mathematical functions (Chap. 12), convenient utilities (Chap. 15), etc.

B.2 Software Architecture

No matter how small or large a given software may be, it is essential to use a good, properly sized *software architecture*. The architecture may contribute to the overall quality of the software more strongly than any other factor. Programming skill and elegance of implementation alone can only augment software quality, not create it. The combination of solid architecture and competent coding ultimately leads to success in real-time C++.

When working in a project with a documented software architecture, one is not merely programming but engaging in software engineering and system design instead. Metaphorically speaking, software architecture comprises the foundation, floors and walls of the project; the code being the plaster, paint and furniture. In the absence of a stable and robust architecture, even good code will, in time, erode and crumble under its own weight.

Designing a software architecture can start with a simple block diagram of the major software layers and components such as the one shown in Fig. B.1. Initially, this can be a rudimentary hand-sketched diagram. Create the corresponding directories and files and fill them with preliminary namespaces, classes and functions that embody the most important interfaces. At first, classes and functions can be incomplete skeletons. Implementation details can be added later. Try to ensure that names of namespaces, classes, functions, etc. have recognizable associations with the architecture sketch.

Software architecture need not be complicated. A straightforward one with a few clearly defined layers is usually best. Consider, once again, the software architecture shown in Fig. B.1. This architecture consists of three layers that have successively higher levels of abstraction.

The MCAL contains microcontroller-specific peripheral drivers such as timer, watchdog or communication interfaces. Intermediate system-level software such as startup routines and monitor functions can be implemented in the System Layer. The Application Layer contains high-level application software. Modules in the application layer should be kept entirely portable. The operating system and project utilities can be used by all three layers in the architecture. Over the years, I have had good results with this kind of layered architecture in numerous projects with varying application size.

When developing a software architecture, try to achieve easy-to-understand modularity and object granularity. Avoid overly long files, classes and subroutines. It may take a few iterations until the architecture and functional granularity *feel*

A Microcontroller Software Architecture

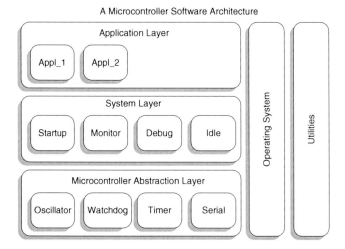

Fig. B.1 A layered microcontroller software architecture is shown

right. Time invested in designing software architecture is, however, time spent well because the architecture provides for long-lasting organization in a project that may potentially be worked on for years.

B.3   Establishing and Adhering to Runtime Limits

Microcontroller programming is time critical and things tend to go wrong if the software has unpredictable timing. For example, a late response from a communication attempt might be just as bad as the wrong response, regardless of its content. To address this problem, it can be helpful to establish runtime limits and adhere to them.

This can be done by identifying the priority classes of tasks and interrupts in the system and defining runtime constraints for them. Table B.1, for example, lists potential runtime limits selected for a system with three priority classes: high-priority interrupts, low-priority interrupts and the task-level priority. The runtime constraints are given in a form indicating a typical value representing the design target and a maximum limit which should never be exceeded and only sporadically neared under worst-case load conditions.

When designing an embedded microcontroller system, the most time consuming software processes should be identified up front and designed with a temporal granularity that facilitates an even distribution of the work load. In general, it is poor form to program with blocking calls that engage the CPU for long time spans such as hundreds of microseconds or even several milliseconds. It is much better to program short, fast sequences in a multitasking environment that process information or

Table B.1 The runtime limits for a system with three priority classes are shown

Priority class	Design target (μs)	Worst-case maximum (μs)
High-priority interrupts	< 10	$\lesssim$ 25
Low-priority interrupts	< 40	$\lesssim$ 100
All tasks	< 500	$\lesssim$ 1,000

service a state machine quickly and rapidly relinquish control to other processes in the system. Interrupt service routines should be held terse and efficient. Keeping the runtime within the established limits generally leads to a more predictable software with higher quality and reliability.

References

1. Programming Research Group, *High-Integrity C++ Coding Standard Manual* (2007), http://www.codingstandard.com/HICPPCM/index.html
2. W. van Hagen, *The Definitive Guide to GCC* (Apress, Berkeley, 2006)

Appendix C
Building and Installing GNU GCC Cross Compilers

There are several reasons one might want to build GCC [4], such as to obtain the newest version of the compilers or to enable additional language features or other languages. This appendix provides step-by-step instructions for building a GNU GCC cross compiler for our target with the 8–bit microcontroller. GCC can be most easily built on *nix-like systems. In this example, the build is done in MinGW/MSYS [6] using standard GNU auto-tools configure scripts and make procedures. The methods in this chapter can easily be adapted for building a cross compiler targeted to another microcontroller architecture.

C.1 The GCC Prerequisites

Building GCC has *prerequisites*, meaning that certain libraries must be installed and available to the build system before GCC can be built. If any prerequisites are missing, these either need to be installed or built from source. At the time this book is written, the prerequisites for building GCC are:

- GMP [5], the GNU multiprecision library.
- MPFR [2,8], the GNU multiprecision floating-point library.
- MPC [7], a C library for the multiprecision arithmetic of complex numbers.
- PPL, the Parma Polyhedra Library [1], for abstract geometrical polyhedron representations.
- Binutils [3], the binary utilities for the cross compiler.

It may seem odd that GCC has prerequisites for such exotic mathematical functions as multiprecision floating-point numbers and geometrical polyhedron representations. The multiprecision functions in GMP, MPFR and MPC are needed by GCC for compile-time calculation of floating-point mathematical expressions. The geometrical polyhedron representations in PPL are used for high-level optimizations including program loop analysis, parallelization and vectorization.

C.M. Kormanyos, *Real-Time C++*, DOI 10.1007/978-3-642-34688-0,
© Springer-Verlag Berlin Heidelberg 2013

Perhaps the binary utilities should be considered part of the compiler rather than a prerequisite. Here, we will call the binary utilities a prerequisite simply because the build of GCC needs to use them. This, in turn, means that the binary utilities need to be built and installed prior to building GCC.

C.2   Getting Started

Building the GCC prerequisites and GCC can take several hours of manual work. At times, this work can be tedious involving intricate command lines, detailed operating system operations and careful monitoring. It may, therefore, be best to undertake building the GCC prerequisites and GCC only if ample time and peace of mind are available for this kind of endeavor. The process of building, installing and using GCC constitutes a rich topic, see [4, 10].

Sometimes building a GNU cross compiler works. At other times, it does not. There are several reasons why building GCC might fail. The prerequisites might be absent or improperly built. The binary utilities or the compiler sources might be flawed for the particular compiler version and target. Very experienced compiler builders often patch the sources of a new compiler version, thereby correcting minor flaws. The strategy thereby is to integrate the patches in a compiler bug-fix in a later subversion.

Middle-of-the-road compiler builders and users should probably avoid such advanced compiler development as patching the sources. It may, therefore, be necessary to do a bit of trial-and-error work in order to find a combination of prerequisites, binary utilities and a compiler version that harmoniously build together. The components selected in this appendix have been successfully built.

The entire build session including all the prerequisites, the binary utilities and GCC can best be organized within a single root directory. It is not a good idea to perform the build of a given component in its own source tree directory. For each component, therefore, we use two directories, one for the component's source tree and another sibling object directory next to the source tree in which the build is carried out.

We begin by creating a root directory for all the builds. Here, for example, we will use the directory /home/tmp as the root directory for performing the builds.

- Create the directory /home/tmp.

C.3   Building GMP

We will now build GMP version 5.0.5 in MinGW/MSYS.

- cd /home/tmp
- Get the GMP sources and unpack them in /home/tmp.

- Perform the command `mkdir objdir-gmp-5.0.5` in order to make the GMP sibling directory.
- `cd objdir-gmp-5.0.5`

The source tree of GMP should be in the GMP source directory:

```
/home/tmp/gmp-5.0.5
```

We should now be in the GMP sibling object directory:

```
/home/tmp/objdir-gmp-5.0.5
```

In the `objdir-gmp-5.0.5` GMP sibling object directory, configure GMP with the following command:

```
../gmp-5.0.5/configure --prefix=/usr/local \
--build=i686-pc-mingw32 --disable-shared \
--enable-static --enable-cxx CPPFLAGS="-fexceptions"
```

This configuration defines the characteristics that will be used when building GMP. It defines the prefix where the build results will be installed, specifies the build system and instructs the build to create static libraries, not dynamic link libraries.

In the `objdir-gmp-5.0.5` GMP sibling object directory, make GMP with the command:

```
make --jobs=2
```

This will take a while. The optional `--jobs=2` flag indicates that two processes should be used to speed up the build. It is also possible to use more processes.

In the `objdir-gmp-5.0.5` GMP sibling object directory, install GMP with the command:

```
make install
```

C.4 Building MPFR

We will now build MPFR version 3.1.1 in MinGW/MSYS.

- `cd /home/tmp`
- Get the MPFR sources and unpack them in `/home/tmp`.
- Perform the command `mkdir objdir-mpfr-3.1.1` in order to make the MPFR sibling directory.
- `cd objdir-mpfr-3.1.1`

The source tree of MPFR should be in the MPFR source directory:

```
/home/tmp/mpfr-3.1.1
```

We should now be in the MPFR sibling object directory:

```
/home/tmp/objdir-mpfr-3.1.1
```

In the `objdir-mpfr-3.1.1` MPFR sibling object directory, configure MPFR with the following command:

```
../mpfr-3.1.1/configure --prefix=/usr/local \
--build=i686-pc-mingw32 --disable-shared \
--enable-static --with-gmp=/usr/local
```

This configuration defines the characteristics that will be used when building MPFR. It defines the prefix where the build results will be installed, specifies the build system and instructs the build to create static libraries, not dynamic link libraries. The configuration also tells the build of MPFR where the installation of GMP can be found.

In the `objdir-mpfr-3.1.1` MPFR sibling object directory, make MPFR with the command:

```
make --jobs=2
```

This will take a while. The optional `--jobs=2` flag indicates that two processes should be used to speed up the build. It is also possible to use more processes.

In the `objdir-mpfr-3.1.1` MPFR sibling object directory, install MPFR with the command:

```
make install
```

C.5 Building MPC

We will now build MPC version 0.9 in MinGW/MSYS.

- `cd /home/tmp`
- Get the MPC sources and unpack them in `/home/tmp`.
- Perform the command `mkdir objdir-mpc-0.9` in order to make the MPC sibling directory.
- `cd objdir-mpc-0.9`

The source tree of MPC should be in the MPC source directory:

```
/home/tmp/mpc-0.9
```

We should now be in the MPC sibling object directory:

```
/home/tmp/objdir-mpc-0.9
```

In the `objdir-mpc-0.9` MPC sibling object directory, configure MPC with the following command:

```
../mpc-0.9/configure --prefix=/usr/local \
--build=i686-pc-mingw32 --disable-shared \
--enable-static --with-gmp=/usr/local \
--with-mpfr=/usr/local
```

This configuration defines the characteristics that will be used when building MPC. It defines the prefix where the build results will be installed, specifies the build system and instructs the build to create static libraries, not dynamic link libraries. The configuration also tells the build of MPC where the installations of GMP and MPFR can be found.

In the `objdir-mpc-0.9` MPC sibling object directory, make MPC with the command:

```
make --jobs=2
```

This will take a while. The optional `--jobs=2` flag indicates that two processes should be used to speed up the build. It is also possible to use more processes.

In the `objdir-mpc-0.9` MPC sibling object directory, install MPC with the command:

```
make install
```

C.6 Building PPL

We will now build PPL version 0.12.1 in MinGW/MSYS.

- `cd /home/tmp`
- Get the PPL sources and unpack them in `/home/tmp`.
- Perform the command `mkdir objdir-ppl-0.12.1` in order to make the PPL sibling directory.
- `cd objdir-ppl-0.12.1`

The source tree of PPL should be in the PPL source directory:

```
/home/tmp/ppl-0.12.1
```

We should now be in the PPL sibling object directory:

```
/home/tmp/objdir-ppl-0.12.1
```

In the `objdir-ppl-0.12.1` PPL sibling object directory, configure PPL with the following command:

```
../ppl-0.12.1/configure --prefix=/usr/local \
--build=i686-pc-mingw32 --disable-shared \
--enable-static CPPFLAGS="-fexceptions" \
--with-gmp=/usr/local
```

This configuration defines the characteristics that will be used when building PPL. It defines the prefix where the build results will be installed, specifies the build system and instructs the build to create static libraries, not dynamic link libraries. The configuration also tells the build of PPL where the installation of GMP can be found.

In the `objdir-ppl-0.12.1` PPL sibling object directory, make PPL with the command:

```
make --jobs=2
```

This will take a while. The optional `--jobs=2` flag indicates that two processes should be used to speed up the build. It is also possible to use more processes.

In the `objdir-ppl-0.12.1` PPL sibling object directory, install PPL with the command:

```
make install
```

C.7 Building the Binary Utilities for the Cross Compiler

We will now build the binary utilities (binutils) version 2.22 in MinGW/MSYS. The binary utilities provide tools needed by the cross compiler such as the assembler, the linker, the library archiver and assorted utilities for manipulating binary files in ELF binary format.

In this example, the binary utilities will be specifically built in preparation for building GCC version 4.6.2 for the `--target=avr-unknown-elf` cross target.

- `cd /home/tmp`
- Get the binutils sources and unpack them in `/home/tmp`.
- Perform `mkdir objdir-binutils-2.22-avr-unknown-elf` in order to make the binutils sibling directory.
- `cd objdir-binutils-2.22-avr-unknown-elf`

The source tree of the binutils should be in the binutils source directory:

```
/home/tmp/binutils-2.22
```

We should now be in the binutils sibling object directory:

```
/home/tmp/objdir-binutils-2.22-avr-unknown-elf
```

In the `objdir-binutils-2.22-avr-unknown-elf` binutils sibling object directory, configure the binutils with the following command:

```
../binutils-2.22/configure \
--prefix=/usr/local/gcc-4.6.2-avr-unknown-elf \
--target=avr-unknown-elf --build=i686-pc-mingw32 \
--disable-__cxa_atexit --disable-nls \
--disable-threads --disable-shared \
--enable-static --disable-win32-registry \
--disable-sjlj-exceptions --with-dwarf2 \
--with-gmp=/usr/local --with-mpfr=/usr/local \
--with-mpc=/usr/local --with-ppl=/usr/local
```

This configuration defines the characteristics that will be used when building the binutils. It defines the prefix where the build results will be installed, specifies the build system and instructs the build to create static libraries, not dynamic link libraries. For building the binutils, there are additional configuration flags for compiler details. The configuration also tells the build of the binutils where the installations of GMP, MPFR, MPC and PPL can be found.

In the `objdir-binutils-2.22-avr-unknown-elf` binutils sibling object directory, make the binutils with the command:

```
make --jobs=2
```

This will take a while. The optional `--jobs=2` flag indicates that two processes should be used to speed up the build. It is also possible to use more processes.

In the `objdir-binutils-2.22-avr-unknown-elf` binutils sibling object directory, install the binutils with the command:

```
make install
```

C.8   Building the Cross Compiler

We will now build GCC version 4.6.2 in MinGW/MSYS. GCC will be built for the `--target=avr-unknown-elf` cross target. GCC will be built with the newlib library [9].

- `cd /home/tmp`
- Get the GCC sources and unpack them in `/home/tmp`.
- Get the newlib sources and unpack them in `/home/tmp`.
- Perform the command `mkdir objdir-gcc-4.6.2-avr-unknown-elf` in order to make the GCC sibling directory.

The source tree of the GCC should be in the GCC source directory:

```
/home/tmp/gcc-4.6.2
```

After unpacking GCC and newlib, the newlib sources need to be copied to the GCC source tree. For newlib version 1.20.0, for example,

```
cd /home/tmp/newlib-1.20.0
cp -r newlib libgloss ../gcc-4.6.2
```

Return to the GCC sibling object directory for building GCC with:

```
cd /home/tmp/objdir-gcc-4.6.2-avr-unknown-elf
```

We should now be in the GCC sibling object directory:

```
/home/tmp/objdir-gcc-4.6.2-avr-unknown-elf
```

In the objdir-gcc-4.6.2-avr-unknown-elf GCC sibling object directory, configure GCC with the following command:

```
../gcc-4.6.2/configure \
--prefix=/usr/local/gcc-4.6.2-avr-unknown-elf \
--target=avr-unknown-elf --build=i686-pc-mingw32 \
--enable-languages=c,c++ --with-newlib \
--disable-__cxa_atexit --disable-nls \
--disable-threads --disable-shared --enable-static \
--disable-win32-registry --disable-sjlj-exceptions \
--with-dwarf2 --with-gmp=/usr/local \
--with-mpfr=/usr/local --with-mpc=/usr/local \
--with-ppl=/usr/local
```

This configuration defines the characteristics that will be used when building GCC. It defines the prefix where the build results will be installed, specifies the build system and instructs the build to create static libraries, not dynamic link libraries. There are additional configuration flags for compiler details including the languages to build (C and C++) and to use newlib. The configuration also tells the build of GCC where the installations of GMP, MPFR, MPC and PPL can be found.

In the objdir-gcc-4.6.2-avr-unknown-elf GCC sibling object directory, make GCC with the command:

```
make --jobs=2
```

This will take a while. The optional --jobs=2 flag indicates that two processes should be used to speed up the build. It is also possible to use more processes.

In the objdir-gcc-4.6.2-avr-unknown-elf GCC sibling object directory, install GCC with the command:

```
make install
```

C.9 Using the Cross Compiler

We will now assume that the work of building the GCC prerequisites and GCC has been successfully completed. If this is the case, the GCC build results should be located in the installation directory:

```
/usr/local/gcc-4.6.2-avr-unknown-elf
```

Note, however, that the `/usr` directory in MinGW/MSYS could be an alias for a directory such as `/msys/1.0`.

We will now investigate the structure of the build results. In particular, two versions of the compiler should have been installed. There should be one version with tools having decorated names and a second version with tools having undecorated, plain names.

In `/usr/local/gcc-4.6.2-avr-unknown-elf`, the installation directory, there should be versions of the tools with decorated names. For example, the version of g++ with a *decorated* name is:

```
bin/avr-unknown-elf-g++.exe
```

In `/usr/local/gcc-4.6.2-avr-unknown-elf`, the installation directory, there should also be versions of the tools with undecorated names. For example, the version of g++ with an *undecorated* name is:

```
avr-unknown-elf/bin/g++.exe
```

Both the decorated version of the tool chain as well as the undecorated one function equivalently. It is, however, best to use only one of them at one time. Consider which version of the tool chain to use for cross development and use it consistently.

When using GCC, it can be convenient to add the path of the compiler executables to the PATH variable of the shell. In MinGW/MSYS, path information for the cross compiler should be added to the PATH variable in the file `/etc/profile`. In other *nix-like systems, path information for the cross compiler can be added to the PATH variable in the file `/home/.bashrc`.

Some developers recommend not moving an installation of GCC. It is, however, possible to move a fully-built installation of GCC to another location provided the entire directory tree of the compiler is moved. In our example, for instance, this means moving all files, directories, etc. in `gcc-4.6.2-avr-unknown-elf/*` from their installed location to another place as a cohesive unit.

A GCC installation that has been built in MinGW/MSYS can also be used outside of the MinGW/MSYS environment, for example, by employing another command line interface. When doing so, it is necessary to include several dynamic link libraries from the MinGW/MSYS installation in the path of the compiler's binaries or in the build environment. This technique is used in the reference project of the companion code.

References

1. BUGSENG, *The Parma Polyhedra Library (PPL)*, http://www.bugseng.com/products/ppl (2012)
2. L. Fousse, G. Hanrot, V. Lefèvre, P. Pélissier, P. Zimmermann, MPFR: a multiple-precision binary floating-point library with correct rounding. ACM Trans. Math. Softw. **33(2)**, pp. 1–15 (2007)
3. Free Software Foundation, *GNU Binutils* (2011), http://www.gnu.org/software/binutils
4. Free Software Foundation, *The GNU Compiler Collection Version 4.6.2* (2012), http://gcc.gnu.org
5. GMP, *The GNU Multiple Precision Arithmetic Library* (2012), http://gmplib.org
6. MinGW, *Minimalist GNU* (2012), http://www.mingw.org
7. MPC, *GNU MPC* (2012), http://www.multiprecision.org
8. MPFR, *The GNU MPFR Library* (2013), http://www.mpfr.org
9. Red Hat, *newlib* (2013), http://sourceware.org/newlib
10. W. van Hagen: *The Definitive Guide to GCC* (Apress, Berkeley, 2006)

Appendix D
Building a Microcontroller Circuit

This appendix provides details on assembling the microcontroller circuit depicted in Fig. 2.1. Information on the circuit, the schematic and assembly on a solderless prototyping breadboard are included.

D.1 The Circuit Schematic

Recall the microcontroller circuit on the prototyping breadboard first presented in Sect. 2.1, Fig. 2.1. The corresponding schematic for this circuit is shown in Fig. D.1 on the following page. This is a simple microcontroller circuit that can be assembled with just a handful of components.

Our microcontroller circuit consists of the following three main circuit groups:

1. 5 V Regulator
2. Microcontroller and Peripheries
3. JTAG Connector

The 5 V regulator group is shown in the upper right of the schematic. It is responsible for converting an input voltage ranging from about +8 V ... 24 V to the +5 V TTL voltage required by the microcontroller. The ideal input voltage range is around +9 V ... 12 V.

Moving counterclockwise, down and to the left, we encounter the second circuit group, which is the microcontroller and its peripheries. This circuit group contains the microcontroller, its crystal quartz oscillator circuit, a reset push-button and the LED D1. Note that the LED D1 in our circuit diagram here is the same LED that was first presented in the LED program of Chap. 1, see Fig. 1.1.

The third circuit group located to the right and above the circuit label is the JTAG connector. This is a six-pin connection that can interface to a commercially available SPI™ programmer or JTAG ICE debugger.

A microcontroller circuit assembled on a breadboard generally does not have the robustness necessary for high-volume production. Circuit assembly on a solderless

C.M. Kormanyos, *Real-Time C++*, DOI 10.1007/978-3-642-34688-0,
© Springer-Verlag Berlin Heidelberg 2013

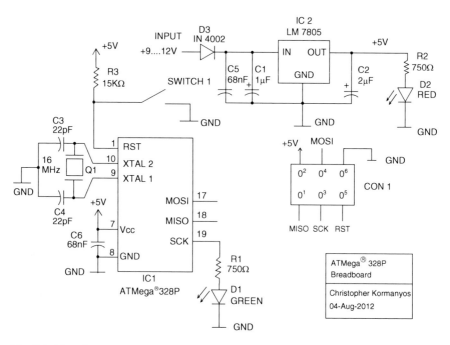

Fig. D.1 The schematic of our target system is shown

prototyping breadboard does, however, provide adequate quality for microcontroller benchmarking and compiler testing.

The part list for our microcontroller circuit is provided in Table D.1. All of the components needed for our microcontroller circuit should be available at any good electronics store.

D.2   Assembling the Circuit on a Breadboard

Our microcontroller circuit assembled with discrete components on a solderless prototyping breadboard is shown in Fig. D.2. The three main circuit groups are highlighted in rectangular boxes.

Circuit assembly uses standard breadboard methods. See, for example, Sects. 3.2 and 3.3 in [2] for additional information on working with a breadboard. An effort should be made to keep wire connections as short as possible and flat on the breadboard. In general, try prevent wire crossings as far as possible. Optionally, a kit containing pre-formed wires, isolated and bent for the breadboard slots, can be conveniently used for some connections.

For other connections, it may be better to make custom-length isolated wires. AWG–22 [3] conducting wire cut to length and appropriately bent for the slots

Table D.1 The discrete components in our microcontroller circuit are listed

Label	Type	Value	Function
D3	1N4002-type rectifier	100 V	Short-circuit protection
IC2	7805 voltage regulator	+5 V	Linear voltage regulator in TO–220 package [5]
C1	Electrolytic capacitor	1 μF	Input stabilization
C2	Electrolytic capacitor	2 μF	+5 V stabilization
R1, R2	1/4 Watt resistor	750 Ω	LED current limitation
D2	LED red	5–10 mA	Power indicator
C5, C6	Ceramic capacitor	68 nF	High-frequency filter
IC1	ATMEL® AVR® ATmega328P [1]	–	8–bit microcontroller in DIL–28 package [4]
D1	LED green	5–10 mA	User LED on pin 17
Q1	Quartz	16 MHz	Oscillator circuit
C3, C4	Ceramic capacitor	10 pF	Oscillator circuit
R3	1/4 Watt resistor	15 kΩ	+5 V pull-up on reset
SWITCH1	Mini push-button	–	Manual reset button
CON1	6-pin 2.54 mm connector	–	SPI^{TM} connector

Fig. D.2 Our microcontroller circuit assembled with discrete components on a breadboard is shown

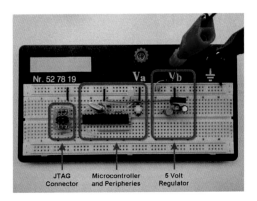

is suitable for breadboard connections. AWG–22 wire has a diameter of approximately 0.6 mm. Custom breadboard wires can be isolated with commercially available skinny, round silicon tubes or small heat-shrink tubing.

Critical circuit components requiring high electromagnetic stability benefit from short, soldered connections. In our circuit on the breadboard, for example, the quartz periphery and the JTAG SPI^{TM} connector have been fitted on secondary snap-on boards built with soldered connections.

In addition, overall stability of the board can be improved by keeping capacitors physically near the components they are meant to stabilize. For example, C1 and C2 are placed near the +5 V voltage regulator, C5 is close to the input rectifier and C6 is tight on the microcontroller VCC and GND pins.

Assembling a microcontroller circuit on a breadboard requires reliable work. It is best to work methodically, properly fitting one circuit group at a time. A volt meter can be used to check the proper placement of the components and their electrical connections.

References

1. ATMEL®, *8-bit ATMEL® Microcontroller with 4/8/16/32K Bytes In-System Programmable Flash (ATmega48A, ATmega48PA, ATmega88A, ATmega88PA, ATmega168A, ATmega168PA, ATmega328, ATmega328P)*, Rev. 8271D–AVR–05/11 (ATMEL®, 2011)
2. M. Schmidt, *ARDUINO®: A Quick-Start Guide* (Pragmatic Programmers, Raleigh, 2011)
3. Wikipedia, *American wire gauge* (2012), http://en.wikipedia.org/wiki/American_wire_gauge
4. Wikipedia, *Dual in-line package* (2012), http://en.wikipedia.org/wiki/Dual_in-line_package
5. Wikipedia, *TO–220* (2012), http://en.wikipedia.org/wiki/TO-220

Glossary

Bootloader   A bootloader is a small program, the job of which is to program another application via communication with another part of memory and/or another device.

Build   Build is the process of building a software project including compiling the sources, linking them, extracting the executable program and optionally programming it into the microcontroller memory.

Debug   Debug means remove the bugs, whereby a bug in this case is a software defect caused by an error in coding, design, timing characteristics or any other mistake.

Flash, Flashing   Flashing is the act of programming an executable program into the FLASH program memory of the microcontroller.

Flashed   Flashed is the state of the FLASH program memory of the microcontroller having undergone flash programming.

Heap   The term heap commonly refers to a pool of computer memory typically used for dynamic memory allocation and deallocation.

Multitasking   Multitasking is a programming technique used to distribute the work of a computer program among more than one task or process, thereby potentially improving program robustness via carefully designed temporal and functional distribution.

Stack   A stack is a linear chunk of computer memory usually used for storing local variables and preserving register contents within one or more (possibly nested) subroutine or interrupt call(s).

Standard Library   The standard library refers to the C++ standard library (as specified in ISO/IEC 14882:2011), which is an extensive collection of types, functions, classes, generic containers and algorithms.

Startup Code   The startup code is the part of the program that runs before the `main()` subroutine and is responsible for initializing RAM and static constructors and subsequently calling `main()`.

C.M. Kormanyos, *Real-Time C++*, DOI 10.1007/978-3-642-34688-0,
© Springer-Verlag Berlin Heidelberg 2013

Index

A

abstract class   57
access control   10
ADC   *See* analog digital converter (ADC)
add() template function   71
<algorithm>   x, 43, 84, 85, 187, 193, 283, 288, 289, 313–317, 324
algorithm (STL)   *See* STL algorithms
algorithmic complexity   100
   linear   100
   logarithmic   100
   quadratic   100
allocator
   std::allocator   177
   and STL containers   176
   custom   119, 176, 177
   ring_allocator   178
analog digital converter (ADC)   112
   optimizing circuit of   113
architecture (of software)   329
   AUTOSAR   12
   layered   330
   MCAL   12
ARDUINO®   19
   bootloader   19, 23
area
   of circle   201, 232, 306
   of rectangle   306
<array>   x, xi, 40, 42–44, 170, 187, 192, 260, 313
   partial implementation of   289
array, C-style   11
   and inner product   90
   and range-based **for**(:)   321
   and std::array   42

assembly
   dedicated file   105
   GCC inline syntax   105
   in startup code   138
   inline   105
assembly listing   102
   from objdump   102
   mangled names in   104
auto keyword   294, 320
AUTOSAR   12
<atomic>   44, 197
__attribute__   61, 116, 117, 154
AWG (American wire gauge)   344

B

bash (*nix shell)   104
big-O notation   100
binutils (binary utilities)   102, 333
   build   338
bit-field   134
bitwise constant   114
bool   35
Boost   278
   Boost.Math   212
   Boost.Regex   325
   Boost.Thread   198
   and C++ standardization   279
   circular_buffer   279
   noncopyable   61
boot
   microcontroller boot time   25
braced initialization syntax   *See* uniform initialization syntax

C.M. Kormanyos, *Real-Time C++*, DOI 10.1007/978-3-642-34688-0,
© Springer-Verlag Berlin Heidelberg 2013